"Midorikawa and Sweeney have committed an exceptional act of literary espionage. English literature owes them a great debt."
— *Financial Times*

"A thought-provoking meditation on literary friendship, as well as engagingly intimate glimpses of four of the world's finest writers in a pursuit that, for women of their times, skirted the edges of decency." — *San Francisco Chronicle*

"*A Secret Sisterhood* is curious about the creative impetus each novelist got from a woman writer beyond her immediate family. Obstacles to intimacy for every pair proved constant—sporadic letters, foiled rendezvous, painful illnesses, misunderstandings. So did an urgent feeling of connection, as this medley of vivid narratives reveals." — *Atlantic*

"Glorious insights into female rivalry and female solidarity and the delicate balancing act required to ensure one doesn't override the other." — *Herald* **(UK)**

"Now that *A Secret Sisterhood* is in print it will be even more difficult than ever before for critics and biographers, male or female, to dismiss, ignore or bury the friendships that literary women have enjoyed. And that's worth cheering!"
— *New York Journal of Books*

"Enthralling, illuminating, and a treat for fans of any of the writers who are covered." —*Booklist,* starred review

"*A Secret Sisterhood* is a marvel. On the strength of a hunch, two friends embark on a research mission that winds up becoming a vital and necessary contribution to women's history, literary history, and the literature of friendship. Beautifully written, rich with insight and feeling, this book is a must-read for anyone who knows that behind every great woman stands a great female friend." —**Kate Bolick,** author of *Spinster: Making a Life of One's Own*

"Rich and revealing . . . these forgotten friendships, from illicit and scandalous to radical and inspiring, are revelations." —*Kirkus Reviews*

"In this wise and exhilarating book, Midorikawa and Sweeney, literary friends themselves, delve into the friendships of women writers, learning lessons along the way about making art, making and keeping friends, and the perils and pleasures of literary life." —**Samantha Ellis,** author of *How to Be a Heroine: Or, What I've Learned from Reading Too Much*

"[An] evocative and well-researched ode to female solidarity." —*Publishers Weekly*

"*A Secret Sisterhood* offers a clever new perspective on established literary figures. While we may inherit family and circumstances, we get to choose our friends; and those these famous women writers have chosen reveal much that is fresh and fascinating about their lives and their work."

—**Tracy Chevalier,** author of *Girl with a Pearl Earring* and editor of *Reader, I Married Him*

A *Secret* Sisterhood

A *Secret* Sisterhood

The Literary Friendships of

 Jane Austen,
Charlotte Brontë,
George Eliot
& Virginia Woolf

EMILY MIDORIKAWA &
EMMA CLAIRE SWEENEY

Mariner Books
Houghton Mifflin Harcourt
BOSTON   NEW YORK

First Mariner Books edition 2018

Copyright © 2017 by Emily Midorikawa and Emma Claire Sweeney
Foreword © 2017 by Margaret Atwood

First published in the U.K. in 2017 by Aurum Press Ltd.

For information about permission to reproduce selections from this book, write
to trade.permissions@hmhco.com or to Permissions, Houghton Mifflin Harcourt
Publishing Company, 3 Park Avenue, 19th Floor, New York, New York 10016.

hmhco.com

Library of Congress Cataloging-in-Publication Data
Names: Midorikawa, Emily, author. | Sweeney, Emma Claire, author. |
Atwood, Margaret, 1939– writer of foreword.
Title: A secret sisterhood : the literary friendships of Jane Austen,
Charlotte Brontë, George Eliot, and Virginia Woolf / Emily Midorikawa,
Emma Claire Sweeney ; foreword by Margaret Atwood.
Other titles: Literary friendships of Jane Austen, Charlotte Brontë,
George Eliot, and Virginia Woolf
Description: Boston : Houghton Mifflin Harcourt, 2017. |
Includes bibliographical references and index.
Identifiers: LCCN 2017044906 (print) | LCCN 2017050302 (ebook) |
ISBN 9780544883789 (ebook) | ISBN 9780544883734 (hardback) |
ISBN 9781328532381 (pbk.)
Subjects: LCSH: Women authors, English — 19th century — Biography. | Women
authors, English — 20th century — Biography. | Austen, Jane, 1775–1817 — Friends
and associates. | Eliot, George, 1819–1880 — Friends and associates. | Brontë,
Charlotte, 1816–1855 — Friends and associates. | Woolf, Virginia, 1882–1941 —
Friends and associates. | Novelists, English — Biography. | Female friendship —
Great Britain — History. | Authorship — Collaboration — History. | Women and
literature — Great Britain — History. | BISAC: BIOGRAPHY & AUTOBIOGRAPHY
/ Literary. | BIOGRAPHY & AUTOBIOGRAPHY / Women. | FAMILY &
RELATIONSHIPS / Friendship.
Classification: LCC PR119 (ebook) | LCC PR119 .M53 2017 (print) |
DDC 820.9/9287—dc23
LC record available at https://lccn.loc.gov/2017044906

Book design by Jackie Shepherd

Printed in the United States of America
DOC 10 9 8 7 6 5 4 3 2 1

Contents

Foreword by Margaret Atwood　*ix*

Introduction: In Search of a Secret Sisterhood　*xiii*

JANE AUSTEN & ANNE SHARP

1. A Circle of Single Women　3

2. Rebellion Behind Closed Doors　23

3. Closing Ranks　41

CHARLOTTE BRONTË & MARY TAYLOR

4. Three's a Crowd　63

5. Two Adventurous Spirits　81

6. One Great Myth　103

GEORGE ELIOT & HARRIET BEECHER STOWE

7. The Stuff of Legend　129

8. The Specter of Scandal　147

9. An Act of Betrayal　168

KATHERINE MANSFIELD & VIRGINIA WOOLF

10. Friends or Foes?　187

11. Cat-and-Mouse　207

12. Life and Death　227

Epilogue: A Web of Literary Connections　*253*

Acknowledgments　*264*

Notes　*269*

Select Bibliography　*310*

Index　*317*

To Jack and Jonathan,
for support from the wings of the stage

Foreword

LASTING JOYS the man attend / Who has a faithful female friend," said the Victorian poetaster Cornelius Whur. The role of the female friend, for a male writer, was to soothe, to sympathize, and to admire; if more than a friend, to be beautiful, and perhaps to play the Muse by inspiring. And to refrain from turning writer herself: competition from such a direction might be crippling to the male ego.

And damaging to the woman herself, since it was a received opinion throughout the past two millennia, up to and including much of the twentieth century, that women, if they were to write at all, should not attempt anything heavier than an etiquette guide. They were naturally without talent, since all their energy was channeled into their reproductive organs, not their tiny brains, and they lacked the larger experience that men could easily acquire. To write seriously was immodest for a woman, and even if she did manage to squeeze out a literary effusion, it was bound to be stunted and inferior. If against all odds she managed to enter the literary world, she would be deemed abnormal. Female writers were reclusive, tormented, neurotic, even morbid. Best not to try.

But many women did try, and many succeeded. In the

eighteenth and nineteenth centuries they turned out quantities of light verse, patriotic songs, social and gothic novels, histories and biographies. They could sell their work more easily if they remained anonymous or wrote under a male pseudonym—no publisher need meet them face to face—and the prospect of making some money of their own was a not inconsiderable motive. Unlike other means of earning a livelihood, writing was something they could do at home.

Some of these female writers became very popular. Nathaniel Hawthorne wrote resentfully about "that damned mob of scribbling women" who were taking up market space that should rightfully have been his. George Eliot wrote the acidic essay "Silly Novels by Lady Novelists," denouncing the frivolity of such novels, of which by 1856 there were many. A woman writer with higher standards would have to write very well indeed to overcome the belief that she couldn't do it, that she shouldn't do it, and even if she did do it, she could not do it well.

This book is about four women who did overcome: Jane Austen, Charlotte Brontë, George Eliot, and Virginia Woolf. Where could a great talent—if female—turn for support? A man might play a sustaining role—George Henry Lewes for George Eliot, Leonard Woolf for Virginia—but for Charlotte Brontë and Jane Austen such a figure was lacking. There might be sympathetic siblings—her sister Cassandra for Jane Austen, Emily and Anne for Charlotte Brontë—but there might not.

In accounts of the lives of male writers, peer-to-peer friendships, not unmixed with rivalry, often loom large—Byron and Shelley, Charles Dickens and Wilkie Collins, Hemingway and Fitzgerald. But female literary friendships have been overlooked, partly because they were actively suppressed by surviving relatives, as with Jane Austen, or overshadowed by better-known family bonds, as with Charlotte Brontë, or passed over by biographers, as with George Eliot and Harriet Beecher Stowe, or interpreted as merely spiteful hissy-fights by commentators, as with Woolf and Mansfield.

In digging up the forgotten friendships chronicled in *A Secret Sisterhood,* Emily Midorikawa and Emma Claire Sweeney have done much service to literary history. We are reminded how hard it was for two of these writers to make their way when they were young and as yet unpublished. The physical privation, lack of status, and financial desperation endured by Charlotte Brontë, and the shrunken circumstances in which Jane Austen found herself after the death of her father, are recounted here in painful detail. But for each of these writers there was a secret sharer. The energetic Mary Taylor—an aspiring writer herself—pushed the diffident Charlotte Brontë to exploit her talent; Anne Sharp, a nascent playwright, shared Jane Austen's passion for writing in a way that Jane's sister, Cassandra, could not.

George Eliot and Harriet Beecher Stowe, and Virginia Woolf and Katherine Mansfield are somewhat different, as all four were published and already part of the literary world when the friendships began. These friendships were trickier, as matters of relative literary success and thus resentment were bound to intrude.

In all four of these friendships, there were cooling periods, misunderstandings, perceived slights, hurt feelings, and silences. A betrayal by a female writing friend must have seemed a triple betrayal—of friendship, of female solidarity in the face of a powerful society dominated by men, and of writing itself. Many readers will recognize the delicate dances these writers perform through their letters to one another: complimenting here, hinting there, ignoring subjects that they can't comment on without causing pain. How much should be expected of a friend—how much tact, how much empathy, how much honesty, how much praise? It's still an open question.

Once people become famous their images tend to congeal. They become engravings of themselves, and we think of them as always having been grown-up and respectable. *A Secret Sisterhood* reminds us that this is not the case. Sweeney and Midorikawa take us back to formative years, retrace forgotten footsteps, and tap into emotional undercurrents in these writers that we had not suspected. These four women, however iconic they have now become, were not two-dimensional icons, nor were they plaster angels: they were real people, with all the neediness, anxiety, ardor, and complexity that come with the territory.

Margaret Atwood

Introduction:
In Search of a Secret Sisterhood

LITERARY FRIENDSHIPS are the stuff of legend. The image of Samuel Taylor Coleridge and William Wordsworth tramping the Lakeland Fells has long been entwined with their joint collection of groundbreaking poems. The tangled sexual escapades of the later Romantics Lord Byron and Percy Bysshe Shelley fueled gossip in their own time, and remain a source of endless fascination. By the mid-nineteenth century, Charles Dickens was taking Wilkie Collins under his wing: publishing the younger writer's stories, acting in his household theatricals, initiating excursions to bawdy music halls. And the memoirs of Ernest Hemingway offer readers a ringside view of his riotous drinking sprees with F. Scott Fitzgerald, thereby securing the pair's Jazz Age friendship its place in literary lore.

But while these male duos have gone down in history, the world's most celebrated female authors are mythologized as solitary eccentrics or isolated geniuses. The Jane Austen of popular imagination is a genteel spinster, modestly covering her manuscript with blotting paper when anyone enters the room. Charlotte Brontë is cast as one of three long-suffering sisters, scribbling away in a drafty parsonage on the edge of the wind-swept moors. George Eliot is remembered as an aloof intellectual who shunned conventional Victorian ladies. And Virginia Woolf haunts the collective memory as a depressive, loading her pockets with stones before stepping into the River Ouse.

Our own experiences, as writer friends, led us to question these accounts of extreme seclusion. We met in the summer of 2001, when we were in our early twenties—part of a group of several hundred graduates who would soon be taking up teaching posts in Japan. On the surface, back then, we had little in common. Emily's razor-slashed dark hair had recently been streaked blond, and she wore a T-shirt and cropped trousers bought while visiting relatives in Tokyo. Emma's fair locks, in contrast, flowed down her back, and she was dressed in a long skirt and sandals. We had both been allocated jobs in the rural prefecture of Ehime. Emma positively embraced the prospect of a year in the remote village to which she had been assigned. But Emily, despite having been placed in the region's capital, fretted about returning to "small-town" life after her university years in London. And while Emily remembers that, of all the people she encountered that day, the young woman in the long skirt and sandals was the one with whom she felt an instant connection, Emma's feelings were less certain. She couldn't decide whether our differences would always loom large, or whether we'd end up the best of friends.

Looking back, we laugh about this, and wonder how we managed to detect in each other a hidden similarity that would eventually draw us together. Though we both kept it secret, we shared the same ambition: to write books and see them published.

We settled into our new lives in Japan, and it wasn't long before we were regularly making the ninety-minute drive along the mountain highway that divided our homes, and planning weekend road trips far and wide. At parties held by other English teachers, we'd frequently find ourselves drifting off from the group, sipping Asahi beers in the corner, happily engrossed in our own conversation.

After almost a year of friendship, we had not yet shared our hopes of becoming published writers. Emma had decided by then to leave her mountain village, while Emily—who'd enjoyed life in her "small town" after all—would be remaining for another twelve months. When we arranged to meet for a farewell dinner, we had no idea that we'd come to look back on this evening as a key moment in our friendship.

We chose a garlic-themed restaurant in Emily's local shopping mall, which had become, by then, an eccentric favorite of ours. Seated at a table covered in a checkered plastic cloth, we talked about news from home, plans for the future, the books we loved. And then, over the course of the next hour, while twisting strands of spaghetti around our forks, we "came out" to each other as aspiring authors. Neither of us had much to show for these aims just yet: diaries kept over the past year, a few short stories. We understood next to nothing about the book industry either. But nonetheless, by the time we laid our cutlery down, we had something perhaps more precious: we knew that we had a friend with the same dream, and that by supporting each other, we could follow it together.

During the years ahead, we would come to rely on each other: critiquing early drafts, passing on news of writing courses and contests, exchanging details of literary agents. As we trod our joint path, sharing moments of both celebration and consolation, we found ourselves wondering whether some of our favorite female authors of the past had enjoyed this kind of support.

The research we'd end up undertaking would offer us sustenance during our long years of striving to become published authors. We had, by our thirties, found jobs as lecturers at the same university, but we'd never studied together. And so, now spending much of our free time scouring library archives, we relished this second stab at studenthood. This joint work would lead us — via bundles of letters yellowing with age, neglected wartime diaries, and personal mementos stored in temperature-controlled rooms — to a treasure-trove of hidden alliances.

We would make the surprise discovery that, in the early nineteenth century — the era of Wordsworth's treks with Coleridge, and Byron's adventures with Shelley — Jane Austen forged a rather more unlikely bond. Ignoring the raised eyebrows of her relatives, she befriended one of the family's servants. Anne Sharp, the governess of Jane's niece, penned household plays in between teaching lessons. Though separated by the mighty class divide, the pair shared the status of amateur writer, and this acted, for a time, as an important social leveler. Yet the differences in their circumstances always threatened to open a gulf between them. The audacity of these two intelligent single women, who built their relationship against the odds, upturns the well-worn version of Jane as a conservative maiden aunt, devoted above all else to kith and kin.

Charlotte Brontë is rarely imagined outside the world of her Yorkshire village, where she dwelt with her literary siblings. But we'd learn that she enjoyed a lively friendship with the pioneering feminist writer Mary Taylor, whom she had met at boarding school in 1831. From frictions during these early days, to daring adventures as young women, to a shock announcement from Mary, these two weathered many storms. Their relationship paints a picture of two courageous individuals, groping to find a space for themselves in the rapidly changing Victorian world.

Unlike Jane and Anne, and Charlotte and Mary—writer friends who enjoyed vastly different levels of recognition—George Eliot and Harriet Beecher Stowe shared an unusual status as the most famous female authors of their day. In the mid-nineteenth century—as Dickens was fêting the work of Collins—Eliot heaped public praise on this far-off American author who had written *Uncle Tom's Cabin,* the era's great antislavery novel. And so, in 1869, Eliot felt delighted to receive an unexpected letter from Harriet's home, set amid an orange grove in Florida. She thrilled to her correspondent's ebullient personality, and—overcoming vast differences in character, opposing views on religion, and the social stigma of Eliot's "living in sin"—they would soon form a deeply personal attachment. But somehow, despite the enduring fame of both women, this compelling friendship remains little known.

Of all the historical collaborations that we have explored, the most complex, perhaps, is that of Virginia Woolf and Katherine Mansfield, who met during the dark days of the First World War, not long before Fitzgerald and Hemingway became friends. Unlike the pairs who came before them, the relationship between Virginia and Katherine, an outsider to the Bloomsbury group, *has* gone down in history. But for all the wrong reasons. Despite the many affectionate letters and thoughtful gifts they exchanged, their simmering creative rivalry frequently threatened to boil over. And so—while Hemingway and Fitzgerald have been remembered as combative friends—these women are often regarded solely as bitter foes. Yet Katherine and Virginia in fact enjoyed a powerful partnership that would profoundly influence the course of English literature.

When the two of us began searching out details of these female friendships, we had very little light to guide us and no clear destination. As we uncovered more and more facts about these four relationships, we gradually came to realize that each of these stories presented its own challenges.

Although many references to her friend crop up in the correspondence of Jane Austen, only one letter from her to Anne Sharp survives. But we caught glimpses of their creative collaboration in a rich variety of archival sources. Chief among these were the unpublished diaries and letters of Jane's beloved niece, Fanny Austen. As the pupil of Anne, who was the family governess, Fanny was a regular observer of exchanges between her teacher and her aunt. Yet as invaluable as her writings are, they remain the words of a child. Fanny watched the comings and goings of the adults not from the bright-lit heart of the action, but from the darkened wings of the stage. We often had to read between the lines of Fanny's childish scrawl to decipher its truths. At times this meant questioning received wisdoms about Jane's life, some of which have become so entrenched that they seem almost impossible to dispute.

Correspondence between Charlotte Brontë and Mary Taylor is similarly limited, since Mary destroyed almost all missives from her friend "in a fit of caution," to protect the women's reputations. But mentions of Mary litter Charlotte's wider communications, and that of other individuals close to this pair. We soon grew used to dealing with the inevitable contradictions and inconsistencies of opinions expressed to different people at different times. To work out the most likely versions of events, we had to weigh one clue against another, careful not to take sources at face value.

Willingness to look beyond first impressions was important too when we considered the transatlantic friendship of

George Eliot and Harriet Beecher Stowe. Too many critics have written them off as mere acquaintances, lacking genuine closeness since they never met — and, unbelievably, despite the fame of these women, a significant proportion of their correspondence remains unpublished. But once we had read all the letters and placed them within the framework of the authors' lives, a startlingly different picture emerged.

Reams of Virginia Woolf's and Katherine Mansfield's diary jottings and correspondence have survived, and these women were part of a self-mythologizing milieu that prized conversational candor. But instead of finding a certain frankness in their personal writing, the more we read, the more we learned to be wary of each woman's inclination toward verbal performance. Rather than fixate on each woman's much-quoted insults about the other, we tried to view their words — both kind and cruel — within the context of their game of literary cat-and-mouse.

As writers today, we know that we owe a great debt to the lives and works of female authors of the past. In setting out to discover more about the friendships of Jane Austen, Charlotte Brontë, George Eliot, and Virginia Woolf, we hoped to learn valuable lessons about how we could sustain our own friendship in the years to come. We'd always considered ourselves fortunate to have met at the start of our careers, allowing us to celebrate early achievements together and to commiserate as publishers' rejection slips stacked up. But it had long been a nagging worry that we might be driven apart by the success of one of us before the other. In our research, we have witnessed just such moments from the past, gleaning warnings about these kinds of pitfalls as well as heartening examples of trust.

In their friendships, these women overcame differences in worldly success and social class, as well as personal schisms and public scandal. But they could not prevent family members and biographers from missing, ignoring, or even willfully covering up their treasured collaborations.

In piecing together the lost stories of these four trailblazing pairs, we have found alliances that were sometimes illicit, scandalous, and volatile; sometimes supportive, radical, or inspiring—but, until now, tantalizingly consigned to the shadows.

JANE AUSTEN
&
ANNE SHARP

The men think us incapable of real friendship, you know,
and I am determined to show them the difference

JANE AUSTEN, *NORTHANGER ABBEY*

1

A Circle of Single Women

IN THE MOST FAMOUS PORTRAIT of Jane Austen, she wears a gauzy dress and frilled cap, and sits demurely, gazing into the middle distance. In 1869, half a century after her death, her nephew James Edward Austen-Leigh commissioned this romanticized watercolor for his commemorative biography of Jane. The posthumous image took inspiration from a sketch drawn by her sister, Cassandra, in around 1810, when the novelist was in her mid-thirties. Her plain dress in this informal portrait is a far cry from the blue ribbons and diaphanous fabric of the painting used to create the frontispiece to *A Memoir of Jane Austen*. And the woman who stares from the original sketch conveys an uncompromising demeanor: a wry look in her eyes, her lips pursed and arms defiantly crossed.

Like the later picture favored by her nephew, his sanitized book — written with the assistance of siblings and one of his cousins — scoured Jane's personality of all its grittier qualities. Conveniently ignoring their aunt's sharp tongue, they preferred to emphasize the neatness of her handwriting, the precision with which she dropped sealing wax onto her letters, the matchless nature of her needlework.

Not only was this younger generation of Austens keen to

appeal to high-minded Victorian ideals about propriety, they were also hampered by fading childhood recollections and a dearth of surviving documentation. Here, Cassandra must take some blame. In the 1840s, the elderly woman read each letter she'd received from her sister one last time. Whenever she came across anything particularly intimate or revealing, she paused, committed Jane's words to memory, and then fed the pages into the parlor's blazing fire. And so their most private confidences curled and flared and finally darkened to ash.

Cassandra's eldest niece, Fanny, followed her aunt's example. She refused to collaborate with her cousins on the memoir and failed to preserve the letters that her father had received from Jane, as well as the vast majority of her own. This stealth begs the question: what secrets could Fanny and Cassandra have been at such pains to hide?

In 1926, *The Times* of London published two previously unseen letters, one from Jane and one from Cassandra, both addressed to a woman little known to fans and critics alike. Subtitled "Devoted Friends," the article introduced readers to "a shadowy figure" named Anne Sharp "for whom Jane Austen had no ordinary affection." That this woman had not appeared, even fleetingly, in the authorized version of Jane's life would have seemed strange to readers. From Jane's opening greeting of "my dearest Anne" to the warmth of the private jokes, family gossip, and heartfelt confidences that followed, it is clear that the recipient was a most treasured confidante.

It might seem curious that the Austen family had been so keen to exclude a figure like Anne, on whose "tender" feelings Jane had come to depend and to whom she considered herself forever "attached." After all, by the Georgian era the British had moved so far from the classical ideal of friendship as an exclusively male domain that they especially prized such bonds between women. But Jane's letter, passed down by acquaintances of Anne through their female descendants, calls into question the Austen family's genteel portrayal of their famous aunt. For Anne was employed as the governess of Jane's niece, Fanny. Here was a relationship that belied the *Memoir*'s image of a woman content solely with the company of her family and whose refined acquaintances "constituted the very class from which she took her imaginary characters."

The uptight tone of Cassandra's letter to this same Anne Sharp hints at another reason for family disapproval. She accused Anne of "ardent feelings" and made a point of asserting her own greater claim on Jane. Cassandra's possessiveness and the younger generation's snobbery speak volumes about why this correspondent appears to us today only as a ghostly apparition, absent from official portraits of the novelist's life.

But unpublished papers stowed deep in library archives still whisper of this woman and the bond she shared with Jane. To understand why Anne has been excluded from histories of her close friend, we must turn to the words of Jane's niece, Fanny. Keen as she was to get rid of her father's documents, Fanny kept her own crimson leather-bound pocket diaries, in which she made meticulous entries from the tender age of ten. Along with a cache of her correspondence, they have been passed down to us unscathed.

These unpublished notebooks and letters, largely unmined by literary critics, shed light on what must have lain at the heart of the deep affection between Fanny's governess and aunt: like Jane, Anne was a writer.

The child's entry for a Saturday early in 1804 transports us to a time before she knew anything of Anne's literary bent. On January 21, the governess was on her way to Godmersham Park — the grand home of Jane's far wealthier brother — to take up employment teaching Fanny. Anne's overnight journey took her through neat Kent villages and land scarred by freshly dug ditches that divided commons and heaths—these regimented fields worlds away from the bustle of London, where she had been born thirty-one years earlier.

History has shown such scant interest in Anne that, until we discovered her name in an old baptismal ledger, even the year of her birth was unknown. And, as with most working women of her generation, no portrait nor any direct record of her words has ever been unearthed. Despite the wealth of information we have found, our reconstruction of Anne's life must largely rely on Austen family papers, most notably the account of Fanny, a privileged child born into the landed gentry, trained to regard household staff with kindly condescension.

Fanny's letters show that she awaited the arrival of her new teacher with both eagerness and nerves—mixed feelings that Anne surely shared. As the coach carrying the governess reached Godmersham Park, it would have halted at the boundary of the Austens' estate, its driver dismounting with his key before leading the horses onto the driveway, the towering iron gates closing behind them. As the carriage continued through the estate's deer park, a break in the trees offered Anne a glimpse of the red-bricked façade of the house, a place already so familiar to Jane: the hatching across its countless windows; the decorative masonry above the pillared entrance; the pleasing symmetry of its flanking pavilions, which had been so fashionably added just twenty-five years before.

On approaching the coach-turning circle, it became clear that one of the new pavilions housed a huge reading room— surely a cheering sight for a woman who penned theatricals. This library, where Jane enjoyed many an hour of solitude during her lengthy but occasional visits, dwarfed the size of the entrance hall and rivaled the ballroom, creating the impression, at least, that its owners were great lovers of literature. Beyond its checkered windows stood floor-to-ceiling bookshelves whose volumes would have offered something of a sanctuary to the intellectually curious.

From the moment Anne's feet touched Godmersham's black-and-white marble flagstones, all eyes would have been upon her, the brood of children trying to get the measure of her, while the footmen and lady's maids sized her up for signs of haughtiness—a characteristic considered common in governesses, who, though gentlewomen, were often paid little more than other household staff. *The Times,* whose later interest in Anne would stem only from her connection with Jane, would compare such a role to "a kind of shuttlecock between servants and mistresses, and the butt of both."

Unbeknownst to Anne at this time, Jane too had never felt at ease during her stays at Godmersham—despite its being the home of her brother. The employees could tell she was a poor relation; the housemaids learned not to expect much in the way of tips from Jane, and the visiting hairdresser offered her a discount rate. Even the family of the house could at times be disparaging, sneering at Jane's unfashionable attire. She and Cassandra tended to dress dowdily, in matching clogs and bonnets. And on occasions when they marked a bereavement, they had to pick stitches from old bombazine or crepe pelisses, soak the fabric in black dye, then resew it into gowns. For the sister of a landowner, such apparent lack of refinement was cause for embarrassment. But no one would raise an eyebrow at a new governess showing up in makeshift mourning garb, and with an air of genteel impoverishment.

Anne's engagement with the Austens had likely been necessitated by misfortune. Fanny recorded that her new governess had suffered a bereavement, but failed to mention for whom she grieved. "I think Miss Sharpe pretty but not strikingly so," she noted, before adding: "she is in mourning & I think it becomes her." With the era's casual disregard for consistent spelling, the girl added an *e* to her new teacher's surname—a mistake that Jane would also make throughout her long friendship with Anne. A woman with Anne's mother's name, Elizabeth Sharpe, had been buried in London in April 1803, and so it appears that the governess had lost a parent. In the early nineteenth century, a single woman in her position, without affluent male relatives to support her, would face the unenviable task of securing a respectable way to earn her keep.

Anne's employment had gotten off to a late start. She should have taken up her role as governess to young Fanny some months earlier, but a dangerous bout of ill health—perhaps exacerbated by her recent bereavement—had delayed her arrival. Her new home in a busy household would hardly have proved a suitable place for convalescing. Her pupil, Fanny, was the eldest of five boys and four girls—the youngest a sweet-natured but noisy newborn—and the stuccoed ceiling of the entrance hall forever rang with the sounds of Edward's and Elizabeth's many relatives being welcomed in or waved off.

Both master and mistress hailed from large families; each had seven siblings. In all other ways, however, their backgrounds contrasted. Edward had been brought up with Jane in a Hampshire rectory, where their father supplemented his modest clergyman's income by running a farm and taking paying pupils into his home. Elizabeth, on the other hand, had been raised at Goodnestone Park—an estate almost as grand as her current home, the neighboring Godmersham. This unlikely match had come about through Edward's adoption as an adolescent by the Austen family's landlord and distant cousin, Thomas Knight, who owned grand homes in Hampshire and Kent. Such an arrangement suited all concerned. The wealthy couple gained a longed-for child, while their tenants, who negotiated to continue educating Edward at home with his siblings, saw their third-born rise from a mere rector's son to the inheritor of three lucrative estates. By 1804, when Anne joined the staff at Godmersham, Edward had become firmly entrenched in the landed gentry, his lifestyle a far cry from that of his sister Jane, who could count hardly a penny to her name.

Edward enjoyed his fortune, taking his children to extravagant firework displays; treating his guests to delicacies such as French wine, lobster, and ices; and encouraging his wife and daughters to purchase colored Persian silks, muslin neckerchiefs, and hats stylishly ornamented with artificial fruit. But he was also keenly aware of the responsibilities incumbent on a landowner to preserve his assets for the next generation. Encouraged by his wife, it would appear, his generosity fell short at times when it came to his less fortunate sisters—strait-laced Cassandra and sharp-tongued Jane.

Anne's early days at Godmersham Park boded well, however, since the first Monday of her employment fell on her pupil's eleventh birthday, and the lady of the house invited the governess to join the family for the exchange of gifts, special meals, and games of cards. And so, at ten o'clock in the morning of January 23, 1804, Anne sat down with her master, mistress, and Fanny in a wood-paneled parlor, where a table was set with fine china.

During her own visits, Jane would marvel at this leisurely lifestyle, describing such lazy days as "*a la* Godmersham." But on this particular morning, the twenty-eight-year-old was 150 miles away with her parents and sister in Bath. It was her custom to rise early, preparing a breakfast of tea and toast for her family before taking up her quill. She had been writing since childhood, when she used to read aloud her stories and plays to the high-spirited glee of her household audience. By now, just shy of thirty, she had produced reams of such entertainments, and even three full-length novels—books that sent up the snobbery and sense of entitlement she'd witnessed as an outsider looking on at the "happy Indifference of East Kent wealth." But, like the governess who was about to enter her life, Jane had not experienced the pleasure of seeing her words in print.

On the morning of her pupil's birthday, Anne was about to witness the kind of seemingly trivial incident that would provide fodder for Jane's works-in-progress. Following the pleasures of a gourmet breakfast—treats at the time included ginger-spiced plum cake, buttered brioche, and hot chocolate poured from a silver-spouted pot—the mistress of the house offered her daughter the gift of a pretty sandalwood box containing toothpicks. Readers of *Sense and Sensibility* would one day encounter just such a decorative object: a symbol in the novel for the extravagance and conceit of those with surplus wealth. Jane had embarked on the story some years earlier, but she would continue to revise it for several more, the final version bearing the influence of Godmersham in far more significant ways.

If Jane raised a wry smile at the expense of her brother's family, they also seemed to view her with suspicion. Her sister-in-law certainly did not take kindly to intellectual conversation; her main interests ranged from her beloved children and cherished mare to the dress patterns and rolls of muslin that she liked to order from traveling salesmen or through friends in town. At Godmersham, Jane's talk often fell on unappreciative ears. As one of her nieces would recall in later life, Elizabeth—for whom "a little talent went a long way . . . & much must have gone a long way too far"—was not overly fond of her bookish sister-in-law.

During the months that followed Anne's arrival, the illusion of scholarship conveyed by the lofty library was swiftly dispelled. Elizabeth canceled lessons with such frequency that it appeared she did not want her eldest daughter to receive much of an education, and Edward spent his days hunting and fishing and settling neighborhood disputes. It was also his responsibility to inspect the troop of volunteer soldiers whom he permitted to exercise at the top of his parkland, for rumors abounded that Napoleon Bonaparte's French forces were planning to invade English shores via the local Kentish coastline.

Such grave worries were offset by the cheerfulness of family life. Anne would have quickly gotten to know the younger children, who still came under the nursemaid's care: William, a six-year-old, who loved to practice shuttlecock for hours on end; Lizzy, a bright little thing already taken to needlework at just four years of age; Marianne, a toddler, easily identifiable by the traces of a mark on her neck (the causes of which Fanny would later white out from her letters during the more squeamish Victorian era); Charles, a curly-haired child who carried with him a doll that he called his wife; and the youngest, Louisa, a black-eyed infant with a loud cry and an infectious smile. In time, Anne would also meet the elder boys, who boarded at Eltham School: Henry, Edward, and George.

Anne and Fanny soon fell into a pleasing routine. They usually met in the schoolroom at ten, where they began the working day by breakfasting à deux. The governess then heard her charge recite her lessons, testing Fanny's knowledge of French conjugations, picking out distant lands on the globe, and discussing the books Anne had selected from Godmersham's library. They punctuated their studies with strolls along the lane to take tea with the child's great-aunt, or more boisterous expeditions into "the Wilderness"—an overgrown area made treacherous by exposed roots and low-hanging boughs. On fine days, they sometimes allowed themselves to be lured from their studies by the entreaties of Fanny's brothers, or even her mama and papa, to join them on cross-country rides or fishing for pike on the serpentine—a bend in the river at the south-easterly edge of the park.

Almost six months passed by in this manner, the sharp frost of January giving way to sunbursts of daffodils in spring. And, just as the plants shrugged off the darkness of previous months, so Anne too must have felt revived. What bliss, after the hardships of the previous year, to find her health returned.

While Anne gamely threw herself into family frolics, she had less time alone than she might have preferred. The hectic frivolity of Edward Austen's huge household allowed for few solitary hours in the library. Even nightfall failed to bring a respite from Anne's duties. She could not read or write by candlelight lest she disturb Fanny, for her role as governess involved sharing her bed most nights with her pupil—a common practice during this era, although one that Anne might well have hoped to avoid when she secured employment in a house of such a respectable size.

But over the coming year, she must have managed to steal some time for herself, perhaps rising early while the housemaid was still pumping bellows to reignite the embers in the kitchen hearth. With the dawn light climbing up the library walls, Anne may have dipped her quill in ink to work secretly on her play scripts instead of turning to the correspondence that gentlewomen ordinarily dealt with during the quiet pre-breakfast hours. In the same vast, empty room where Jane also holed up during visits, Anne could have taken her pick of the five library tables and the room's twenty-eight chairs. She had surely heard by now of her young pupil's paternal aunts: Cassandra, the favorite, such a help with the children, and Jane, who thought herself so very clever with her own made-up stories and plays.

Over in Bath, Jane was finding it difficult to carve out the time and solitude she required for her literary work, because, like Anne, she had endured an upheaval. Three years earlier, her clergyman father had announced his intention to retire from Steventon Rectory in Hampshire. It occurred to neither Reverend nor Mrs. Austen to consult with their unmarried daughters, both of whom still resided with them, about their intended relocation to a spa town over fifty miles away. No thought was given to the effect of wrenching Jane and Cassandra from their female friends—members of the Bigg-Wither and Lloyd families—or from their longstanding creative and domestic routines. The expectation that Jane should accompany her family to fashionable tearooms, opulent bathhouses, and chandeliered balls kept her from writing as much as she might have liked. Despite the enjoyment of such distractions, she longed for her former Hampshire hillside.

Though her father's decision had cost Jane her creative haven, he had always been a staunch supporter of her work. Back in 1797, when she was just twenty-one, the Reverend George Austen had sent one of her manuscripts to Cadell and Davies, a leading London bookseller. He clearly paid no heed to those who deemed it improper for women to publish. Nor was he browbeaten by the repressive tendencies of the wartime era, when any writing that criticized the British status quo was deemed dangerous. This was a charge that could have been leveled against Jane. *First Impressions*, the novel that she would later rename *Pride and Prejudice*, dared to criticize the behavior of the king's soldiers, and it also questioned women's lack of economic independence. Whether or not Thomas Cadell found such subject matter troubling, he certainly failed to predict that this book would become one of the world's most beloved works. He turned it down by return post.

Jane held her nerve, though, and in 1803 — the year Anne had agreed to join the large household staff at Godmersham — she'd sought publication of another of her novels, known today as *Northanger Abbey*. On this occasion, she had cause for celebration. Benjamin Crosby of Crosby & Co. in London purchased her satirical story's copyright, albeit for just ten pounds — a sum with which Jane could have purchased a fur-trimmed shawl or two, along with a velvet cloak and bonnet. Despite the paltry fee, she must have felt overjoyed to learn that this great man of letters had advertised her book's forthcoming publication in his annual catalog of gothic romances. After a decade and a half of writing, she would finally see one of her novels ushered into the wider world.

Throughout 1804, while Jane was anticipating her first publication, her home life had taken a downward turn. When the lease expired on the family's house in Bath's fashionable Sydney Place, overlooking the pleasure gardens, the Austens were forced to move to quarters in the far less desirable western fringe of town. Just three years earlier, they had rejected this low-lying area close to slum housing on account of the dampness of the buildings and "reports of discontented families & putrid fevers."

Anne was experiencing difficulties too. By early summer, her illness had reared up once more. On June 19, the children of Godmersham were in fine fettle; the kitchen garden had yielded the season's first strawberries, and the cook had whipped up vast quantities of the dairy's fresh cream. But despite all this good cheer, Anne could not hide from Fanny the fact that she was "not quite well."

The next day, the two met in the schoolroom. Anne was hopeful that she had endured the worst, but soon she began to feel faint. As she gradually lost track of the lesson, shadows cast the light from her eyes, her legs gave way beneath her, and she fell to the floor.

When she stirred she found herself in the arms of Susannah Sackree, Godmersham's nursemaid, who helped the governess to her feet and then guided her slowly upstairs. On entering her room, Anne flung herself onto the bed, entirely spent. Here, she was administered a draft of laudanum before being left alone to sleep. But despite the sedation, Anne found herself wakeful.

The hours passed in a haze until the house came alive with the sounds of dinner. Before too long, she heard a knock at the door, and then little Fanny appeared, proffering a bowl of whipped syllabub. Its sickly scent of sugar, sherry, and cream made Anne's stomach turn, but she took the curative dessert from the child and gathered all her strength to get up, so that the maid could change her bedding. Try as she might, though, she couldn't raise so much as a spoonful of syllabub to her mouth.

During this period, Anne received sympathetic treatment from her employers and fellow staff. But as the months wore on and she kept suffering intermittently from similar spells of ill health, she must have grown anxious about retaining her position. After all, the Godmersham Austens were known for high turnover of household staff. It could only be a matter of time before Edward and Elizabeth dismissed a governess who so frequently took to her sickbed.

This period was marked by trepidation not only for Anne,

but also for Jane. Having waited in vain for two years to see *Northanger Abbey* go to print, the eager writer could only speculate that Crosby & Co. might have had second thoughts about bringing to press a satire that sent up the gothic genre in which the firm specialized. In fact, the publishing company had simply run into financial trouble. Regardless, Jane's disappointment at the lack of progress must have been crushing. She'd prioritized writing over courtship and domestic responsibilities, turning down at least one proposal of marriage, eschewing invitations whenever possible, and allowing her sister to take on more than her fair share of family duties. Now Jane had to suffer the ignominy of yet another rejection of her work. Ultimately, though, she was undeterred. She simply picked up her quill and continued drafting a new novel, provisionally titled *The Watsons.*

But then a catastrophe befell the Austen household. Ever since moving into the damp-ridden house in Green Park Buildings, her father had been suffering from weakness and fevers. On January 19, 1805, he endured a violent seizure, and within days he passed away.

His death robbed all the Austen women of an affectionate father and husband, and Jane of an enthusiastic admirer of her work. Since women could not inherit a church pension, Mrs. Austen and her daughters also lost their main source of income. The only wellspring of hope that Jane could draw from these saddest of circumstances was the possibility that she might now return to surroundings more conducive to her creativity. Thank goodness for her brother Edward's adoption by the wealthy Knights. His estates in Hampshire and Kent each comprised dozens of properties, and his inherited fortune would surely stretch to subsidizing his mother and sisters for the loss of Reverend Austen's retirement fund. And yet, perhaps Jane always harbored some doubt about her brother and sister-in-law's generosity. *Sense and Sensibility* would later portray a buffoonish brother and his self-serving wife who cruelly neglect a mother and her daughters after the death of the family patriarch.

Neither Jane nor any of her books' heroines faced the prospect of fending for themselves. But, like Anne, she was now similarly reliant on the purse of Godmersham's owner—a man who guarded his wealth from all but his wife and children.

Edward and the rest of Jane's brothers consulted on their womenfolk's financial affairs and presented their mother with a fait accompli: between the six of them, they would pool a sufficient annual income to allow her and her daughters to winter in serviceable lodgings in Bath and summer between the abodes of more affluent relations, including themselves. This plan seemed to suit Mrs. Austen well enough, but once again, no one gave a thought to the wishes of her daughters. Despite Edward's own vast fortune, he promised his mother and sisters a yearly stipend of only one hundred pounds—no more than that offered by one of his younger brothers, Frank, a less prosperous naval man recently engaged to a penniless girl. Jane put a brave face on it, but her exploration of fraternal betrayal in *Sense and Sensibility* suggests that she felt badly let down.

The Austen women soon came to realize that their modest finances could not cover the rent for Green Park Buildings. And so, just two months after her father's death, Jane and her grieving sister and mother had to relocate to still cheaper lodgings, ten minutes' walk away at 25 Gay Street.

It was during this period, in April 1805, that a governess friend named "Miss Sharpe" first crops up in Jane's surviving correspondence. Within four months, she would be writing warmly of Fanny's teacher "Miss Sharpe" in her letters, and throughout the rest of her life, references to this governess friend would litter Jane's missives. But surprisingly, an annotation tucked away at the back of the authoritative edition of Jane Austen's letters insists that the Miss Sharpe first mentioned in April 1805 could not possibly be the same woman to whom Jane would grow so attached. *This* governess friend cannot be Anne, so the story goes, because she and Jane could not yet have met. There's no evidence that Jane had paid a visit to her Kentish relatives during the fifteen months of Anne's employment. And Anne must have been at Godmersham throughout that time.

But this, in fact, was not the case. Young Fanny's metal-clasped diaries and wax-sealed letters reveal that during that spring of 1805, her teacher was away from home. These unpublished manuscripts show that Anne's month-long absence coincides with the same period of Jane's removal from Green Park Buildings to her poky new rented abode.

Fanny waved off her governess during the week commencing March 18, and Anne didn't return for almost a month. So it seems possible that Edward sent her to assist the Austen women with their move, and that Jane and Anne grew fond of each other far from the watchful eyes of the owners of Godmersham.

If so, this was not the first time that Anne had been told to cancel lessons and fit herself into other family plans. She was regularly instructed to work outside the schoolroom: sent to drop off the boys at their boarding schools at the beginning of term and pick them up at its close, and called on at times to chaperone her employer's guests on their journeys. But any inconvenience to Anne must have been outweighed by Edward's promise to stop in London during their travels, so that she could consult a doctor about her eyes, which had been troubling her ever since her collapse.

Within the spacious drawing room of Green Park Building East, Anne would have been greeted by Cassandra, Jane, and their mother, all dressed in mourning garb only slightly less shabby than the outfit she herself had worn when she began her employment at Godmersham. Cassandra was a polite woman, outwardly reserved. But the younger sister, like her mother, was a much more spirited character, whose love of literature sustained her through difficult times. Packing up the household together, she and Anne would have found plenty of opportunity for literary conversation, such as trading thoughts on favorite books by the likes of Maria Edgeworth and Frances Burney.

At some point, this flicker of friendship ignited to flame, their difficulties perhaps giving each woman a reason for trading confidences. Anne's persistent headaches and eye problems must have hampered her attempts at devising plays, and Jane had not been able to concentrate on her new novel during the months since her father's death. In the years to come, these women would find all sorts of ways to support each other's endeavors, but on this occasion, the pair could have barely gotten to know each other before they had to part—Anne returning to Godmersham and Jane remaining in Bath.

At the right moment on April 9, 1805, Jane would have been easy to spot, picking her way among the crowds that thronged Gay Street—her parasol, dyed dark for mourning, out of tempo with the cheerful hubbub in this part of town. Sedan chairs, shouldered by one man at the front and another at the rear, carried visitors down the steep hill to take the waters in the Grand Pump Room nearby. In this spa town, Jane was surrounded by holidaymakers and husband hunters, with whom she found little in common. Whereas *she* had to call Bath home, most women of her age and class were just passing through.

When Jane stepped inside 25 Gay Street that morning, she would have found the rooms especially quiet, since her sister had gone to Hampshire to help nurse the terminally ill mother of their old friend Martha Lloyd. Jane soon settled down to continue a letter to Cassandra that she'd started the day before. Dipping her quill into the homemade ink, she began with a wish that the mercy of death might come to Mrs. Lloyd as swiftly as it had settled on their father. Just as she gave in to the flow of her words, a visitor was announced: a Miss Colbourne, the lady who owned the school on Lansdown Crescent.

As Jane would admit when she resumed her letter, this interruption made her hackles rise. She knew that her dark rooms were a world apart from Miss Colbourne's grand institution on a hill above town. And Jane had, in fact, long harbored negative feelings about schools. At seven years of age, she'd been sent to Oxford to boarding school, along with her sister and cousin. All three girls contracted a dangerous fever, and their lives hung in the balance. They managed to get word out to Jane's aunt, who fetched them immediately and eventually nursed them back to health. But in the process of saving the girls, she caught the disease herself, and for her it proved fatal. Despite this trauma, after a year at home Jane had been sent off to another school—this time her life was not endangered, but she received little in the way of learning.

Miss Colbourne had come to enquire after the character

of one of the Austen women's former maids, whom—thanks to Edward's parsimony—they could no longer afford to keep on. The brothers had decided that their mother could "reduce her establishment to one female domestic" instead of the three she had previously employed. Jane had no choice in the matter, and now she felt that this school owner was condescending to her. These days, it couldn't escape Jane's notice that guests often seemed to look down on her—though, she drolly noted, they were more than happy to partake of her precious supplies of tea leaves and sugar.

And yet both sisters saw some opportunities in their new impoverishment. In Jane's next surviving letter, she would discuss with Cassandra the intention to invite their childhood friend Martha to join their new household. The sisters had been keeping this plan from their family, but now that Mrs. Lloyd's death was imminent, the time had come, Jane wrote, to let others know of these hopes. Martha's meager finances could supplement theirs, and her skills as an amateur cook and apothecary would be welcome indeed. But more than anything, it was her friendship they held dear.

A line buried in this same letter suggests that friendship was also at the heart of another of Jane's schemes. Her note to Cassandra gives the impression that she had been looking for work on Anne's behalf—an endeavor that would have involved going behind her brother's back, prioritizing the bond she shared with his governess over the loyalty she owed to him. And now it seemed her efforts had met with success. The daughter of an acquaintance, she revealed, was soon "to take lessons of Miss Sharpe"—surely the same governess whose company Jane would prize in the years to come. For all her pleasure at the prospect of establishing a close female circle in

Bath, she nonetheless knew to proceed with caution. "Among so many friends," she mused, "it will be well if I do not get into a scrape."

Scrapes aplenty did indeed await her as she tried to bring the keen playwright into her group of intelligent single women —the others all avid readers of Jane's novels in draft, but none of them able to offer quite the creative solidarity of a fellow writer like Anne.

2

Rebellion Behind Closed Doors

IN JUNE 1805, two months after Jane Austen sought employment for Anne Sharp in Bath, the pair were indeed together.
But they were not among the crowds of women at one of the
city's circulating libraries, laden with conduct books, sermons,
and popular novels. Nor were they huddled over the fire in
the parlor at the Austen women's new quarters in Gay Street,
discussing their writing over tea and Bath buns covered with
sugar-coated caraway seeds. For reasons lost to history, Jane's
plan to include Anne in her circle in Bath had clearly not come
to pass. The unlikely friends had to resort to meeting up within
the walls of the Godmersham Park estate in East Kent. For despite Jane's efforts to secure Anne a new post, the governess remained an employee of Edward Austen.

On June 19, the diary of Anne's pupil, Fanny, mentions
the arrival at six o'clock in the evening of "Grandmama Austen, Aunts Cassandra & Jane," along with two of Fanny's favorite cousins, both twelve years old, like her. As the women's
carriage came into view, the sun was still high in the sky. Anne
would have had the perfect excuse to join her charge at the
coach-turning circle. But it would hardly have been the done
thing for Jane to greet her brother's employee with affection,

and even her mother and sister might have raised their eyebrows at such intimacy, particularly given Anne's humble roots.

In later years, the governess would keep quiet about her past, a decision made understandable in light of evidence in that neglected baptismal ledger. London ecclesiastical records show that only one baby to share a name with the governess was christened in the city during the weeks following her birth. The father is noted as a gardener, and though street addresses are included for the other infants christened in February 1773 at St. Paul's Church in Deptford, this baby is simply recorded as "from WH"—a common abbreviation for the workhouse. Such an institution might have offered Anne an unusual level of education for a girl of her modest background, but this proximity to urban paupers was worlds away from the rural parsonage upbringing of the Austen siblings. And yet, with hardly a penny to her name, Jane was in a situation somewhat comparable to Anne's.

Jane, who had come to stay at Godmersham for the whole summer, was deeply in need of a friend. Her situation had gone from bad to worse in the two months since her removal to Gay Street. Still grieving for their husband and father, the Austen women had now discovered that even their modest new dwelling was rather beyond their means. They had been left with no choice but to withdraw their tenancy and impose on the hospitality of their relations while they worked out what they could afford to rent in Bath on their return. The disruption of one house move and the prospect of yet another, not to mention the melancholy brought on by the loss of her father, had sapped Jane of her creative vigor. And with one book rejected and another having languished for two years in a publisher's drawer, she had no reason to believe that her writing would ever reach a readership beyond her close family and friends—

especially since she'd arrived at Godmersham having made the decision to abandon her novel-in-progress, *The Watsons.*

The activities of the next few days must have lifted Jane's spirits: gathering around the brand-new pianoforte, trips in the chaise to Canterbury, pony rides around the estate, inspection of the canary's freshly laid eggs. What's more, Jane sometimes got to enjoy these escapades with Anne. The governess canceled lessons the day after the Austen women arrived. Instead, the three cousins and their aunts all boisterously baptized one of Fanny's dolls by anointing its forehead with water and staging grand entertainments to celebrate its christening.

Such diversions could offer a temporary balm, but they would hardly cure Jane's unaccustomed artistic lethargy. As a writer herself, Anne was better placed to help than even Jane's dear sister, Cassandra. But the governess and the houseguest couldn't have risked spending too much time engaging in literary conversations without irritating Godmersham's mistress, Elizabeth.

This time the pair would cement their bond within the unthreatening environs of the schoolroom: the one place where Anne held sway. Fanny's entry in her lady's pocket diary on June 26, 1805, escapes into the columns usually reserved for records of money received or spent. Her account of the day's antics fizzes with joy at the memory of dressing up and playing at school along with her governess, aunts, mother, grandmother, and her cousins Fanny Cage and Anna Austen. Such games of make-believe were just what the two visiting girls needed, since both were in need of affection. Over the past six months, Fanny Cage had lost both her father and mother, and Anna faced further exclusion at home now that her stepmother was expecting a second child.

These forlorn girls decked themselves out in costume, and

to their delight, the adults joined in. In her cross-dressing role as sergeant, Anne issued orders to those who usually held rank over her. Jane and Cassandra were assigned characters strikingly similar to Anne's real-life role—Jane playing the part of Miss Popham, the teacher, and Cassandra cast as Mrs. Teachum, the governess. They needn't have looked far for props; Anne's own chalk and slate would do. Jane's mother and sister-in-law took on characters even lower down the Georgian social scale: Betty Jones, the piewoman, and a nameless seaside-bathing attendant.

Roles assigned, Anne moved between the part of the sergeant and that of the dancing master. This sort of activity appealed to Jane, for she loved cotillions and Scotch reels, and her nimble footwork had long inspired admiration. Jane had inherited her fun-loving, satirical bent from her mother, and so it's easy to picture the sixty-six-year-old widow throwing herself into a country dance, her apron swaying in time with her steps, as she held a rolling pin aloft. Anne's mistress too never shied away from play-acting, so long as it was all just fun and games. And Cassandra, far more reserved than the rest, could not deny her nieces the pleasure of seeing all the adults make a show of themselves.

Later in the day, Anne managed with military precision to maneuver the party from playing school to acting in a drama that she herself had secretly penned. The maids clearing away the dessert dishes from the wood-paneled dining room would have been privy to her suggestion that the children put on a play. Its title, *Virtue Rewarded,* could have given no cause for alarm. This sketch—like most of the era's theatricals for youngsters—would provide moral instruction, the title cried out; there could be nothing clever or troubling here! Perhaps on account of her mistress's distrust of talented women, Anne did not admit that she was the author of this play. And she couldn't even count on support from Jane—a woman who had a tendency toward ridicule and who, in any case, could offer encouragement only with the greatest discretion.

Anne turned her attention to the children—the one interest she could legitimately share with Jane. The orphaned Fanny Cage was appointed Duchess of St. Albans; Anna Austen, black sheep of her family, was transformed into Shepherdess Flora; the daughter of the house became Fairy Serena.

It would be easy to write all this off as no more than a bit of fun, just as the mistress of Godmersham must have done. Certainly, most biographers have deemed it unworthy of scholarly attention that the great Jane Austen shared a rapport with a scribbler of children's entertainments, whose scripts no one thought to save. But the events of the coming months and years reveal that Jane treated Anne as her most trusted literary friend, understanding both the value of the governess's playwriting and the constraints under which she labored, due to the demands of her teaching work.

During the fortnight following the impromptu theatricals, the usual restrictions on Anne's freedom eased off. Now that Fanny had her cousins to keep her company, the governess could pack off the children for adventures in Godmersham's grounds. One day, she allowed them each to choose a gothic novel and then sent them to climb up to the estate's folly, an artificial ruin decoratively situated in the parkland. Here they could devour their stories in a suitably mysterious location. Later that week, loading a basket with books, paper, and pencils so that they could complete their schoolwork wherever they chose, she encouraged them to pretend to be gypsies for the day. And she added a large bottle of water, as well as a loaf and a hunk of cheese so that the girls could stay out as long as they pleased.

But the next day, Fanny was taken ill with a cold and fever. She lost her voice and couldn't recite her lessons. Anne must have felt concerned that the adventures she'd devised to get her pupil out of the house had proven too much for the girl's constitution. Soon afterward, Fanny's mother caught the same complaint—suffering more seriously still—and was also confined for two weeks to her bed. Thankfully, nobody in the family seemed to cast blame on the governess, but it was a worrying time. With the rudimentary medicine of the early nineteenth century, even the common cold could be dangerous.

Anxieties aside, with both employer and charge laid up in the sickroom, the governess could escape her usual duties and steal time with her friend. Jane would come to look back on this summer with Anne as a period of great animation. And the events of the following months suggest that she did all she could to prolong their shared seclusion.

As soon as her sister-in-law rallied, however, Jane was whisked off for dinners at local manor houses, balls in nearby Canterbury and Ashford, and mercy missions to the homes of Elizabeth's ailing relatives. Anne's duties also kept the pair apart throughout much of August and the early weeks of September. She accompanied Fanny on a short break to Canterbury, where they visited the cathedral, feasted on pastries, and listened to the music of traveling bands. Here, she shared a few moments with her friend, who was there simply to switch carriages with Cassandra. Jane was on her way to Goodnestone to take over family nursing duties from her sister, so that Cassandra—always Elizabeth's favorite—could return to Godmersham. It may have been a brief exchange, but Anne made quite an impression on Jane's two companions: Edward's wealthy benefactress, the kindly Catherine Knight, and Molly Milles, a single woman who could empathize with Jane's itinerant lifestyle, since she too had been forced to move from one set of rented quarters to another. Unlike Fanny's first impression of her governess as "pretty but not strikingly so," these women were much struck by Anne's beauty as well as her style of conversation. "Pray say everything kind for us to Miss Sharpe, who could not regret the shortness of our meeting in Canterbury more than we did," wrote Jane in her next letter to Cassandra. "I hope she returned to Godmersham as much pleased with Mrs. Knight's beauty and Miss Milles's judicious remarks as those ladies respectively were with hers."

A plan was already afoot for Anne to accompany Jane and her relatives on holiday, and to spend the entire autumn of 1805 together by the sea — not at the nearby Kent coast but on the far side of the Downs in Worthing. The odds of success, however, did not look good. Jane's mother and sister would not necessarily share her enthusiasm for including Anne on their sojourn. What's more, how could Godmersham's master and mistress be persuaded to do without their daughter's governess for weeks on end?

A holiday at the seaside for the Austen women might have seemed a reasonable request. After all, they had to spend their autumn somewhere, Jane may have reminded her brother, and they could hardly impose themselves much longer at Godmersham. But she faced a difficult challenge when it came to convincing Edward to allow his daughter's governess to accompany them.

And yet he did acquiesce to the plan, even though it involved agreeing to the six-week absence of an important member of the household staff. Perhaps Jane had made the argument that the coastal air would do Miss Sharp a world of good and that she would return to Godmersham in the best of health, her debilitating headaches a thing of the past. In letters,

Fanny cited these reasons to explain the prolonged absence of her governess. But Anne's migraines and eyestrain hadn't seemed to trouble her quite so much of late, and so perhaps Edward's reasons for agreeing had more to do with guilt. With so many properties at his disposal, it hardly reflected well on him that his own mother and sisters lacked a place to call home. The seaside holiday may have helped him to convince himself that he was not neglecting them—and Anne, as his employee, could provide the women with invaluable help.

Edward could offer this kind of assistance without risking the wrath of his wife. After all, she hardly wanted Fanny to grow overly learned, and it must have been rather trying to share her home with a good-looking woman of quick wit—a quality of Anne's noted even by James Edward Austen-Leigh, Jane's nephew and first biographer, who later left Anne out of his account of his aunt's life. In a note to his half sister, Anna, dated 1820—fifteen years after the letter's recipient had played the role of Shepherdess Flora in Anne's play—he described the governess as "horridly affected." But even he couldn't deny that she was also "rather amusing."

Although Jane's seaside plan had succeeded, by the time the convoy of coaches made its way from Kent to Worthing, the group's initial enthusiasm had begun to wane. Near the abbey at Battle, their intended stopping-off point, they were unable to find accommodation to house the entire traveling party, which included Fanny, her parents and grandmother, her two aunts and governess, and also the Austens' childhood friend Martha Lloyd. She was a cheery woman, ten years Jane's senior, and the pair had long enjoyed conversing late into the night. They were forced to ride on to Horsebridge, a further fifteen miles across the South Downs. Fortunately, here they secured rooms before darkness descended. And it turned out that a good night's sleep was all they needed to revive their spirits for the final leg of the trip.

The knocks and bumps of the journey paled to insignificance at the first sight of the sea. They had made good time, and the September sun shone sufficiently bright to afford a pleasant afternoon in Brighton. Here they would have noticed the vast riding school and stables being constructed in Indian style around the pavilion where the Prince of Wales, later to become George IV, was reputed to indulge in hedonistic pursuits. Jane, in particular, found such extravagance distasteful. How could the prince justify constructing a pleasure palace when the Napoleonic Wars had inflated the price of bread to an all-time high and the British fleet under Admiral Lord Nelson was preparing for battle against the combined forces of France and Spain? Surely coastal towns should be investing in fortifications.

The weather held up, and after arriving in Worthing and settling into their rental property, the whole party took an evening walk on the sands. Summer may have been fading to autumn, but hope was abloom: at least temporarily, the household of intelligent women of which Jane had dreamed was about to come to pass.

Five days later, once her brother and sister-in-law had departed, there would be plenty of time for creative work: early mornings of writing, strolls with Anne, lamp-lit hours poring over books. In the meantime, the pair had much else to enjoy: dawn trips to the beach to purchase fish from the freshly caught haul; the invigorating shock of the waves when the bathing attendant lowered them by rope from a mobile hut into the sea; afternoons lounging in the town's warm salt baths; evenings at the raffle, where Jane won seventeen shillings—enough to buy as many four-pound loaves.

Soon enough, Jane, her mother, her sister, Martha, and Anne would be left in peace. It's tempting to imagine that, in these favorable circumstances, Jane put pen to paper once more. She may well have written up a clean copy of one of her early novellas, *Lady Susan,* a story about a scheming widow, since the clean manuscript is on paper watermarked with the date 1805. Such an exercise would have eased her back into her work. She could trick herself that she was simply transcribing, but no writer with Jane's stamina for revision could have resisted making changes as she went along. Anne too apparently put her time to good use because it wasn't long before she had in her possession a revised version of her play.

The two must have felt that these weeks of writing and creative companionship were nothing short of a coup. And yet the way that Jane had removed Anne from Godmersham bordered on the meddlesomeness of Emma, Jane's future heroine who attempts to "improve" the lot of a less fortunate friend. In real life, Jane was gambling with Anne's future security for her own short-term gain. While the two women were reveling in their freedom, Anne's employment at Godmersham had moved onto shaky ground.

While Anne was with Jane in Worthing, Fanny had invited her former governess, Dorothy Chapman, to leave the home of her married sister, where she now resided, to return to her old workplace for a while. Fanny's mother encouraged this scheme—a self-serving act of hospitality if ever there was one. While Fanny breakfasted with her parents over the coming weeks, and was permitted to sleep downstairs in the closet adjoining her mother's boudoir, Miss Chapman's presence meant that Anne's absence didn't cause much inconvenience. The master and mistress of the house could go out riding whenever they chose, leaving their daughter in the hands of her dear former governess. And what capable hands they were! Far from stealing solitary hours in the library or taking to her bed with recurring headaches, Miss Chapman roped Fanny and the younger children into gardening duties, showed them how to make pets of dormice, took them off to gather nuts from the estate's trees, and even managed to press her former charge to complete more needlework than ever before.

But Anne had not been entirely forgotten—at least not by Fanny, who spent her governess's six-week holiday stitching an elaborately embroidered neckerchief to present to her upon her return. It was the first of November by the time Anne went back to Godmersham, the crisp leaves of autumn dampening into mulch.

After the novelty of her time away with Jane, Anne returned to find that not much had changed. Lessons were still punctuated by visits from traveling salesmen, the writing of letters, and walks in the parkland—where they had to take good care, since Edward's regiment of volunteer soldiers continued to use the grounds as a firing range in preparation for an attack by France. But small alterations soon emerged: Fanny's garden looked far neater, and a dormouse now resided in a box in the schoolroom. Someone as astute as Anne might even have sensed the tension rising among Edward and his troop of soldiers, for word had it that a great sea battle would soon commence. If the navy failed to hold back the French ships, the people of Kent expected to feel the full force of a Gallic invasion—an assault that could come any day.

While great tensions were occurring on a national level, Anne's extended time away had apparently cured her of the pressures that had been afflicting her body. According to

Fanny's diary, her governess seemed to her "uncommonly well," and Anne assured the child that she thought herself "better for her stay at Worthing." The pair soon fell back into their routine of breakfasting together in the schoolroom—a far cry from the quiet mornings enjoyed by Jane, who rose before the rest of her household.

Within days of Anne's return, further news from the outside world made its way through the gates of Godmersham. The British had won a great victory, but Nelson had been fatally wounded. It had taken a fortnight for the outcome of the Battle of Trafalgar to reach the householders of Kent, who could sleep easy in the knowledge that, at least for now, the threat of a French invasion had passed.

But, as it turned out, Anne was to enjoy only three days free of worry. During this reprieve, Miss Crow—a professional "paintress," as Fanny would refer to her within the covers of her pocketbook—arrived at Godmersham to make portraits of the household. With the wintry light streaming in through the floor-to-ceiling windows, Miss Crow's eyes moved from Anne to the page and back to Anne, as she sketched the contours of the governess's face. Miss Crow's current task required her to study her subject intently, and she could afford to take her time, since she'd be staying at Godmersham for a few days.

Fanny and Anne ended up exchanging their finished portraits as keepsakes, but it seems these works have not survived. Neither has turned up in an auction catalog or a jumble sale. But just like the famous watercolor of Jane, Anne's likeness reportedly conveyed little sense of her true appearance. "We are all quite *sick* of Miss Crow's pictures," Fanny complained. "They are no more like than, *the man in the moon*; mine was the most like but that Miss Sharpe has got. I have hers which might

as well be called mine, for Miss S. has not such a very *silly* countenance as Miss C. has chosen to give her, neither such *sleepy
eyes,* such a *mumped up* mouth, in short they are all detestable,
& fit for nothing but to be *thrown in the fire."*

But Miss Crow's watchful gaze may have spotted something in the governess's face that her employers and pupil had
missed. One of Anne's headaches was brewing, perhaps drawing the light from her eyes and causing tension around her
mouth. Over the following days, her migraine reached its peak,
with pain far worse than any she had known before. On the
day of the visiting painter's departure, a specialist doctor, Mr.
Lascelles, had to be called to Godmersham, and he advised the
governess to take measures so drastic it would require his presence in the house for the next seven days.

It was mid-November 1805, and the fires roaring in the
grates at Godmersham could not quite mask the chill in the air.
Fanny had been removed from the bedroom she shared with
her governess, returning temporarily to her mother's downstairs closet. The twelve-year-old had been told the undiluted
truth about the operation that the doctor had recommended
for her governess: a suture to the nape of the neck. But it isn't
known whether word of the ordeal had reached Trim Street
in Bath, where, insufficiently supported by Edward, the Austen
women were making do in dark quarters in an especially noisy
and polluted part of town.

In Anne's room at Godmersham, the doctor ground ingredients such as extract of Spanish fly and mustard seeds, before stirring the powder with plaster until it became a smooth
paste. Once the ointment was to Mr. Lascelles's liking, he spread
it on Anne's exposed nape, her hair pinned out of the way.
Once applied, the lotion would have swiftly caused a burning

sensation, causing a blister to form. Mr. Lascelles then used a needle to pierce it, and tightly closed the sore with a suture known as a seton stitch — a constriction intended to release pressure elsewhere.

During the days that followed, the mistress of the house ate breakfast with her children and stepped in for the governess by hearing Fanny's lessons. The high spirits occasioned by the baby's first steps, so soon before her first birthday, must have been tempered by the knowledge that Anne writhed in agony upstairs. She had to keep the seton stitch in her neck for as long as she could endure it. But, as Fanny wrote to Miss Chapman a week after the operation, the stitch was giving Anne such "exquisite torture" that it seemed unlikely she could bear to keep it in for many days more.

As time dragged on, Anne continued to be dogged by pain. But at the end of the doctor's planned week of treatment, she emerged from her room to take dinner downstairs for the first time since the beginning of the attack. Within two days, she was expected to resume her full duties, sharing her bed with Fanny once more. Edward and Elizabeth even left their eldest daughter with Anne while they went off for a week's stay with relations in another part of Kent. Throughout all this, she stoically kept the seton stitch in her blistered nape, insisting, as she told Fanny, "her eyes much benefitted by it."

Throughout December's cycle of snow and melt, Anne recovered sufficiently to rehearse a series of plays and monologues with the children. In between carol singing, treats of Spanish licorice, and games of snapdragon, duck apple, and blindman's buff, she prepared the Austen children for a festive performance. The theatricals stood out to Fanny as the highlight of 1805. She mentioned them in a letter, and a jotting in her diary on December 20 referred to her participation in "a delightful play & several pieces." Claiming that "they were too long to be detailed here," she revealed that she had "given the account of them as a piece of paper to be found in the pocket of this book."

Although the diaries themselves have been carefully cataloged, this paper is absent from any library records because archivists assumed it had been lost. But in fact, hidden within Fanny's tiny calfskin books, we discovered cardboard pouches as brittle as late-autumn leaves. The glue that had originally attached them to the inside covers has lost its grip, but one fragile pocket of Fanny's 1805 diary still contains her detailed account of Anne's theatricals—just as it has for well over two hundred years.

According to the child's report, the production went off with aplomb. At six o'clock in the evening, seven-year-old William rounded up the family servants, and then positioned himself at the door, passing out programs to those who entered and crying out their contents for all to hear. The children acted in a play titled "Alfred," which they'd found within the marbled covers of the schoolroom's copy of *Evenings at Home*—a compendium "consisting of a variety of miscellaneous pieces for the instruction and amusement of young persons." This patriotic drama about Alfred the Great's successful defense of his kingdom against the Viking invasion was timely indeed, given Britain's recent victory at Trafalgar. They then performed a scene from *Douglas,* a popular blank-verse tragedy, which, years later, Jane would archly cite in *Mansfield Park* as an appropriate play for household performance. The entertainments culminated in recitations from poetry annuals, and then Elizabeth treated the children to sips of tea and games of lottery. Fanny went to bed happy, believing that the "pieces were performed *uncommonly well* as we were afterwards told."

In the aftermath of the evening's success, Anne grew more ambitious for the children's theatricals. By the twelfth night of Christmas, Fanny was once more penning letters about yet another evening of entertainments, and again, she wrote up a detailed account and tucked it into her still-pristine copy of the Daily Lady's Companion, recently purchased for her record of 1806. And yet again, the document has survived.

Anne—whom Fanny now referred to interchangeably as "Miss Sharpe" and "Anny"—created great anticipation for the performance on January 4, 1806. Keep it a secret, she told the children, from everyone other than your parents. She stage-managed the whole affair, as well as embroidering the costumes. Elizabeth and her sisters agreed to play the musical accompaniment, and Anne rustled up an audience of servants and guests. The spectators who congregated in the breakfast parlor found the actors positioned in front of a curtain. The nursemaid and cook, footman and lady's maid were subjected to repeats of the pre-Christmas recitations, but toward the end of the evening, the children went on to act out a redrafted version of the drama they had staged with Jane and Cassandra the previous summer. By now Anne had revised this play of hers, not least by changing its name from *Virtue Rewarded* to *Pride Punished or Innocence Rewarded*—a title later echoed by that of Jane's most famous novel, *Pride and Prejudice*, which at this time was still called *First Impressions*.

According to Fanny, the evening was a great success. No doubt encouraged, Anne owned up to being its author—a mistake, perhaps, given what happened next.

Before the week was out, Anne's employment at Godmersham had come to an end. Fanny was distraught. As she wrote in a letter to her former governess, Miss Chapman, "I *as-*

sure you I regard it as much more than a *disagreeable ceremony,* for I hardly know how I shall bear it, she has been so long with us, & uncommonly kind to me!"

Despite the admirable way Anne had coped after her excruciating operation, the Kentish Austens cited ill health as the official reason for the cessation of her employment. Whatever the truth, she would urgently need to find new work, since the ongoing war had inflated the costs of both food and rent.

This time, Jane could not come to Anne's rescue with another attempt to relocate her to Bath. By now, the Austen women's hold on the city was diminishing. Their cramped rooms in Trim Street—an area they'd categorically ruled out of their house search just five years earlier—could not even accommodate their family friend Martha. So much for Jane's dream of an intelligent circle of single women.

And so in 1806 Jane was living an ignominious existence, still unpublished, her one writer friend sundered from her. Although she lacked worldly success, Jane could at least enjoy the support of her sister and mother. Their keenness to offer opinions on her work and their willingness to relieve her of all but the most undemanding of household tasks allowed her to keep writing the novels that would finally make her name.

Unlike Jane, Anne received no such support for her artistic leanings, and the demands of earning her keep meant that writing could never play a central role in her life. While Jane, through her novels, still speaks loud and clear, Anne's voice as a writer has been forever stifled. It appears that her plays were never staged outside the schoolroom, and her scripts, diaries, and letters have never been discovered.

Surely filled with anxiety, Anne left Godmersham for the last time on January 18, 1806, just three days after her thirty-third birthday. Her departure took her away from the schoolroom and library where she'd enjoyed such animated times, along the avenue of limes that led through the deer park, and finally between the tall iron gates, which closed behind her, shutting her even farther away from Jane.

3

Closing Ranks

WITHIN TWO MONTHS of leaving Godmersham Park, Anne Sharp was working once more, this time employed by a Mrs. Raikes to teach her six-year-old daughter. But before the spring of 1806 was out, the governess would have to leave this job as well, required to work as the paid companion of her mistress's frail unmarried sister. Anne now moved in with this new employer, Miss Bailey, who lived in Hinckley — a bustling market town in the Midlands.

Reliant on the goodwill of her brothers, Jane likewise had little say over where she lived. The Austen sisters had recently relocated to Southampton — almost 150 miles from Hinckley — where they were now sharing the marital home of one of their sailor brothers. Frank removed them from Bath's squalid Trim Street, further emphasizing the neglect of their elder and far wealthier brother, Edward, who had failed to offer the women accommodation on any of his vast estates. The forces that had separated Jane and Anne could so easily have triumphed during this time. But the two amateur writers managed to sustain their friendship in the way they knew best: by putting pen to paper.

Almost three years into the correspondence that the pair

established following Anne's departure from Godmersham, Jane found herself forced to write a most unexpected letter. Anne's former mistress, Elizabeth Austen, had died suddenly on October 10, 1808, just three days after the safe delivery of her eleventh child. The poor eldest daughter, Fanny, at just fifteen years of age, now bore the responsibility of mothering the newborn and consoling her bereft father. Knowing that the girl's former governess would be well placed to offer comfort, Jane wrote to Anne with the sad news. She also exchanged a series of letters with Cassandra, who had been staying at Godmersham to help with the confinement, but she made a point of refusing to dwell for too long on the late Elizabeth's qualities or to write a "Panegyric on the Departed," as she put it. Beyond inquiring about the state of the corpse, Jane focused her thoughts less on her late sister-in-law and more on the recently bereaved children. Even if no love had been lost between Jane and Elizabeth, Jane indeed felt shocked by the suddenness of the death. By all accounts, the thirty-five-year-old had recovered well from the birth and had been tucking into a hearty meal just half an hour before her fatal collapse.

Fanny's bad fortune likely was the cause of a surprising upturn in Jane's luck. Tellingly, less than a fortnight after his wife's death, Edward suddenly found it in himself to offer the Austen women lifelong residence in one of the many properties on his land. They chose the former bailiff's cottage at Chawton, an opportunity to return to their Hampshire roots. The house was also big enough to accommodate Jane and Cassandra's childhood friend Martha Lloyd.

Renovations were completed by the summer of 1809, and the women wasted no time in making the move. Here, Mrs. Austen enjoyed watering the shrubbery of sweet williams and columbines, picking apricots in the orchard, and even donning a laborer's green outfit to dig up potatoes from the kitchen garden. Now approaching seventy, she let the younger generation take over most of the domestic management. In an extraordinary act of generosity and faith in Jane's writing, her sister, Cassandra, and their friend, Martha, exempted the aspiring author from the more onerous household chores. Jane did take responsibility for the tea caddy, however, which she kept under lock and key, eking out the leaves and sugar—expensive commodities during those long years of war. She continued to rise early, practicing the piano before spearing slices of bread with a fork, then holding them close to the glowing embers until the smell of toast drew the others downstairs. But for the most part, Jane was free to work at her tiny walnut table, poring over the manuscript of *Sense and Sensibility*—the novel about a neglectful brother and sister-in-law that she had begun almost fifteen years earlier. Absorbed in her revising, she could be wrenched from her fictional world only by the creak of the parlor door.

In such conducive conditions, Jane began to enjoy a time of creative industry comparable to the period of intense composition prior to her move to Bath. But Anne continued to endure a litany of troubles. She confided in Jane about her strained relations with her mistress, whose physical impairments required the ministrations of a full-time companion. It couldn't have helped that, while attending to Miss Bailey, Anne's own symptoms had flared up once more. The seton stitch in the nape of her neck failed to achieve any lasting improvement to her headaches and eyestrain, so Anne had resorted to a new-fangled treatment. Her hair shorn and electrodes attached to her skull, she underwent an early form of electrotherapy. As Fanny would report, Anne's "eyes have been worse than ever, & she had all her hair cut off, & continual blisters on her head all to no purpose."

Knowing that the deterioration in Anne's health made writing difficult and that the shift from governess to companion robbed her of a ready-made cast and audience for her plays, Jane must have braced herself to share her own good news. With the help of her favorite brother, Henry, a military man turned banker, she had secured her first publishing deal. After fifteen years of intermittent work on *Sense and Sensibility,* such news, which she received as 1810 drew to a close, was cause indeed for celebration. But Jane's achievement represented only a modest success. As its name would suggest, the Military Library, Whitehall, specialized in books about warfare. Such a publisher was hardly the ideal choice for a love story exploring the injustice of primogeniture. To make matters worse, Jane had to agree to a contract that forced her to take all the financial risk yet granted the publisher a share of any profits, and so she was faced with the daunting prospect of taking a loss as well as the delightful anticipation of possible success. From Henry's London home, Jane wrote to Cassandra of *Sense and Sensibility,* "I can no more forget it, than a mother can forget her sucking child."

While Jane was apprehensively awaiting the book's publication, now back in Hampshire, she pulled out another early manuscript, the novel she would rename *Pride and Prejudice.* Among all this literary endeavor, she yearned to converse in person once again with her long-distance friend. And so, when a set of prospective houseguests canceled their visit to Chawton Cottage at the end of May 1811, Jane spotted the opportunity to welcome Anne for an extended stay. First she had to convince the rest of the household to agree to this "magnificent project," as she referred to it in her letter to her sister. Brimming with excitement, she set out the logistical reasons for extending the invitation: Anne had already scheduled holiday leave for right around this time; they could host her at Chawton for a lengthy duration before the arrival of the next party of guests; she could share transportation with Cassandra and Martha, their own comings and goings set to coincide with the former governess's prospective travel plans. Time was of the essence, so Jane contacted both her sister and their childhood friend, telling them to "write by return of post if you have any reason for not wishing it done." To be on the safe side, in a postscript, she added, "I shall consider Silence as Consent."

But neither woman held her tongue, each raising objections to the proposal. Jane's frustration simmered beneath the politeness of her reply: "I have given up all idea of Miss Sharpe's travelling with you & Martha, for tho' you are both all compliance with my scheme, yet as *you* knock off a week from the end of her visit, & *Martha* rather more from the beginning, the thing is out of the question."

Cassandra and Martha would have had grounds to feel aggrieved by the strength of Jane's admiration for her fellow writer. After all, through their efficient household management, they did more than anyone else to facilitate Jane's creative work. But the soon-to-be-published novelist, never one to give up without a fight, would win them round before long. A throwaway line in the pocketbook of Mary Lloyd—the sister of Martha and the wife of Jane's eldest brother, James—reveals that Anne came to stay in August of 1811.

Every day, Collyer's public stagecoach, drawn by six horses, passed so close to Chawton Cottage that it caused the windows to rattle, the spectacle offering Mrs. Austen a never-ending source of entertainment and the travelers a glimpse of the women's parlor. It was here that Anne descended from the carriage to the Austens' new home, in its idyllic setting: a reed pond opposite, Edward's Great House towering over the village in the distance, roofs of thatch all around. How glorious the cottage's interior must have seemed to Anne: a pianoforte in the large sitting room, books from the local circulating library, the tiny twelve-sided walnut table at which her friend wrote beside the parlor's fire.

While Jane looked forward to finally seeing her name in print, Anne also had some good news of her own. She had secured a new position as governess to the four daughters of the recently widowed Lady Pilkington, and would be relocating to Chevet Hall, a Yorkshire estate of even higher status than Godmersham. It was perhaps no coincidence that Jane's fellow inhabitants of Chawton Cottage welcomed Anne just when she was about to take up employment at the home of an aristocrat. Whatever the reason, this acceptance of the amateur playwright allowed Jane to enjoy her last months as an unpublished author alongside all four of the women who'd most supported her work.

When *Sense and Sensibility* came out in October 1811 it was to little fanfare. Jane Austen herself only stumbled across an advertisement for the work a month after it had been published. Still, she was thrilled to see the title of her book listed side by side with that of one of her favorite authors, Maria Edgeworth, whose novels explored then-taboo issues such as interracial relationships, women's rights, and same-sex desire. Jane's own name did not feature in the announcement or on the cover of her book. She had opted to publish anonymously, her writing authored "By a Lady." Although the book had not been entirely ignored, reviewers expressed only rather subdued praise. Not until February 1812 did an article appear in the *Crit-*

ical Review, which concluded that "the characters are in genteel life, naturally drawn, and judiciously supported." By this time, however, the novel was beginning to be passed around among members of the upper classes, and although the print run had been small—likely a thousand or so copies—it eventually sold out. Jane made a profit of 140 pounds, and through Henry, secured an advance of 110 pounds for the publication of *Pride and Prejudice*—albeit still with the same small military press.

Enjoying the unaccustomed feeling of her own earnings in her purse, in May 1813, a few months after the publication of *Pride and Prejudice,* the thirty-seven-year-old author indulged in a trip to London—the like of which Anne could only dream. En route, she treated herself to a new pair of gloves, picking them up at a bargain price. And once she arrived in the nation's capital, she dashed from linen-drapers to jewelers on errands for her relatives: fine silk sarsenet for the lining of her mother's gown; a hard-wearing striped dimity cotton for the motherless Fanny; a plain gold locket for her sister at a higher cost than either of them had expected.

When Jane did manage to steal some time for herself, she headed to an art exhibition at Somerset House, indulging in an unusual literary quest. Speeding along the Strand in Henry's barouche, its top concertinaed open, she felt on the verge of laughter, amused to find herself riding in a low-slung carriage on this personal victory parade about town.

She'd decided to entertain herself by searching the great galleries of London for a portrait that might resemble Elizabeth Bennet of *Pride and Prejudice*. Although Jane had scoured the watercolors and oils on display in both Spring Gardens and at the British Institution in Pall Mall, she'd failed to find an image that might resemble her heroine, whom the author herself remarked was "as delightful a creature as ever appeared in print."

She *did* have every right to feel proud of herself. Some critics had compared the anonymous author to William Shakespeare, and such compliments must have been fresh in Jane's mind as she rushed about town. The *Critical Review* had proclaimed her book "very superior to any novel we have lately met with," and the famed dramatist Richard Sheridan urged a friend to purchase a copy immediately, describing it as "one of the cleverest things" he had ever read. Jane must have felt buoyed up by the enthusiasm for a novel that had been turned down out of hand sixteen years earlier and, even now, had been brought out by a little-known press. She was determined to look on the bright side, squeezing every bit of pleasure from her modest triumph.

When Jane stepped from the barouche onto the vast courtyard of the newly built Somerset House, its Grecian-style columns towering above her, she had still to come across a portrait of anyone who bore much resemblance to Elizabeth Bennet. In the first gallery she'd visited that day, she had come across a small painting that looked just like the image in her mind's eye of her heroine's elder sister. That evening, in a letter to her own sister, Jane would marvel that in "size, shaped face, features & sweetness; there never was a greater likeness." The young woman in the picture, she explained, was dressed "in a white gown with green ornaments, which convinces me of what I had always supposed, that green was a favourite colour with her." Since these fictional characters had inhabited Jane's mind for over seventeen years, it was hardly surprising that they had taken on such a life of their own.

It was perhaps as she paused at one of the decorated landings of the staircase that wound up to the Royal Academy Exhibition Room that she resolved to search for a painting of a woman in yellow. Unlike the green clothing suited to the demure eldest Miss Bennet, her creator felt that her Elizabeth would be drawn to something buttercup-bright. Walking beneath the ornate painted ceiling, Jane's eyes flitted from one portrait to the next—so many canvases packed on the walls. Her search was, once more, in vain. Although disappointed, she consoled herself with the notion that "Mr. D. prizes any Picture of her too much to like it should be exposed to the public eye." Yes, that would be his feeling, she later wrote to Cassandra, "that mixture of Love, Pride & Delicacy."

Although she published anonymously, Jane reveled in the opportunity to share her children—as she continued to think of her novels—with doting friends and strangers alike. Anne was in on the secret, of course, and she felt delighted to see Jane's words in print. Their affection burned as strong as ever, with no hint of envy from the unpublished writer, who was still toiling in the schoolroom. She, of course, did not have a land-owning brother to provide a roof over her head or female relatives to help her carve out time to write. And yet she rejoiced in Jane's achievements. The letter Anne sent to Jane in November 1813, following the publication of *Pride and Prejudice,* caused the novelist to swell with pride: "—Oh! I have more of such sweet flattery from Miss Sharpe!—She is an excellent kind friend."

Ever one for a scheme, Jane dreamed that Anne might receive a proposal of marriage from Sir William Pilkington, her employer's wealthy brother-in-law. "Oh! Sir Wm," Jane joked in a letter to Cassandra, "how I will love you, if you will love Miss Sharp!" Such were the lack of opportunities for a woman like Anne to improve her lot that her friend had to resort to these kinds of lighthearted matchmaking fantasies.

But by 1813 Jane's own dreams were coming true. She'd begun to feel more confident about her status as a novelist. By now, most of Chawton knew that the creator of *Sense and*

Sensibility and *Pride and Prejudice* lived among them—a fact that she treated with characteristic levity. Before Cassandra returned from a trip to Kent, her sister felt obliged to warn her that the secret had gotten out. "I know your starched Notions," Jane teased, "but you must be prepared for the Neighbourhood being perhaps already informed of there being such a Work in the World, & in the Chawton World!" This disclosure offered some amusements, such as a letter from Fanny, which mischievously addressed her aunt as if she were Mr. Darcy's sister. And Jane rather enjoyed the fact that her identity was also beginning to reach readers far and wide: the daughter of a wealthy gentleman known for his radical politics, the wife of an Irish judge, an elderly lady whom the novelist imagined as clever and good.

After some positive responses to *Sense and Sensibility* and great interest in *Pride and Prejudice*—both revisions of novels she'd begun in her youth—the thirty-seven-year-old nurtured high hopes for her third book. Bringing all her mature powers to bear on this work, which she'd begun to write at Chawton, she felt that *Mansfield Park* was her best yet. But when it came out in the spring of 1814, it did not receive a single review. Presumably finding the silence unbearable, Jane begged Anne to give her an honest assessment of the novel. The response, which the novelist later jotted down, is as close as history comes to recording Anne's voice. She praised "its good sense & moral Tendency" as well as singling out the "natural & just" characterization. But the pair's bond was strong enough to cope with criticism too. "As you beg me to be perfectly honest," Anne ventured, "I confess I prefer P. & P." Rather than offer the kind of bounteous praise she'd served up on *Pride and Prejudice,* Anne now assessed the weaknesses as well as the strengths of her friend's work, and Jane valued this support. After all, despite Jane's modicum of fame, Anne remained her only writer friend.

Such a collaboration—unlike those of the male Lake Poets, for instance—could go on only behind closed doors. At least Anne was now welcome at Chawton Cottage, where she may have had this conversation with Jane about *Mansfield Park* during a visit in June 1815. While she was staying with the Austen women, official intelligence traveled from the far-off battlefields at Waterloo to the woodlands and footpaths of Hampshire: the Duke of Wellington's forces had triumphed. At last, twenty-two years after war was waged with France, these women could look forward to the simple pleasures and privileges of peace: an end to the ever-increasing price of food, a release from the constant threat of invasion, a relaxing of the tendency in society and government to regard any criticism of the status quo as sedition.

Amid the celebrations, Jane was charting her own plan of attack, which she would implement soon after her friend bade her farewell. In an attempt to revitalize her literary career, Jane turned once more to Henry. This same brother would later feel obliged to memorialize his sister as an unassuming lady scribbler concerned with neither "fame nor profit." But in fact, he helped her to carry out a plan to achieve both recognition and remuneration. As the summer of 1815 seeped into autumn, Henry agreed to send out his sister's fourth novel, *Emma*. This time, they submitted it to John Murray, one of the most influential publishers of the day, renowned for bringing out work by writers as celebrated as Lord Byron and Sir Walter Scott. The siblings' audacity paid off, for the publisher got back to them swiftly, proposing to purchase not only Jane's new novel,

Emma, but also the copyrights for *Mansfield Park* and *Sense and Sensibility*—which, unlike rights for *Pride and Prejudice,* she had not ceded to the military press.

Jane did have some bargaining power by now, since her novels had begun to draw the attention of London's high society. And so it came to pass that—just weeks after these successful negotiations—she found herself back on Pall Mall, that street along which she'd ridden in her brother's barouche two years earlier. It was November 13, 1815, and she was now stepping inside the Prince Regent's royal residence, no less.

Here was a relationship that her successors would be happy to explore. Jane's correspondence with the prince's librarian, James Stanier Clarke, has been passed down the generations, as has his *Friendship Book,* an album in which he painted watercolors of his acquaintances, including one portrait that some claim depicts Jane Austen. Along with extant presentation copies of *Emma,* this image of a strikingly fashionable woman, her black hat festooned with flowers and feathers, is among the artifacts that shed light on Jane's visit to Carlton House and its aftermath.

On arrival at the royal residence, this cottage-dwelling daughter of a country clergyman did not convey any sense of awe. The invitation by royal command to roam these decadent chambers of Carlton House—plush Persian carpets underfoot and crystal chandeliers overhead—had, in fact, caused her great anguish. She could not abide the Prince Regent, who had failed to steer the country with care during his father's bout of insanity. It was ten years now since Jane and Anne had seen the prince's pleasure palace being constructed when they stopped in Brighton en route to their seaside holiday. There, as here, the future George IV had indulged his love of ornate furnishings, decorating cornices and pillars with gilt and displaying his vast collections of lacquered chinoiserie. Not only was he profligate with the nation's dwindling wealth, he was careless in his marital affairs too—something about which Jane was privately livid. In a letter to Martha, she had taken the side of his estranged wife, "because she *is* a woman, & because I hate her Husband." But Jane could not risk spurning this man she so despised, and, thus summoned, she was left with little choice but to accept his sumptuous hospitality and hold her sharp tongue.

Jane must have been relieved to discover that the librarian, in lieu of the prince, would show her around. And so, here she was, in a scarlet-curtained anteroom, greeting this rather obsequious courtier. The prince, the librarian told her, had left instructions for him to pass on his admiration for all her novels, sets of which he kept in each of his residences. The librarian was also himself a particular fan. "Your late Works, Madam, and in particular Mansfield Park reflect the highest honour on your Genius and your Principles," he would insist by letter a few days later; "in every new work your mind seems to increase in energy and powers of discrimination."

If the portrait in the courtier's Friendship Book is anything to go by, Jane's white gauze gown would have whispered down the elegant double staircase as he escorted her in the direction of the library. She may not have been feeling particularly comfortable in her unaccustomed finery, but she would enter home territory on setting foot among the bookshelves.

Here, with the landscaped gardens visible through the French doors, St. James's Park and the towers of Westminster Abbey beyond, the librarian had an important piece of information to impart. He told Jane that she should feel at liberty to dedicate any future work to the prince. There would be no necessity to seek His Royal Highness's approval.

This proposal nagged at Jane over the coming days. She wrote to ask the librarian whether it was "incumbent" upon her to inscribe her new novel to the prince. His reassurance that "it is certainly not *incumbent* on you" did little to persuade Jane that she was off the hook, especially since he went on to add that "if you wish to do the Regent that honour, either now or at any future period, I am happy to send you that permission which need not require any more trouble or solicitation on your Part."

Anyone would be reluctant to risk making an enemy of the prince. However much she detested his way of life, Jane was also shrewd enough to understand that such a dedication could give her leverage with her publisher and printer, thereby increasing her public acclaim. So, with mixed feelings, she acquiesced, contacting her editor to request the simplest of inscriptions on the title page: "Dedicated by Permission to H.R.H. The Prince Regent." John Murray informed her that protocol required something rather more elaborate, insisting on devoting an entire page to the dedication and including the assurance that the author was His Royal Highness's "most dutiful and obedient humble servant." To add insult to injury, Jane was required to purchase from her own pocket a bound presentation copy of *Emma* to furnish the prince's main library at Carlton House. At great personal expense, she had the three volumes of her novel bound in red morocco, the goatskin decorated with gilding and embossed with the regent's hallmark badge of feathers.

At least Jane could divert herself with the more pleasurable task of devising a list of recipients to whom she genuinely desired to send the remaining eleven presentation copies. These gifts, though delivered with real affection, she could not afford to bind. She set aside most of them for family members, but kept two of her dozen copies for fellow female writers. Yet her reasons for wishing to share her work with each of these women couldn't have been more different.

An endorsement from the bestselling writer Maria Edgeworth could have propelled Jane to much greater literary acclaim and financial success. "The authoress of Pride and Prejudice has been so good as to send me a new novel just published, *Emma,*" wrote Edgeworth in January 1816. But she did not feel at all inclined to extend the hand of friendship, failing even to acknowledge receipt of the gift. She did find time, however, to complain to a friend that she found *Emma* unbearably dull. Two years later, she would outline to her aunt what she considered the failings of the finally published *Northanger Abbey,* making no comment on the fact that it contained an extremely complimentary reference to Edgeworth's own most controversial book. *Belinda,* the narrator of Jane's novel insists, is written in "best-chosen language" and conveys "the greatest powers of the mind" and "the liveliest effusions of wit and humour." The failure of Jane's attempts to woo the celebrated author might be explained away by unfortunate timing, or perhaps Edgeworth was guarding her space at the top. For although she did not care for *Northanger Abbey,* in that same letter of 1818 to her aunt, she admitted to a deep admiration for Jane's final completed novel *Persuasion.* In contrast to Jane, though, she would never publicly praise her literary peer.

Unlike the presentation copy sent to Edgeworth, the one Jane set aside for Anne would be given without any self-serving designs. The governess and amateur playwright, whom she'd favored over her brother Edward when choosing her twelve recipients, clearly couldn't help her to achieve the fame and fortune she so desired. Here was a gesture that spoke simply of Jane's gratitude for Anne's consolation during those long years when she too had been unpublished, as well as the celebrations they'd since enjoyed.

Appreciating the value of this gift, Anne must have scrimped and saved to pay for the binding of the three-volume novel, using economical marbled card to protect the covers, with just enough calfskin for the spines and corners. And yet her gratitude did not make her obsequious. Far from it. Of *Emma,* Anne admitted to Jane that she liked it "better than M.P. —but not so well as P. & P." Jane jotted down her friend's responses to some of the characters, which the author recorded as "pleased with the Heroine for her Originality, delighted with Mr. K—& called Mrs. Elton beyond praise." Yet Anne had to concede that she was not convinced by the portrait of Jane Fairfax, who dreads the future mapped out for her as a governess. It's a telling criticism, since Anne was so well placed to judge. In *Emma,* the inhabitants of the village feel aghast that one of the most elegant and accomplished among them should be destined to labor in the schoolroom, the shackles of the governess's "human intellect" being likened almost to the sale of "human flesh." While such comparisons demonstrate Jane's sympathy for the likes of Anne, they also underscore the vast gulf between them.

In September 1816, only nine months after Anne received her precious presentation copy, Jane unexpectedly allowed her tongue to turn against her longstanding friend. Gossiping in a letter to her sister, who was taking the waters in Cheltenham, Jane complained about Anne's having sent "quite one of her Letters." The governess had been plagued once more by ill health, but her account of her treatment had irked Jane, who wrote off such complaints as hypochondria. She sarcastically summarized the governess's suffering to Cassandra: "she has been again obliged to exert herself more than ever—in a more distressing, more harassed state—& has met with another excellent old Physician & his wife with every virtue under Heaven, who takes to her & cures her from pure Love and Benevolence."

Forty-year-old Jane was suffering herself—in her case, from backache—but she was taking an approach very different from Anne's. While the governess put her faith in physicians, Jane was attempting to regulate her own health, assuring Cassandra that she was "nursing myself up now into as beautiful a state as I can" and insisting that "my Back has given me scarcely any pain for many days." But in reality, Jane's self-administered regimen of moonlit walks and curative doses of rhubarb was failing to have the desired effect.

As the autumn of 1816 progressed, the lilacs in the garden at Chawton hanging on their spent flower heads, Jane continued to be tormented by ill health. In addition to the backache, she was experiencing nausea, diarrhea, muscle weakness, and fatigue. Her illness worsening, she began to reassess her recent attitude toward Anne: fellow spinster, fellow sufferer, and most of all, fellow writer, whose astute literary opinions she'd so often sought.

By May 22, 1817, Jane had been bedridden for at least a month, and Anne was still very much on her mind. Pleased to have regained sufficient strength to prop herself up with bolster pillows, she resolved to write a letter to the friend she had come to take for granted. Candor had formed such a central part of their relationship that, sharpened quill in hand, she was left with a conundrum: how honest should she be about the state of her health? Curled up behind the bed's floor-length curtains, she put nib to paper to address Miss Sharp as "my dearest Anne," admitting to the severity of the recent "attack of my sad complaint," but thanking the Almighty that "My head was always clear, & I had scarcely any pain; my cheif sufferings were from feverish nights, weakness & Languor." Jane reassured her friend that her health was improving, yet at the same time, she was clearly writing a prolonged adieu.

This would prove to be the last letter Jane ever sent from Chawton Cottage. Within two days, she would travel in her sister-in-law's carriage to the cathedral town of Winchester, each jolt on the fifteen-mile journey surely causing her much discomfort. Here, under the specialist care of a local apothecary and surgeon, Jane would see out her final twenty-five days.

Notified of the death of her dear friend, Anne asked Cassandra to send her a lock of Jane's hair. Just four days after the funeral, the beloved sister took the time to fulfill Anne's wish, adding a pair of Jane's belt clasps to the package, along with her silver needle. Although these humble mementos speak of the tenderness shared between women of modest means, Cassandra's accompanying note has a barbed quality. On her deathbed Jane turned to Anne, but her sister by birth continued to distrust the friend who had been singled out. Jane had loved and been loved by both these intelligent women, who in their different ways had supported her literary endeavors, but Cassandra couldn't help but assert her greater claim to intimacy. "What I have lost," she reminded the governess, "no one but myself can know." She did bring herself to acknowledge that Anne too was "not ignorant of her merits" but asserted that no one else could possibly "judge how I estimated them." Worse still, she insisted that "I am much more tranquil than with your ardent feelings you could suppose possible."

If only Anne's letter to Cassandra had also survived, we could measure for ourselves the friend's "ardent feelings" against the sister's "starched Notions," as Jane had once referred to Cassandra's sense of propriety.

Cassandra's words were freighted with conflicting emotions: her desire to honor her sister's highly valued relationship competing with a touch of snobbery and envy. She felt compelled to offer to see the woman Jane so loved: "If any thing should ever bring you into attainable distance from me we must meet my dear Miss Sharp." But she did not go out of her way to visit the friend her sister called "my dearest Anne," nor did she offer any specific hospitality.

How surprising, then, to discover that Anne returned to Chawton Cottage for several weeks, three years later, in 1820, and that she and Cassandra remained connected for many decades to come. In 1843, twenty-six years after Jane's death, at about the same time that a seventy-year-old Cassandra destroyed most of her late sister's letters, she also left thirty pounds in her will to the elderly Anne. How did the pair move from competition to compassion? What took them from a half-hearted offer to meet to staying under the same roof? How did their relationship develop and change during this time? These tantalizing questions remain in part because the lives of working women were seen as unworthy of record and because Jane's family actively whitewashed this friendship from accounts of her life.

Anne too must take some of the blame. By 1823, perhaps through assistance from her former employer Lady Pilkington, she had come into sufficient funds to give up her post as a governess and establish her own boarding school on York Terrace —a prosperous street, perched wind-whistlingly high above the city of Liverpool, with views across the River Mersey to Birkenhead beyond. According to the 1841 census, Anne at this point employed three teachers and as many family servants, and eleven girls attended the school. Over the years, she would come to be considered one of the area's wisest and most formidable inhabitants. As Mrs. Creaghe-Howard of Ottery St. Mary wrote of Miss Sharp in *The Times,* following the publication of Jane's deathbed letter to Anne: "She was very reticent about her early life before coming to Liverpool, and also made a mystery of her age."

Such reluctance to share the experiences of her days as a governess must have contributed to the secrecy that built up around her literary friendship with Jane. But as Anne accumulated far greater wealth and worldly chattels than her novelist friend could ever have dreamed, she continued to cherish private memories of Jane—which she passed down, albeit obliquely, by arranging for her presentation copy of *Emma* and Jane's deathbed letter to be left to two of her most reliable friends. Over two centuries, these treasured items would be bequeathed from one pair of hands to the next, reaching today's generation intact, allowing these long-silenced tales finally to be deciphered.

CHARLOTTE BRONTË
&
MARY TAYLOR

No one understood them as they understood each other

MARY TAYLOR, *MISS MILES*

4

Three's a Crowd

THE ROUTE FROM HAWORTH to Mirfield is about twenty miles, a daunting day's slog for an anxious fourteen-year-old in a horse-drawn carrier cart. One chill morning in January 1831, the young Charlotte Brontë set off from her father's parsonage, bound for Roe Head School. She was leaving behind a small Yorkshire mill town on the edge of the moors—a cluster of soot-blackened buildings around a steep central street, its tilted gutters flowing with waste from the shops and the nearest outdoor privies.

Once away from these unsanitary yet comfortingly familiar surroundings, the girl's extreme short-sightedness intensified her inevitable bewilderment. The rugged hills that gradually gave way to green valleys and woods all passed by as a blur. The wagon's cover could protect Charlotte from rain and the worst of the wind, but not the jolt of the wheels over the rough ground. For a frail girl suffering from nerves and cold, each bump along the country lanes must have added to her discomfort.

This wouldn't be her first experience of formal education. Six years earlier, she'd spent some ten months at the Clergy Daughters' School at Cowan Bridge—the future model of the nightmarish Lowood Institution in her most famous book, *Jane Eyre*. Charlotte would always remain haunted by the harsh conditions she'd endured: the school's overbearing discipline, its dirty kitchen and the careless cook's disgusting food, the feverish agonies of sickly fellow boarders. Her own older sisters, Maria and Elizabeth, had both died of pulmonary tuberculosis after a serious outbreak of illness at the school. Having brought each girl back to Haworth to die, their grieving father then rushed to collect Charlotte and little Emily before the consumptive disease could lodge itself inside them too.

After such trauma, it might seem strange that the Reverend Patrick Brontë would put his eldest surviving daughter through another potentially similar ordeal. But as a widower in his fifties, he could no longer avoid the fact that, upon his death, his parsonage would fall into the hands of another clergyman and his children might be left unsupported. It must have been some comfort to know that if she received the right sort of learning, Charlotte would be able to earn her own living —although in the early nineteenth century, as in Anne Sharp's day, job prospects for impoverished young women of their class remained few and far between. Charlotte's best hope, of course, was to "marry up," and becoming more "accomplished" might support that possibility. Failing that, the training she'd receive at a school like Roe Head would at least equip her to find work as a schoolmistress, still one of the few respectable careers open to women.

As she approached her destination, the cart trundled over Roe Head's curving drive, then came to a stop at last. Warily stepping from the cart, squinting at the gray stone house set back from rolling green lawns, a frozen Charlotte would have just made out the school's arched bow windows, but not the little crowd that must have assembled within, to witness her shuffling dismount. Neither could she know that among Roe Head's ten or so pupils was one with a forthright personality who would eventually challenge her entire way of looking at the world.

Mary Taylor, the future author of the feminist novel *Miss Miles,* was immediately intrigued by Charlotte. To Mary, the girl looked miserable, her clothing antiquated—a sharp contrast with the fashionable young ladies of the school.

At almost fourteen, and ten months younger than Charlotte, Mary was an attractive young woman with rosy cheeks—"too pretty to live," according to Margaret Wooler, Roe Head's well-liked headmistress. But like the newcomer, Mary and her boisterous sister, Martha, were far from stylish. The blue cloth coats they wore outdoors were too short for them, their black beaver bonnets only plainly trimmed. They even had to stitch over new pairs of gloves, to make them last longer. The state of their wardrobe reflected a much larger story. Britain's first major industrial slump had hit the Taylor family hard. The girls' father, once a prosperous woolen mill owner, had accumulated heavy debts. The other students assumed that the popular Taylor sisters cheerfully accepted the consequences of their reduced circumstances, so visibly apparent in their clothing. But Mary's inner feelings of humiliation apparently cut deeper than her schoolmates could guess. Still, rather than empathize with Charlotte, Mary scorned the girl's outdated dress and cowed demeanor. Why, she noted to herself, she looks like "a little old woman."

Later, in the airy schoolroom, Mary was quick to notice that Charlotte had changed into a different frock, this one just as old. The new girl's timidity and her wildly seeking, side-to-side glances were another source of amusement. From her chair, Mary observed Charlotte hunched over her desk, knowing that this would not do either for the middle-aged Miss Wooler, reminiscent of an abbess in her embroidered white gowns, or for the other Wooler sisters who helped at the school.

Sure enough, when Charlotte's posture was noticed, she was told to raise her head. She complied, but in order to keep reading, she raised the book in the air too. There it stayed, close to her nose, until the roomful of girls couldn't help but laugh. Charlotte's lilting voice, with what Mary took for an Irish inflection, also sounded strange to her classmates. Their amusement could only have compounded Charlotte's feeling of isolation.

It was all so different from the intense, creative atmosphere of Haworth Parsonage, where she and her remaining siblings—Branwell, Emily, and Anne—had flourished. Along with her brother and sisters, Charlotte had enjoyed a rigorous and free-ranging home curriculum guided by their intellectual father, while their practical aunt, who also lived with them, instructed the girls in household matters. In addition to these lessons, the children regularly produced poems and short stories for their own entertainment, including a series of manuscripts in minuscule writing, barely decipherable without the aid of a magnifying glass and thereby largely rendering them out of bounds to prying adults. Many of these works were set in the confederation of Glass Town, an imaginary world inspired first by the four's childhood games and later their precocious literary tastes. Charlotte had come away to school knowing that, in her absence, her siblings would continue their joint writings without her—that by the time she returned to Haworth, their collaborative fantasy landscapes might be utterly changed.

While the unfettered style of Charlotte's home schooling had made her well-versed in areas out of the range of Miss Wooler's lessons, it had left her largely ignorant in other vital subjects, such as geography or the theory of grammar. At playground games too she was considered inept, possessing a physical feebleness that an incredulous Mary put down to Charlotte's self-denying refusal to eat meat—an unusual stance for anyone of her time.

In those early days at the school, Charlotte felt compelled to put in many extra hours of private study, warned by Miss Wooler that unless she caught up with those of her own age, she would be forced to sit with the younger ones. Although the other students believed Charlotte to be very ignorant, Mary was beginning to understand that there might be more to the new girl than the oddness that first struck Mary. Charlotte's reserve couldn't hide her talents for long. Soon she would impress her classmates with her drawing ability and her much-envied skill at writing in italics, a technique honed for the Brontës' household magazines, which were made up of the children's stories and poems. Eventually, she would overcome her shyness, gaining the confidence to weave ghostly tales in the dormitory at night, holding her nightdress-clad audience in the throes of terror.

Charlotte's expectations were surely raised when, one day at the school, the attractive Mary approached her to talk. Even in her short time at Roe Head, Charlotte would have gleaned an understanding of Mary's keen intelligence. Now she may have dared to dream that her schoolmate had sensed similar qualities in her.

But while Mary would eventually warm to the new girl, those initial feelings of condescension hadn't yet disappeared. Any fanciful hopes on Charlotte's part were dashed when Mary pronounced, in her typically blunt manner, "You are very ugly."

With her pale, dry skin and untamed frizz of hair, Charlotte had never been considered conventionally beautiful, but having been brought up in a deeply religious home, she would have been encouraged not to dwell on such vanities. Nonetheless, Mary's words bruised Charlotte, leaving her forever aware of her unlovely looks, the gauntness of her frame. And though Mary would never cease to be outspoken, she would eventually regret this youthful cruelty.

Years later, when Mary eventually apologized, Charlotte's reply suppressed her pain. Describing this adult conversation to her friend's first biographer, Elizabeth Gaskell, Mary would recall that Charlotte told her not to repent of her words, that Mary had done her "a great deal of good."

Still, the insult was burned into Charlotte's consciousness. In 1843, twelve years after this crushing incident, Charlotte—who'd allowed a cousin of Mary to make a portrait of her—warned the young woman that the picture would not "yield pleasure to Mary Taylor":"do not give it to her, or if you do—do not expect thanks in return—she likes me well enough—but my face she can dispense with." Charlotte knew full well that Mary would flatly tell her cousin this if asked, although the opinion would be given in the "sincere and truthful language" that Charlotte had by then grown to admire.

Back in her earliest days at Roe Head, during that period when the two were still warily circling each other, another new girl showed up. Ellen Nussey arrived a week after the official start of term. Like Mary, she was about a year younger than Charlotte and considered attractive. A portrait made at around this time shows a fair-complexioned girl with ringlets and an atmosphere of gentle serenity.

Decades later, Ellen would remember stepping down outside the schoolhouse while the other students were at play in the gardens—all except Charlotte, who, too short-sighted to join in with the games, had been left to her own devices.

Ellen was shown into the silent classroom. Believing she was all alone, she took in her surroundings, noting that they seemed pleasant enough. A length of crimson cloth covered the long table in the room's center, and a series of shelves took the weight of rows of serious books. Beyond the walls, she could hear the lively voices of the girls. Looking at the volumes on the shelves, Ellen allowed herself, fleetingly, to admit to feeling overawed.

Only then did she notice the small, dark shape by the bow window, weeping without a sound. Feeling both touched and troubled, Ellen took a few steps forward. The figure shrank back as she approached. When Ellen asked after the source of her distress, the girl managed to explain that she was missing home. And Ellen answered kindly that "by and by," she would perhaps be homesick too. Then a quiver of a smile came over the face of the crying girl. Wordlessly they took each other's hands. They would remain there, still and silent, until they heard the approaching footsteps of the other pupils coming in.

Much as Charlotte needed such warm acceptance, as the weeks went by, she couldn't help but find Ellen dull in comparison to Mary. In fact, she considered the well-bred newcomer quite devoid of imagination. Far into later life, she would deride Ellen's eager but unmelodic recitations of poetry and her faltering attempts to talk with Charlotte about books. And yet it didn't take long for the pair to become inseparable.

Epistolary evidence suggests that they shared a bed at school—still a common practice among young female friends and siblings in this era. In Ellen and Charlotte's case too there would have been something almost inevitable about it, since, unlike Mary and her sister Martha and most of the other girls, they had turned up at Roe Head without a sleeping partner.

Bit by bit, Charlotte's relations with Mary also improved,

their shared intelligence and common interests quelling any initial antagonism. Mary and Charlotte—who had allegedly taken an interest in the goings on of Parliament since the age of five—were avid followers of the political maneuvering of the Reform Bill of 1831, which sought to clean up an irregular franchise system and extend voting rights for men, although not for women. They also discovered that they had similar literary leanings. Charlotte's early promise to show Mary one of the magazines she'd created with her siblings at the parsonage gave her schoolfellow the hope that she would be allowed to enter into this secret fantasy world. In time, she and Charlotte would become good friends, forming a tight-knit threesome with Ellen. Overshadowed today by the more famous trio of the Brontë sisters, often thought to be so devoted to each other that they had no need for anyone else, Charlotte's triangular relationship with Ellen and Mary was also of profound importance to her.

Thanks to the diligent private study Miss Wooler demanded of her, Charlotte's efforts would end up carrying her to the top of the school, where she vied for first place with her two friends. For all Charlotte's dismissiveness of her intellect, Ellen was a clever young woman; during her time at Roe Head at least, she was more than able to hold her own with Mary and Charlotte. Ellen even carried off one of the school's most coveted prizes—admittedly for neatness—but her mild, accepting ways meant that, in Charlotte's estimation, she was no match for the politically engaged Mary.

On some deep level, Mary and Charlotte understood that they could challenge each other's thinking. Charlotte's passionate creativity helped the more down-to-earth Mary to see the world afresh. Similarly, the conservative Charlotte came to value the thorny questions of the day raised by Mary, who hailed from a radical family of nonconformists.

The Taylors and the Nusseys were distantly related, but when Charlotte visited the home of each friend, the experiences could not have been more different. Although, like the Taylors, Ellen's family had suffered financially through the recent economic decline, they had been prosperous landowners in the district for generations. At this stage, they were still clinging to their home, Rydings, not far from Roe Head. When Charlotte visited she was met with the grandeur of a castellated building surrounded by towering chestnut trees, one of which had been savagely split apart in a storm. These surroundings, magnificent in comparison to the parsonage at Haworth, made a lasting impact on Charlotte. Like the Brontë girls' first school, Ellen's home became a source of inspiration for *Jane Eyre*. Thornfield Hall, the country seat of Charlotte's Byronic hero, Mr. Rochester, was inspired in part by Rydings—a place that, on the surface, seemed the embodiment of wealthy respectability.

The Red House in neighboring Gomersal, where Mary lived, was less overawing, though Charlotte found it similarly captivating. On the wall of the back parlor, a framed picture of an erupting Mount Vesuvius reminded visitors that, Taylor ancestors had traveled in Italy. Two stained glass windows, through which the sunlight glittered, cast hues of purple and amber on the comfortable room. It's hardly surprising that Charlotte fell under the spell of this house as well. Other than the strained relations between the emotionally stifled Mrs. Taylor and her two daughters, interactions between other family members were as vibrant as the furnishings.

Within the Taylors' welcoming home, the then relatively

conventional clergyman's daughter found herself outnumbered by Mary and her outspoken siblings. Outwardly reserved, Charlotte usually kept quiet during their arguments; but while others might have mistaken her silence for agreement, Mary was not fooled. She knew that when conditions were right, Charlotte could show as much fire as any one of them. Mary would always hold fast to a memory of the schoolgirl Charlotte being drawn into a spirited defense of her hero, the Duke of Wellington, who'd defeated Napoleon Bonaparte's French forces at the Battle of Waterloo about fifteen years before. Charlotte, who considered herself a Tory, had long followed the duke's warring escapades in the popular press, incorporating him as a dashing character into the household games and writings she enjoyed with her brother and sisters. She, then, had many facts to support her argument. Mary, though, while vehemently sure she ought to oppose the duke, found herself unusually speechless since she knew so little about him.

Arguments like these remained good-natured, but quarrels between the two young women could sometimes turn deeply personal. Though the reasons for it have long been obscured by the passage of time, at one point during their schooldays the pair fell out so bitterly that for weeks they didn't speak to each other. Ellen, who remained friends with both throughout the standoff, was puzzled by its cause. Charlotte too claimed to be none the wiser, though clues exist, pointing to an unspoken reason for the conflict.

Though Charlotte admired the bold, independent Mary, her feelings for Ellen were tenderer. While she debated the pressing issues of the era with Mary and shared her literary leanings, in the evenings, when the lamps were low, she retreated to the bed she must have shared with her other close friend. She and Ellen would slide under the covers in their nightdresses, into a space where, undisturbed, they could trade in secrets.

Mary treasured the friendship of both her classmates, and had done her best to make amends for her early cruelty. But as 1831 progressed, the strangely brilliant Charlotte still remained infuriatingly reticent. Despite Mary's interest in the stories and games Charlotte played at home with the Brontë siblings, her friend had now gone back on the promise to let her see one of the household magazines. Worse than that, Charlotte had become inseparable from Ellen, so that Mary surely felt excluded. These situations may have created the impasse that was a mystery to all others at the school.

Charlotte could certainly be possessive of Ellen, and perhaps it was inevitable that the strength of her feelings for the girl would lead to friction with Mary. Though the two eventually made up, with Charlotte presumably realizing that she needed Mary's abrasive energy just as much as Ellen's soothing charm, the complex emotions that bound all three together became both stronger and knottier as they matured into women.

Charlotte and Ellen would continue their habit of sharing a bed during overnight visits well into adulthood. Referring to Ellen as her "bed-fellow," Charlotte would later enthuse about the "calm sleep" that only nights with her friend could bring.

By the mid-nineteenth century, romantic friendships between young women had become idealized, and effusively affectionate correspondence between female friends was commonplace. Yet perhaps a stronger charge lights up Charlotte's letters to Ellen. By 1836, when she had reached the age of twenty, her writing, for a while, took on the passionate tone of a lover driven to distraction by her sweetheart. "My darling," she confided in one such letter, "I have lavished the warmest affections of a very hot, tenacious heart 'upon you'—if you grow cold—its over."

By this stage in life, with her father's finances dwindling, Charlotte had been forced to return to her old school to take up a teaching position. Once more uprooted from her parsonage home, her yearning for Ellen began to combine with the dream of a future together. Recently, she'd even related to her friend a fantasy about sharing a home: "I wish I could live with you always," she'd confided. "If we had a cottage and a competency of our own I do think we might live and love on till *Death* without being dependent on any third person for happiness."

If Mary picked up on the mood between her two friends, she must have felt like the third wheel. And yet, while Charlotte's desire for Ellen intensified, she simultaneously grew more inspired by the candid conversations she enjoyed with Mary. From daring discussions about women's rights to Mary's frustration at what she saw as Charlotte's personal lethargy, theirs was a far more intellectually stimulating and politicized friendship than the one she enjoyed with Ellen, or even in some ways, with her siblings. In the letter describing Charlotte's dream of living with Ellen, she went on to make a second confession. Claiming that she had been in one of her "sentimental humours" the previous Sunday, she admitted to Ellen that she had penned her a note that she had later discarded. Without divulging its contents, she said that she had realized that she ought not to have written it to anyone but Mary, "who is nearly as mad as myself."

Charlotte would come to rely on Mary's "madness"—presumably referring to her unconventionally outspoken nature—and never more so than during her stint as an impatient, resentful teacher. In a sense, a return to Roe Head had seemed the ideal job for Charlotte. The familiarity of the place made it more appealing than work as a private governess: she liked and respected Miss Wooler, and would even be replacing one of the other Wooler sister schoolmistresses, who'd left to be wed — proof that such a position could indeed lead to the chief prize of marriage. This time around, Charlotte wouldn't even have to cope without her family. Emily would accompany her, with Charlotte's wages contributing to her younger sister's tuition.

But the arrangement did not work out as planned. Sensitive Emily, always chronically reserved, suffered with nerves even more than Charlotte had during her early days at Roe Head. Physically, she began to ail. Still haunted by the school deaths of her two elder sisters, Charlotte begged her father to take Emily back to the parsonage at Haworth. The more stoic Anne replaced her, and these two sisters would stick it out together. But Charlotte's professional role would soon cause her deep anguish.

Capable though she was at her studies, she was not a natural educator. Unlike the patient Miss Wooler, Charlotte often felt enraged by what she saw as the stupidity of her charges — largely middle-class daughters of professionals and merchants, girls who would never have to earn a living. On the surface, Charlotte played the role of dutiful schoolmistress. But she felt starved, almost to breaking point, by the job's restrictions on her writing and thinking time. She voiced her frustrations both in conversations with her friends Ellen and Mary and in private notes. She asked herself, "Am I to spend all the best part of my life in this wretched bondage, forcibly suppressing my rage at the idleness, the apathy and the hyperbolical & most asinine stupidity of those fatheaded oafs, and on compulsion assuming an air of kindness, patience and assiduity?"

Patient Ellen comforted her by post, sending her words of encouragement, and Charlotte often dwelt on them in those rare moments snatched to herself after nightfall.

At one such private hour, she sat alone in the school's dining room as a storm vented its wrath outside. Unable to resist, she fell into a trancelike state, her mind swooping her back to the war-ravaged kingdom of Angria—a more recent addition to the Glass Town saga created with her siblings in childhood. These stories still had a powerful hold on her, and now her mind took her over the crushed groves of a trampled garden, a vast marble terrace shining wet with the rain, and into a room richly decorated with standing lamps and floor-to-ceiling mirrors.

She looked for someone reclining on the chaise longue —a young woman she had seen here before in her imaginings. This figure, conjured from the depths of Charlotte's consciousness, had a book in her hand and an arrogant, self-possessed look. Recording the scene on paper the following night, in tiny writing reminiscent of her childhood manuscripts, Charlotte luxuriated over the woman's "exquisite" appearance: "her small & rosy mouth," her proud brow "wreathed with ringlets, & her neck, which though so slender had the superb curve of a queen's about the snowy throat."

So enthralled was Charlotte that she failed to hear the footsteps outside in the corridor. She reacted with a start when the door to the dining room opened and she came face to face with the more humdrum sight of Miss Wooler—apparently in the middle of some household task—carrying a plate of butter.

"A very stormy night my dear!" Miss Wooler said.

"It is ma'am," a resigned Charlotte replied, the evening's fantasy curtailed.

Charlotte's private writings and her similarly charged

letters to Ellen could only provide temporary reprieve from the frustrations of teaching. But at the same time, the assertive Mary was planting ideas in Charlotte's mind about permanent alternatives to what they both saw as the drudgery of the schoolmistress's lot.

Since she was still living close by, Mary visited Charlotte frequently, and the pair's shared intellectual interests meant she was far better placed than Ellen to understand the full extent of Charlotte's suffering. Knowing how stifling conditions at Roe Head must be, Mary had been known to arrange for her family to send their carriage to collect Charlotte and bring her to the Red House in Gomersal. But on one occasion, Mary instead made it her business to come and see her friend at the school.

It must have been strange for Mary to return to Roe Head and cast a grown-up gaze across its familiar sloping lawns, down toward the surrounding fields in which she once played and the shadowy, wooded lanes beyond.

Perhaps it was to one of these secluded places that Mary led Charlotte for a private conversation about why her friend had taken this job. Or it could be that they were lucky enough to find a corner within the house—in the sleeping quarters upstairs perchance, or one of the rooms leading off from the entrance hallway, with its sweeping oak-paneled staircase.

Their conversation would become embedded in Mary's mind. She would always remember Charlotte telling her that by working hard she hoped to put aside some money for herself. But when pressed, Charlotte admitted that after clothing herself and Anne, there was nothing left.

"How can you give so much of yourself for so little money?" Mary demanded.

"It is not brilliant," Charlotte conceded. "But what can I do?"

This was another rare occasion when Mary, burning with indignation, was struck dumb by Charlotte's words.

Though the letters the pair exchanged at this time have not survived, hints gleaned from Charlotte's milder correspondence to others suggest that, over the following weeks and months, Mary would become privy to the full extent of her friend's misery—confessions Charlotte could not bring herself to make even to Ellen or her beloved siblings.

Mary, who could never tolerate moping, had long argued that Charlotte ought to make more of her literary abilities and explore other possible paths in life than those of a schoolmistress or wife. Her hectoring, though less comforting than the balm of Ellen's commiserations, ultimately encouraged Charlotte to reconsider her own potential.

Since Mary's influence was crucial in firing Charlotte's ambitions, it seems strange that so little is known of her today —especially when Mary's provocations, though not always immediately welcome, were instrumental in propelling her friend to take those tentative first steps toward a career as an author. But the well-worn image of Charlotte as one of three isolated sisters has thrown a cloak over the other important female relationships that she sought outside the home.

When Charlotte was back at Haworth for the holidays of Christmas 1836, those arguments from an exasperated Mary seem to have drowned out her feelings of self-pity. Taking her friend's advice to heart, along with the encouragement of her literary brother, Branwell, Charlotte gathered up the courage to send samples of her verse to none other than Robert Southey, the Poet Laureate.

Close to three months would pass before she received a reply from the great man. As it happened, he'd been away traveling around the south of England when Charlotte sent her letter.

Surely in a state of anticipation, she broke the red sealing wax and bowed her head over the first page to make out the Lake Poet's lines, penned with black ink in a precise script. Her message caught up with him in Hampshire, Southey told her, but being so busy at the time, he had been unable to reply. Now that he had returned to his home, far north in Keswick, he informed her that he had allowed her letter to slip to the bottom of a hefty pile of post accumulated in his absence, "not from disrespect, or indifference to its contents, but in truth, because it is not an easy task to answer it, nor a pleasant one to cast a damp over the high spirits, & the generous desires of youth."

Fearfully, Charlotte read on. It must have been a further blow when, halfway through, she reached Southey's judgment. She did have talent, he acknowledged, but she must abandon any plans in this direction. "Literature cannot be the business of a woman's life," he admonished, "& it ought not to be."

Charlotte must have wondered how best to respond to his sterner words. But it did not take her long to work out a strategy. "I must thank you for the kind & wise advice you have condescended to give me," she wrote, in a tone that Southey—when he received her letter—would heartily approve of. While he would feel assured of her ample contrition, there was also an inner strength to Charlotte that could not be subdued. Having assured the poet that she was careful to concentrate on her proper duties all day, she mischievously added that, in the evenings only, "I confess, I do think." And she signed off with the arch promise that, should the wish ever arise again to see her name in print, she would "look at Southey's letter, and suppress it."

Mary might have worried about her friend's apparent passivity, but these words have a different story to tell. They whisper that a hunger for change and creativity already raged within that meek young woman. Her inner tenacity would hold out for several years, until Mary hatched a bold plan of escape for the two. This opportunity would force Charlotte to choose between the responsibilities she felt she owed to her family and to the sweet-natured Ellen, and the chance to branch out into the world with Mary, for real and literary adventures anew.

5

Two Adventurous Spirits

THE YEAR 1841 would see its share of frustrations and sadness for all three of the old Roe Head schoolmates, making plans for escape both more difficult and more urgent. Ellen Nussey, who back in the mid-1830s had enjoyed a modicum of independence, including a spell living with her brother in London, was again entrenched in her Yorkshire parish—this time at the family's new and more modest home, Brookroyd, a short walk from Rydings, their former, grander residence. The Nusseys, who had become reliant on Ellen's caregiving, regularly prevented her from traveling to Haworth.

For Mary Taylor, the death of her bankrupt father at the end of 1840 still cast a long shadow, exacerbating existing tensions between her three brothers and mother over Mr. Taylor's remaining property and business interests. All the children would eventually disperse from Gomersal, with the youngest two going abroad that year—Waring setting sail for the far-off British colony of New Zealand, and their fun-loving sister, Martha, heading for a finishing school in Brussels, where an uncle and cousin lived close by.

As for Charlotte, now that she'd left two consecutive teaching posts, each with Miss Wooler, she had found work as a private governess. During this employment the twenty-five-year-old entertained hopes of gaining some greater freedom by establishing a school of her own, with her two sisters at the parsonage at Haworth. But a package received from Belgium—where Mary and one of her brothers had accompanied Martha for a month's tour—would transform her ambitions.

It must have been with delight that Charlotte pulled the string from the package, to reveal the elegant black silk scarf and kid gloves sent by Mary. These fine Belgian garments were exotic indeed, a far cry from her usual plain wardrobe. But knowing of the late Mr. Taylor's debts, still yet to be fully repaid, the thought of her friends squandering their precious pocket-money dampened Charlotte's enjoyment. Nonetheless, ensconced within the village home of her current employers, she allowed Mary's letter, which accompanied the gift, to transport her. Gone was the dreariness of her existence with the family of a Bradford merchant: Charlotte's painful timidity in the company of the lady of the house, the hours of sewing that supplemented her teaching duties, the unruliness of the children. These irritations all faded from Charlotte's mind as the beauty of famous works of art and towering cathedral spires emerged in their place—sights borne forth from Mary's words. Before long, Charlotte felt overcome with emotion, a lump forming in her throat as her whole being ached with a "wish for wings."

For a minute or two, the desire "to see—to know—to learn" expanded, unchecked. But then reality intruded once more and everything evaporated. Charlotte determined to refocus her attention on the more manageable ambition of opening a school with Anne and Emily, never to think again of thoughts as foolish as these.

At least this was what she told Ellen initially. But she

would go on to confess in a later letter that Mary had "cast oil on the flames." And so, only seven weeks later, as summer shaded into autumn, Charlotte took up her pen again to write something of a very different nature, this time to her aunt.

Back in 1821, when Charlotte was only five years old, Elizabeth Branwell had arrived at Haworth to help care for her dying sister. After Mrs. Brontë's passing, Aunt Branwell had felt called to remain at the parsonage, to keep house for her clergyman brother-in-law and provide a steady influence in the lives of his young son and daughters. Though never given to displays of warm affection, she liked to indulge in a bit of merrymaking when the mood took her. On Ellen's first visit to the parsonage, she'd shocked the sheltered young woman by jokingly offering her a pinch of snuff from the little gold box she always kept close by. A proud unmarried woman, Aunt Branwell was more than ready to argue her case with Patrick Brontë when they came to occasional disagreements, and she insisted on paying him for her keep. Through careful management of her forty-pounds annuity—particularly an astute investment in the York and North Midland Railway Company in the 1830s—Aunt Branwell had accumulated well over one thousand pounds in savings by the time Charlotte wrote to ask if she would be willing to grant her a loan.

Charlotte told her aunt that friends—presumably Mary and Martha—advised that to ensure the success of her future career as a schoolmistress, she ought first to spend six months in Europe, improving her command of languages. Seated at her writing desk, Charlotte methodically laid out her case, arguing that "In half a year, I could acquire a thorough familiarity with French. I could improve greatly in Italian, and even get a dash of German." These advantages, she pointed out, could be turned "to vast account" when she and her sisters set up their

school. With this end goal thus firmly outlined, Charlotte suggested that Emily, who'd been back at home since 1839 and remained the most reserved and yet most untamable of the sisters,
should accompany her to the continent. The more adaptable
Anne, who, like Charlotte, was living away as a governess, could
take Emily's place at some point in the future, she said.

Charlotte was careful to let Aunt Branwell know that she
had "no other friend in the world to whom I could apply on
this subject except yourself." Appealing to the independent nature of this aunt in her mid-sixties, she continued in a voice
that could almost have come from the bolder Mary: "Papa will
perhaps think it a wild and ambitious scheme; but who ever
rose in the world without ambition? When he left Ireland to
go to Cambridge University, he was as ambitious as I am now.
I want us *all* to go on."

Charlotte's approach must have been convincing for, a
fortnight later, she wrote to Ellen again, this time with the announcement that there could be a chance of her going away after all. Charlotte requested that her confidante keep the information to herself, explaining that Mary had advised her to take
this precaution — something that would have further wounded
the bewildered Ellen, shut away at home in Birstall. How far
arrangements had progressed since Charlotte last wrote to de-
clare that she had quelled all such fanciful thoughts!

Charlotte must have known that Aunt Branwell would
part with 150 pounds of her savings only if she believed it
would be a sound investment. And so, desperate to satisfy her
"wish for wings," Charlotte felt bound to present her plans as
a way to further her job prospects. Somewhere inside, though,
she must have feared that adopting this stance would commit
her to the schoolmistress's path, which had already caused her
such misery. Letters written from the home of her employ-

ers, while less rage-filled than the private jottings she'd penned as a teacher at Roe Head, continued to paint a picture of a deeply unsatisfied young woman who hungered for creative liberty. Still, any worries about where this future would take her were pushed into the background by the excitement of making travel arrangements.

Despite Charlotte's heartfelt entreaties, Ellen, no doubt still smarting from the shock that her friend was really leaving, declined to visit her to say goodbye. Over the past months, she had heard of the plans only through Charlotte's letters, thus failing to realize how seriously the twenty-five-year-old was contemplating a move abroad until it was too late to stop her. The pair had quarreled over the matter. While Ellen insisted that her family prevented her from bidding farewell in person, a comment by Charlotte that she could not "quite enter" into the mindset of the Nusseys suggests that she thought that Ellen was using this as a convenient excuse.

The task of finding a Belgian school that was both suitable and inexpensive offered Charlotte a distraction from her troubles with Ellen. Though still debt-ridden, the Taylor family fortunes remained less immediately precarious than those of the Brontës, and the Château de Koekelberg—where Mary was about to enroll as a pupil along with Martha—was deemed too dear for Charlotte and Emily. Back in Yorkshire after her summer tour, Mary invested a good deal of her own time and money in sending her friend information. As ever, her supportive words did much to rally Charlotte's spirits. After the intercession of various others, including the wife of the British chaplain in Brussels, who helped put Patrick's mind at rest, they eventually settled on the Pensionnat de Demoiselles Heger-Parent, situated close to the heart of Brussels and run by the respectable Monsieur and Madame Heger.

What must the townspeople of Haworth have thought when three of the most eccentric of their community set off that day in February 1842? The melancholic reverend, with his soldierly posture, would accompany his daughters on their trip. He, along with the willowy Emily, whose shifting blue-gray eyes refused to meet the gaze of onlookers, and the smaller, bespectacled Charlotte, would have made a sight indeed, laden with their locked trunks.

Their first major stop would be Leeds railway station, where they'd arranged to join Mary and her clever older brother Joe, an experienced traveler and much admired by Charlotte. Following the eleven-hour journey to London, the next three days before their departure by steamship was a whirl of activity. But Charlotte's and Mary's recollections of this time could not have been more different.

For Charlotte, who'd long dreamed of visiting the capital city, the prospect of even a short stay filled her with awe. This was, for her, the start of the adventure and a chance to steep herself in London's great works of art. The group's lodgings at the Chapter Coffee House on Paternoster Row lay within the shade of St. Paul's. Like Lucy Snowe, the heroine of her future novel, *Villette*, when Charlotte woke in the morning and looked out on the blue cathedral dome, she felt the wings of her spirit beginning to shake themselves loose.

St. Paul's was the one landmark that would leave a lasting impression on Mary too. Despite her similar enthusiasm for sightseeing, expressed only months earlier, she now cast a jaded eye over Charlotte's excitement. The urbane Joe gamely volunteered himself as the group's guide, but Mary merely tagged along with the Brontë sisters and their father. While Charlotte, and even the often taciturn Emily, had much to say about what they saw, the more worldly Mary could only look forward to the months ahead when, along with Martha, the young women would all be unchaperoned in Brussels.

Following the sea crossing and arduous journey by stage-coach, the party arrived in the Belgian city after dark. As Mary would remember it at least, all three young women were much preoccupied and gloomy by the time they set off the next morning for their different schools: Mary heading with Joe for the Château de Koekelberg to the northwest of the city, and Charlotte, Emily, and their father making their way to the Pensionnat Heger.

The arrival of the Brontë sisters was the first quiet link in a chain of events that would judder on for decades, ultimately drowning out other aspects of Charlotte's time in Brussels, including Mary's important role in bringing it about. But on that dull February morning, Charlotte and Emily must have seemed a most unassuming pair, hardly the type who could bring notoriety to the pensionnat. All that distinguished them from the other schoolgirls was the relative ripeness of their years — at twenty-five and twenty-three — and their unfashionable garb. The large collars and huge sleeves of Charlotte's frock did nothing for her diminutive frame, while the lack of fullness to Emily's skirts only served to accentuate her straight-up-and-down figure. The sisters and their father had been accompanied for this last part of the journey by the British chaplain of Brussels, who had family connections in Yorkshire. It's likely he did most of the talking, introducing his charges first to the female porter at the door, and then to Monsieur and Madame Heger. This would have given Charlotte and the still shyer Emily the chance to quietly appraise the couple, their three children, and the strange surroundings that would become their new home.

The two-floor building on the Rue d'Isabelle included

rooms for the school's three classes and a dining hall with a pair of long tables, an oil lamp hanging over each. On the level above, a communal dormitory was lined with small beds shrouded in individual white curtains. The school's walled garden was hidden from the street. Amid this peaceful oasis filled with ancient fruit trees, a wilderness took up one side — a dark, brooding mass of foliage with an air of the illicit. A decade later, this spot, which had lingered in Charlotte's mind ever since, would appear in *Villette,* in only lightly fictionalized form.

Claire Zoë Heger, the director, had set up the school prior to her marriage. She was an attractive, hugely capable woman in her late thirties, but it was her husband, the younger Constantin Heger, who made the stronger impression on Charlotte. Short of stature and with a dark complexion, this teacher of rhetoric struck her as ugly and with something of a wild animal about him. At least, this was how she would attempt to rationalize her early reactions to a man who awakened the kind of strong emotions that she'd previously poured into her fevered writings set in the fantasy kingdom of Angria.

While, across town, Mary was finding her bearings at the Château de Koekelberg, Charlotte and Emily struggled to adjust to life at the Pensionnat Heger. They shied away from socializing with their younger schoolmates, who soon came to regard them as excessively earnest. With the permission of Madame and Monsieur Heger, the sisters completely curtained off their corner of the twenty-person dormitory to attain a greater degree of privacy.

In April 1842, once the Easter holidays arrived, it must have been a relief to finally have time to pay a visit to the Taylors' school in leafy Koekelberg, on the city's outskirts. Ahead of this much-anticipated reunion, Mary had written a newsy letter to Ellen, which was waiting to be posted. In her neat, flowing script, she talked of the activity of her days and how, in the evenings, she went to bed "sometimes at nine o'clock heartily tired & without a word to throw at any one." In her usual outspoken manner, Mary laughed at the lack of language skills of her fellow pupils, mimicking a French girl speaking English and declaring that "the Germans make a mess of both languages the german teacher worst of all." These sweeping statements betray the casual stereotyping that would also feature in several of Charlotte's Belgian letters. But Mary's vivid depictions of the finishing school atmosphere—so alien to the independent life path she was determined to forge for herself—give a taste of the burgeoning creativity that would come to bear years later in *Miss Miles,* her feminist novel that celebrates the importance of female friendship.

Mary's letter painted quite a picture of the Château's community. Monsieur Huard, the drawing master, was "a man of some talent, a good judgement, & an intelligible manner of teaching," who she said would have been her favorite "if he did not smell so of bad tobacco." Having mocked her own lack of grace in dancing class, and praised Martha's improvement, Mary continued, "All our awkwardnesses however are thrown into the shade by those of a belgian girl who does not know right foot from left & obstinately dances with her mouth open."

Mary had folded the large sheet of paper in half. Having written her message to Ellen on either side of that first page, she showed Charlotte the space left for her and Martha. When Charlotte sat down to write, her words did not flow; in fact, they were uncharacteristically stilted. No doubt she was still hurt by the lack of a proper goodbye. Gone is the tone of reconciliation that marked early communications in which she tried to make Ellen understand her reasons for leaving. In just half a page, in comparison to Mary's two, she wrote that she and Emily were comfortable, that Mary and Martha were unchanged, and, most tellingly, that Ellen had not been forgotten "as you feared you would be."

Several days later, while Mary sat staring fiercely at a German dictionary, the far less diligent Martha would finish her portion of the letter. Her note, also brief, though less so than Charlotte's, remarked that "there is a very sweet, ladylike, elegant girl here, who has undertaken to civilise our *dragon*," meaning Mary. Martha joked that her sister was "actually improving a little under her hands."

In reality, as Ellen probably guessed, nothing could have been further from the truth. Over the next months, while Charlotte knuckled down to the regime of lessons in French and the rigors of the Pensionnat Heger's curriculum, Mary, true to her restless nature, tired of what she regarded as the hypocrisy of the refined Château. When Martha returned home for an extended visit to Yorkshire in late spring 1842, Mary declined to accompany her. By September, she was preparing to move on to Germany, to continue studying German and music and to earn her keep by teaching English.

Despite having done so much to bring Charlotte to Brussels, Mary, ever eager for new experiences, apparently gave little thought to how her friend would fare without her. Under different circumstances, Charlotte might have felt let down, but by then she was positively thriving at the Pensionnat Heger. Although she and Emily had failed to build a rapport with the other students, their intelligence had drawn the attention of the temperamental Monsieur Heger, who singled them out for private lessons—an act that increased the other students' animosity toward the sisters. But this recognition filled Charlotte with pride and pleasure. She and Emily made such good progress that, with their half year at the school almost up, Madame Heger said she would let them stay on as pupils on the condition that Charlotte take over the English lessons, allowing the director to save money by dismissing the English master. The frequently homesick Emily would be employed to teach music, and although neither young woman would receive a salary, their own lessons in French and German, and their board at the pensionnat, would be free.

On balance, Charlotte considered it a good offer. Both sisters had supposedly begun this European escapade in order to increase their future standing as heads of their own school, but neither had missed her past existence as classroom teacher or governess. Charlotte, in particular, thanks to her love of studying and her growing admiration for Monsieur Heger, felt a strong pull to remain in Brussels. Missing home at times, she occasionally wavered—writing to the unenthusiastic Ellen back in Britain for her views. Overall, though, like her friend across town at the Château de Koekelberg, this was a time of great hope for Charlotte.

But then Mary's sister, Martha, suddenly fell ill. When she'd come back to Belgium from Yorkshire, the twenty-three-year-old had appeared as healthy as ever. By late September, however, she was showing signs of what was subsequently identified as cholera—that ghastly waterborne disease. Its grip tightened so quickly that Mary, preoccupied by this nightmare, did not at first send word to the Brontë sisters. But as soon as Charlotte heard the news, she set off for the Taylors' school. Armed with only scant information about Martha's condition, she arrived at the Château expecting to see both her friends but found only Mary, waiting with the terrible news that Martha had died the previous evening.

The revelation came as a great shock to Charlotte, who

wondered how a young woman as vibrant and full of life as Martha could suddenly be gone. Despite her own early experience of losing Maria and Elizabeth, the thought that death could be on the horizon for Mary's sister had not occurred to Charlotte. To someone raised in nineteenth-century England, cholera was no unfamiliar specter. Charlotte knew of the agonies borne by its sufferers: the extreme sickness, dehydration, and muscle cramping, the terrible awareness that there remained no cure. And yet it was still utterly bewildering to be all these hundreds of miles away from Yorkshire and now without the vivacious Martha.

In the somber atmosphere of the Château, Charlotte gleaned something of the extraordinary level of care Mary had given to her sister. Practical and determined, in the weeks to come, she'd show no hint of letting go of her emotions, striking Charlotte as the very epitome of self-control.

Charlotte, of course, would have been aware that to simply get on with things, on the surface at least, was very much her friend's way. Shortly afterward, Mary's relatives, the Dixons, who lived close by, took her into their home and would have gladly allowed her to remain there for a while. But she still had her sights set on Germany and, tempting though the Dixons' offer must have been, she continued to make the necessary arrangements.

With a visit to Martha's grave at the city's Protestant cemetery still fresh in her mind, a grieving Charlotte once again received distressing news, this time from the home she'd left behind. Aunt Branwell had fallen dangerously ill. Emily and Charlotte decided to depart for Britain at once, but a second letter arrived the next morning bringing the further blow that the woman who'd financed this life-changing trip had passed away. Like Martha, who'd seemed a picture of health, Aunt

Branwell had always had a strong constitution. It appeared simply unbelievable to Charlotte that she would never again see either of these two women who'd played such important roles in bringing about her foreign adventure.

While Mary never seriously entertained the possibility of returning to Gomersal after her sister's death, both Charlotte and Emily felt compelled to go back to Haworth as planned to pay their respects to their aunt. They arrived, too late for the funeral, to find their father much subdued and their brother Branwell, who'd been at his aunt's side in her last days, in a severe state of grief. As Anne had also returned temporarily from her post as governess to take over the running of the household, the four siblings were at least able to draw strength from one another, even under these sad circumstances.

Still in Brussels for now, Mary must have worried about Charlotte, wondering if she would throw away her current freedom for a return to the limitations of her former existence. Mary perhaps envisioned her friend settled with her family within the gray stone walls of the parsonage, a place the Taylors had visited in happier times. Or, like Elizabeth Gaskell in her biography some years later, she may have pictured the Brontë sisters walking the rough tracks of the snow-crusted moors, and contemplated whether the life Charlotte had left behind in Brussels now seemed merely an incredible dream.

Charlotte's tutor, Monsieur Heger, who'd been so entranced by the abilities of his British students, apparently had similar fears. He'd given them a letter, written in French, to pass on to their father, expressing sympathies for the family's loss and praising Emily's and Charlotte's talents. The good character traits the young women had learned at the parsonage, he wrote, were largely responsible for their progress at the pensionnat. Yet Monsieur Heger also stressed that the sisters ought to return to

Brussels in order to complete their education. Just one more year was needed, he said, for Charlotte to gain the confidence and poise to succeed in teaching French. He couldn't bring himself to be quite this effusive in his praise for Emily, but she too, he claimed, was losing some of her natural shyness.

It can't have come as a surprise to her father that Emily showed little eagerness to return to Belgium. Unlike her sister, she'd never embraced Monsieur Heger's exacting teaching methods. While Charlotte seemed happy to exercise her literary artistry by throwing herself into the writing of French essays, Emily had yearned for the familiar landscapes of home and for more time to work on the Gondal saga, which she and Anne had developed from the Brontës' original Glass Town writings and which she had continued into adulthood. Charlotte, on the other hand, decided to do as her tutor suggested — guided by that "wish for wings" that Mary encouraged, and also, perhaps, by the enthusiasm of Monsieur Heger and her deepening attraction to him. But if she set off from Haworth with high hopes for the next year, the arduous journey to Belgium now reads like a bad omen for what was to come.

This time, the security of traveling as part of a group was not on offer. Charlotte, a still outwardly timid twenty-six-year-old, gathered her nerves to take the train to London alone. Due to severe delays, she did not arrive until ten at night and, fearing the possible censure of turning up at the Chapter Coffee House at that improper hour, the inexperienced traveler decided it would be safer to take a horse-drawn cab to London Bridge Wharf. Here, the steamship for Ostend waited, ready to set sail in the morning.

It must have been a shock for the crew members on deck when a female voice called out from a small boat that had appeared in the dark beside their vessel. Having persuaded a waterman to row her out from the dock, the tiny Charlotte shivered in the January air: cold, crisp, and damp all around. Wary though she was of making demands, it was a thrill to be out at this time on the river, with the lamps and hushed noise of London distant in the background.

From the ship, a sneering male voice responded, "No passengers might sleep on board."

But with the boldness that she had learned from Mary and the determination of mind that was very much her own, Charlotte rose precariously to her feet as choppy waves lapped the sides of the waterman's boat. Standing as tall as her short height allowed, she called back that she wished to speak to someone in authority. Much consternation ensued, but when, eventually, such a person arrived on deck, Charlotte's quiet resolution so impressed the man that he allowed her to come aboard and take up residence in a berth.

On her arrival back at the pensionnat, Madame Heger greeted the sole returning sister with kindness, but it wasn't long before Charlotte's gratitude toward the director began to ebb. In a letter to Ellen, five months later, she would tell of her extreme isolation, especially during the holidays, when other teachers and pupils spent time away from the school. Had Mary still been in Brussels, Charlotte could have made plans to see her. Instead, it sometimes happened, she said, that she was left for hours alone—"with 4 great desolate classrooms at my disposition—I try to read, I try to write but in vain I then wander about from room to room—but the silence and loneliness of all the house weighs down one's spirits like lead." In her days as a teacher at Roe Head, she'd craved solitude. But now it brought on a depression that blocked her creativity.

There were, though, important differences between now and then. At Roe Head, Charlotte had been accompanied

much of the time by either Anne or Emily, and her two closest friends lived within an easy distance. Here in Brussels, Ellen
was five hundred miles away, and Mary across the German border. Despite Charlotte's many frustrations with life under Miss
Wooler's rules, her former headmistress had been a steadying
presence. The same could not be said of Madame Heger or her
volatile husband, whom Charlotte nicknamed the Black Swan
and whose influence can be felt in the dark-complexioned appearance and explosive moods of the character Monsieur Paul
Emanuel in *Villette*. Monsieur Heger's gifts of books and the
rigorous demands of his teaching would have a lasting impact
on his student, helping to refine her writing style. The effect
he had on her secret erotic self was more immediate still, for in
the months when Charlotte was alone in Brussels, her feelings
for her tutor deepened. What had once been an excited revulsion, then a strong admiration, would eventually become an
all-consuming passion.

Perhaps unsurprisingly, given the sensually charged relations between them in the past, Charlotte said nothing of these
emotions to the more conventional Ellen, who had never been
in favor of Charlotte's European adventure. Whether she spoke
of them to her other, worldlier friend we cannot know, because Mary — apparently fearful that they might fall into the
wrong hands — would later destroy almost all of Charlotte's
letters. We can discern, however, that Mary had become concerned enough to ask her cousin, Mary Dixon, to keep up a
relationship with Charlotte. Not long afterward, the two Brussels expatriates would pose as portrait models for each other —
leading to that request by Charlotte that her finished picture
not be shown to Mary Taylor, who would find no pleasure in it.

While Mary worried about Charlotte during this period,

Charlotte also worried about Mary. She had sensed from the letters she'd received from Germany—which also have not survived—that though her valiant friend never complained, neither was she enjoying herself as much as she pretended. Since an extant letter from Mary to Ellen in early 1843 was full of enthusiastic declarations about her new life, this leaves the niggling question of what details Charlotte and Mary shared in their private communications. Charlotte knew, from the haunting early experience of losing her own sisters, that despite Mary's resolution to put the trauma of Martha's death out of her mind, the wounds of bereavement take a long time to heal. Likewise, Mary may have had at least an inkling of the true reason for Charlotte's distress.

By the summer, Mary Dixon had departed from Brussels for reasons of health, to undergo bracing cold-water treatments first in Germany and then back in Yorkshire. In August, now more isolated than ever, Charlotte begged Ellen to write to her, calling on her friend's sense of Christian charity to send a "long, long letter—fill it with the minutest details." Homesickness kept creeping over her, she said: "I cannot shake it off."

Another missive, penned a month later, this time to Emily, painted a desolate image of the life of which Charlotte had once dreamed. She would "fall into the gulf of low spirits," she told her sister, if she stayed on her own at the pensionnat, "so I go out and traverse the Boulevards and streets of Bruxelles sometimes for hours together."

Coming back after one such walk, she felt so overcome by feelings of revulsion that she set off again, winding her aimless way through the streets surrounding the Rue d'Isabelle, ending up outside St. Gudule's Catholic church, just at the tolling of the evening bell. For some reason unfathomable to her

—the nineteenth-century daughter of a Protestant preacher, with the era's commonplace prejudice against Catholicism— she found herself drawn inside its great doors.

Here she wandered alone along the aisles, past round columns on either side, the stained glass of the windows casting colored shadows on the gray stone walls. A few elderly women were bent in prayer, waiting for vespers to begin. Charlotte stayed to watch and listen. When the priest's final words had been said, she still could not bring herself to go home. To either side of the church stood ornately carved confessionals. She noticed a few people crouching down in the available spots on the dark wood steps outside each one. Suddenly, she was seized by a "freak" desire to do something—anything—to "vary my life and yield a moment's interest." Having watched a couple of penitents go through the process, and now feeling ready herself to whisper through the bars to the priest within, she approached one of the confessionals.

In another scene that would make it into the pages of *Villette,* Charlotte knelt down. After a short wait, the small door covering the grating was opened, and she understood that this was the sign for her to begin. But Charlotte had no idea what to say. As she would later relate to Emily, she saw herself back alone on the Thames in the waterman's boat, in the dark by the steamship.

At last, she managed to find her tongue, telling the priest, in French, that she was a foreigner, and that she had been brought up a Protestant.

"Are you still a Protestant?" came the reply of the unseen figure.

She could not bring herself to lie. "Yes," she said.

He told her that she could not then enjoy the privilege of confession.

But just as she had that chill night on the river, Charlotte mustered the strength to stay her course. And in the end, the priest relented. It was his hope, he said, that this might be the first step in her return to the true church. So Charlotte leaned close to the grate and, in a voice no doubt tightened by nerves, began to confess.

What she told the priest remains unknown, but it is tempting to speculate that, within the secrecy of the confessional, her growing feelings for Monsieur Heger at least informed her words. As Mary seemed to sense, even from Germany, her friend's life at the pensionnat had become increasingly untenable, Charlotte having become greatly distrustful of Madame Heger. This resentment was no doubt magnified by her growing attachment to Madame's husband—something an astute woman like the head of the school could have hardly failed to notice. Charlotte's duties, when she'd first returned to Brussels, had included teaching English to Monsieur Heger and his brother-in-law. These sessions, though, had been discontinued, and the French tutorials Monsieur Heger gave to Charlotte had been significantly limited. But not long after her extraordinary evening at the Catholic church, when the desolate young schoolmistress attempted to hand in her notice, she was stopped by the force of the man's determination that she remain. He might have been willing to bend, presumably, to his wife's demands that he curtail the time he spent with his protégée, but the thought that he might lose her altogether seems to have come as a wrench he could not bear.

There were so few joys in Charlotte's life at this time —the sight of the young Queen Victoria's carriage passing through the Rue Royale while on an official visit in September 1843 providing a rare moment of excitement. Mary, ever mindful of her friend's suffering, sent a letter from Hagen in

Germany, urging Charlotte to join her across the border. Mary too had found a job teaching English to men—controversially, in her case, to young, unmarried ones. She had begun studying piano with the well-known Friedrich Halle—father of the conductor Charles Hallé, who later added an acute accent to the family name. Mary admired her teacher's expertise but tried his patience by arguing persistently over what she believed was his over-enthusiasm for Beethoven. She had also begun studying algebra, which she liked because "it is odd in a woman to learn it, and I like to establish my right to be doing odd things."

When Mary wrote to Charlotte, she must have hoped that the strength of her words would shake her friend into action. Indeed, it seems that they gave Charlotte the final push she needed to insist that Monsieur Heger accept her notice. Yet Mary must have been disappointed to learn that Charlotte's next destination was not to be Germany. Instead, she would be returning to her old moorland home.

Before Charlotte left Brussels for good, Monsieur Heger gave her a sealed diploma, certifying her competencies as a teacher. He had even suggested she take one of his small daughters with her as a first pupil for her planned school. Though this arrangement would have allowed them to maintain contact, Charlotte turned down his proposal, citing Madame Heger's likely disapproval.

Back at the parsonage once more, Charlotte wrote a mournful letter to Ellen. She mused that "there are times now when it appears to me as if all my ideas and feelings except a few friendships and affections are changed from what they used to be." It was good to have Emily's company again, but her father's noticeable age and his failing eyesight, which had worsened significantly in her absence, were matters of great concern. What she wished for now, she confided in Ellen, was "active exertion—a stake in life." Haworth seemed to her "such a lonely, quiet spot, buried away from the world," but she couldn't bear the thought of leaving her father again.

With Anne returned to her employment as a governess, any plans for Charlotte and her sisters to set up a school were also put on hold. Mary, who understood better than anyone else how ill-suited Charlotte was to the life of a teacher, could at least be pleased at that. But it would have distressed her to learn that, back at Haworth, Charlotte had once again fallen into the habit of restraining her own desires and bending to the needs of others.

Still, spring brought the welcome relief of a reunion between the trio of school friends. When Mary returned for a month from Germany, Charlotte hastened to Gomersal to meet her, as did Ellen, who arrived in the evening. Later, Ellen would recall her feelings as she entered the gardens of the Red House, where, because of the fading light, she could make out only the silhouettes of two female figures.

Walking among the shadowed shrubs and flowers and talking "with all their might," they certainly looked like Mary and Charlotte. But from this distance Ellen could not recognize the pair's voices and so could not identify them for certain. The force of their conversation was evident even in the shadows of dusk, which may have caused Ellen to approach cautiously.

When Charlotte and Mary noticed Ellen's silhouette, they were thrown similarly off guard. Into the blackness they squinted until finally they realized who it was and called out glad greetings of welcome, suddenly full to the brim with warmth.

Ellen would never learn of the words that passed between her two friends that night, and as in the case of Charlotte's church confession, we too remain out of earshot. But we know that it was an impassioned conversation. And we know that Charlotte, who'd soon begin an astonishingly frank and yearning sequence of letters to Monsieur Heger, was deeply dissatisfied with her current situation. We know too that both of these unusual and ambitious young women still hungered for genuine adventure. Perhaps that evening Charlotte spoke of some of her unfulfilled dreams, and Mary, in her brusque but kindly way, tried once again to persuade Charlotte to join her in Germany.

Whatever the truth, *this* we know for sure: just months later, in the autumn of 1844, Mary sent Charlotte a letter that shocked her to the core. She wrote with the news that she intended to go through with something she'd fantasized about before, but that her friend had never believed would happen. Mary planned to leave the Northern Hemisphere and immigrate to New Zealand. It was, as a stunned Charlotte would relate to Ellen, as if "a great planet" had fallen from the sky.

§ 6 §

One Great Myth

ON A MILD WINTER'S DAY in June 1848, Mary Taylor set off from her lodgings in the small settlement of Wellington with a single clear purpose. She had in mind an important letter—as yet unwritten—containing a stern message for her friend Charlotte Brontë. Heading away from the town's few streets of timber houses, Mary followed the curve of the eastern shore, walking in typically determined fashion in the direction of Mount Victoria. From its top, she hoped to spy a ship that could carry her words all the way back to Britain.

Mary's route would take her along rougher roads and over swampland before she reached the base of the hill. The shipping signal station stood 648 feet above, and it was toward this destination that Mary began her ascent. Four years had passed since that evening in the garden with Ellen Nussey and Charlotte. Like her two friends, at thirty-one years of age, Mary remained unmarried. Unlike them, here in New Zealand, she had carved out the kind of independent living that she could never have hoped to enjoy back in Yorkshire, or even in Belgium or Germany.

Since her arrival in July 1845, Mary had built a five-room house on newly established Cuba Street, which she let out for profit while living elsewhere, supplementing her income by giving piano lessons. And when her brother Waring went away, she took care of the day-to-day running of his import and trading company, honing her innate business skills.

What adventures she'd had since she last saw poor Charlotte! Today Mary must have felt she was every one of the 11,500 miles from her old friend cooped up in the parsonage at Haworth. The last time they'd met, not long before Mary's four-month crossing, she'd been dismayed when Charlotte announced that, though richness and variety of life might be possible for other people, she had given up on such things for herself. Mary had argued otherwise, but what with Charlotte's unerring sense of filial duty, it had been no use. And so it was with a heavy heart for Charlotte's prospects that Mary sailed away for New Zealand.

The two had continued to keep in touch, but seaborne communications were unreliable. Some letters took months to arrive, and others seemingly disappeared en route. Perhaps because of the sporadic communication, Mary's pitiful image of her friend remained embedded in her mind.

Charlotte's return to the parsonage, however, had allowed her to focus on her literary plans. In 1846, in a project she spearheaded, she and her sisters had self-funded the printing of a collection of their poems. But despite good reviews in *The Critic* and *The Athenaeum,* they had managed to sell only two copies. Even before they learned of this sorry outcome, Charlotte had begun seeking a publisher for the trio's novels. Anne's *Agnes Grey* and Emily's *Wuthering Heights* eventually found a firm willing to take them on, but Charlotte's novel, *The Professor*—her first attempt at writing of her experiences in the Brussels home of the Hegers—was turned down multiple times, and would remain unpublished until after her death.

It must have been galling on so many levels. When she was rebuffed by her former tutor—who, no doubt alarmed by her
increasing obsession, had begun to ignore her letters—she'd
been afflicted by fevered sleeplessness and an inability to eat.
And now her book that memorialized him had also been rejected. It is testament to her determination that she pressed on
undeterred, and began a new book, *Jane Eyre,* which she would
complete within the space of a year

Until recently, Mary had not seriously reassessed Charlotte's situation. Even today, as she looked down on the waves
—with all she knew now—Mary still could not shake her belief that her friend was wasting her life. Strange perhaps, when
as Mary had just discovered, in the three years since the pair
had said goodbye, Charlotte had achieved one of her chief ambitions: in the guise of "Currer Bell," she had become a published novelist.

After all her considerable disappointments, the immediate success of *Jane Eyre* had taken Charlotte enormously by
surprise. Her tale of an impoverished and determined young
governess who triumphs over adversity had excited critics and
public alike. Charlotte's weeks were now cheered by heartening news from her London publisher. A third print run had
been commissioned within months, offering Charlotte the
sweet prospect, for the foreseeable future, of no longer needing
to contemplate a return to her former life as a governess. While
controversy raged over the true identity of the book's author
—even Ellen was kept in the dark for months—soon after its
publication in October 1847, Charlotte had parceled up the
three volumes of the first edition and sent them on their long
voyage to New Zealand.

Now that she had finished reading the novel, Mary
stood on the hill, looking down for a suitable vessel. But in

this distant outpost of the British Empire she could see only a small boat with a single mast and the HMS *Fly*, an eighteen-gun sloop. A pity, thought Mary, since normally a passing cattle carrier might have carried her mail. Unfortunately, the recent strong easterly winds had kept much of the usual sea traffic out of the bay.

It would, in fact, be several weeks before a suitable ship arrived—and only after the winds changed again could it depart on its return journey. Almost five additional months would go by before Mary's words reached Haworth. By then, although Charlotte read the letter, more time would pass before she could muster the enthusiasm to reply.

Mary's July missive arrived at Haworth at a terribly difficult time for Charlotte. From Mary's distant vantage point in Wellington, when she thought of her friend's unhappiness she tended to focus on the overbearing demands, as she saw them, of Charlotte's aging father. But in reality, the seventy-one-year-old and his worsening health was not even close to Charlotte's main concern. Recent events at the parsonage had been considerably more traumatic.

Throughout what should have been a joyous period for this newly successful author, Charlotte's brother became a constant worry. Branwell had been living mostly at home since his disgraceful dismissal from his job as a tutor, probably following an affair between him and the mother of his pupil. By the date when Mary made that climb up Mount Victoria, Charlotte was confiding in the geographically closer Ellen that the brother she'd once so admired was "much shattered"—not least by his dependency on alcohol and opium. He had most likely developed tuberculosis. When he died in September 1848, almost a year after the publication of *Jane Eyre,* his sisters had not revealed the secret of their literary success to Branwell. Emily, under the pseudonym Ellis Bell, had published *Wuthering Heights*. Anne, as Acton Bell, had seen both *Agnes Grey* and *The Tenant of Wildfell Hall* make it into print. But, as a bereft Charlotte related to Ellen, "we could not tell him of our efforts for fear of causing him too deep a pang of remorse for his own time misspent, and talents misapplied."

Following Branwell's death, his grief-stricken sisters all fell ill. Charlotte recovered fairly quickly, and Anne—whose health had worried Charlotte since their days at Roe Head —also rallied. But Emily, suffering from what they tried to persuade themselves was merely a cold, continued to ail. By mid-December, when Mary's letter at last reached Charlotte's hands, the family could no longer deny that Emily's condition was serious.

It is no wonder that, in the midst of such emotional turmoil, Charlotte could not summon the strength to respond to Mary straightaway. Within the dimly lit interior of a home shrouded in sadness, Mary's lively descriptions of life in New Zealand must have felt starkly at odds with Charlotte's present circumstances. Here in the quiet parsonage, the presence of Emily seemed to pervade everything: the kitchen where, in better health, she kneaded the bread dough while reading from a book propped up beside her; the dining room, where—in a habit learned from their former headmistress Miss Wooler— the three sisters once walked round and round the table until late in the evenings, discussing their writing; the children's study, now Emily's bedroom, where the young Brontës created their miniature manuscripts. Though Charlotte was no stranger to sorrow, never before had she known agony like this. With Emily now on the verge of death, even the most uplifting parts of Mary's letter could have brought her little delight.

The biggest disappointments came in the opening

paragraphs, in which Mary gave her opinion of Charlotte's novel. While she praised *Jane Eyre* for being "so perfect as a work of art," she criticized it for not having a greater political purpose.

"You are very different from me," Charlotte read, "in having no doctrine to preach." It was, according to Mary, "impossible to squeeze a moral" out of the book. "Has the world gone so well with you that you have no protest to make against its absurdities?"

Across continents and a time lapse of several months, Mary's voice seeped from the blue-tinged paper. Even from half a world away, it had the power to pierce the hush of the parsonage, usually marked only by the muffled voices of servants and the ticking of the grandfather clock in an alcove of the staircase.

Mary's rebuke must have come as a surprise since, among the many positive reviews of *Jane Eyre,* some had criticized its apparently dangerous challenge to the status quo. In the same month that Charlotte received the letter, the *Quarterly Review* had attacked the mysterious Currer Bell's book for being decidedly "anti-Christian." Comparing it to Samuel Richardson's scandalous tale *Pamela,* published over a century earlier, the female reviewer remarked that she thought a hero like Rochester would have "no chance, in the purer taste of the present day." As for Jane, her "pedantry," her "stupidity," her "gross vulgarity" came in for criticism. Throughout the book, which the article doubted could have been written by a woman, there was, it said, "a murmuring against the comforts of the rich and against the privations of the poor, which . . . is a murmuring against God's appointment . . . there is that pervading tone of Godly discontent which is at once the most prominent and the most subtle evil which the law and the pulpit,

which all civilized society in fact has at the present day to con-
tend with."

It is hard to imagine the Tory schoolgirl Mary had known
in the 1830s being accused of holding such supposedly out-
rageous opinions. And so the *Quarterly Review*'s condemna-
tion suggests that, in the sixteen years since, elements of Mary's
radicalism had rubbed off on Charlotte—shaping her thinking and writing, even though the two women were separated
by such a great distance. But Mary, clearly, didn't see this. Instead, her letter complained that, unlike the novels of Charlotte's sisters, Emily and Anne, *Jane Eyre* would do nothing to
challenge readers' lazy assumptions about the established social
order. How could Charlotte have written three volumes, Mary
wanted to know, "without declaring war to the knife against
a few dozen absurd do[ct]rines each of which is supported by
'a large & respectable class of readers'?" Emily, Mary opined,
"seems to have had such a class in her eye when she wrote that
strange thing Wuthering Heights."

Notwithstanding the unjustness of Mary's allegations, her
letter surely instilled more complicated emotions in Charlotte
—momentary envy perhaps at this praise of her sister's work,
mixed with guilt over such feelings at a time when Emily was
sinking irrecoverably into the final all-consuming stages of tuberculosis. Within days, on December 19, she would become
the fourth of the Brontë siblings to die, and the second in the
space of three months.

Back in July 1848, when Mary sealed her letter, she had
no idea of the tragedies that would transpire over the next
few months. And so she felt at liberty to take Charlotte to
task, presumably hoping to encourage her friend to make her
next novel more openly political. As to Mary's own literary

ambitions, she had written 150 or so pages of a novel, but had to admit that she was struggling to get past this point. She'd also sent a few articles to the editor of the radical *Tait's Edinburgh Magazine* but had never heard back from him. Another piece had gone off to *Chambers Edinburgh Journal,* to be met with the reply that the editors felt it was unsuitable for them.

These rejections must have been disheartening, but Charlotte had experienced far severer knockbacks. And, unlike Mary, so distracted by her brave new life in Wellington, she had plowed her creative and personal frustrations into her writing.

As 1849 dawned, though, even Charlotte was finding it hard to concentrate. She and Anne were the only remaining siblings, and their bereaved father increasingly leaned on his eldest daughter as a matter of survival — telling her he should sink if she failed him. Charlotte's worries only increased when she received a letter passed on by Mary's brothers, detailing an earthquake that had occurred in Wellington three weeks after the death of Branwell. Having received no word from her friend since that date, Charlotte fretted about Mary too.

By the time Charlotte confided these fears to Ellen, Mary had, in fact, sealed another letter and sent it off on its long voyage to Haworth. Written in April 1849, it told that she was expecting the arrival of a younger cousin, also called Ellen. Mary had already thought up "dozens of schemes" of occupation — the most ambitious of which was establishing a shop. Mary said that she had written an article about the earthquake and its aftershocks and submitted it to *Chamber's Edinburgh Journal*. This, like the pieces she'd mentioned in her letter posted in July 1848, would remain unpublished. While Mary said that she intended to write more, she seemed to doubt herself. She asked Charlotte not to remind her of this statement in a year's time. "I write at my novel a little," she continued, and talked of another book that she referred to as her baby—a text that she hoped would one day "revolutionise society and faire époque in history." Claiming that, in her case, it was "*active* work" that encouraged her writing, she admitted that she was more currently engaged in "doing a collar in crochet work."

At the best of times, Charlotte would surely have raised an eyebrow at Mary's convenient excuses. Since Branwell's death, Charlotte had experienced obstacles of such magnitude that she had put her new novel aside. But in the end, finishing *Shirley* would become a form of salvation. In the immediate aftermath of Emily's death, Anne's health became a matter of grave concern once more. Like Emily and Branwell before her, she was probably suffering from tuberculosis. Hoping that a change of air would do her good, Anne persuaded her reluctant sister to accompany her to the seaside town of Scarborough. However, on their arrival in May 1849, Anne deteriorated rapidly. At lodgings within sight of the waves, death soon stole the last of Charlotte's siblings. After returning to Haworth, Charlotte buried herself in her manuscript. As she said to her editor, William Smith Williams, whatever its eventual level of success with the public, "writing it has been a boon to me—it took me out of dark and desolate reality to an unreal but happier region."

With the impossibility for fluid communication between her and Mary, Charlotte surely felt glad that she now had people other than her school-day friend with whom she could talk about writing. In addition to her editor, she'd begun to establish relationships with some of the best-known literary figures of the era, including William Makepeace Thackeray, whom she'd met during a visit to London, and George Henry Lewes, who would one day become the partner of George Eliot. With the latter, she had established something of a rapport on the page, even arguing with this well-known critic about

the talents of Jane Austen. Lewes was a great admirer, his essays
—written some decades before James Edward Austen-Leigh's
memoir of his aunt—marking him out as one of the era's rare
readers to appreciate her genius. Charlotte's appraisal, on the
other hand, was decidedly less complimentary. "Why do you
like Miss Austen so very much? I am puzzled on that point,"
she asked. Charlotte compared *Pride and Prejudice* to a "da-
guerreotyped portrait of a common-place face; a carefully-
fenced, highly cultivated garden with neat borders and delicate
flowers—but no glance of a bright vivid physiognomy."

While Thackeray and Lewes would always remain acquaintances of hers rather than close friends, in August 1850,
another popular author of the day entered the life of Charlotte
Brontë—someone who, like Ellen and Mary, would go on to
define her legacy.

In New Zealand it was winter, but in Britain, these were
the last weeks of summer. Contrary to Mary's gloomy imaginings, Charlotte had been far from shut away in Haworth in
recent months. She was not long back from a month's stay in
London, during which she sat for her portrait, followed by a
sightseeing tour of Scotland. Tired though she was, she had
now reluctantly accepted the invitation of new friends, Sir
James and Lady Janet Kay-Shuttleworth, to stay at a house they
had rented high above the misty banks of Lake Windermere.
On August 19, after a long and trying northbound journey, it
was eight o'clock in the evening by the time Charlotte arrived
at the small station. Sir James was waiting for her with his carriage, ready to drive them through the wooded lanes that led
to Briery Close. Despite her tiredness, Charlotte—who from
her days of writing to the Lake Poet Robert Southey had romanticized this part of the world—was struck by the brooding
beauty of the Cumbrian fells.

She was not the only guest invited. The next evening, Elizabeth Gaskell, who had written *Mary Barton,* would arrive at the house. She and Charlotte had never met, but since the publication of *Jane Eyre,* Elizabeth, like so many others, had been following rumors about the real identity of its author.

After *Shirley* came out in October 1849, "Currer Bell" had sent Elizabeth a copy of the novel through her publisher, leading to an exchange of one letter each between the pair. Though Charlotte's missive had not divulged her name, it had let Elizabeth in on the tantalizing truth that she was a woman. Some months afterward, during one of her stays in London, Charlotte had come face to face with several well-known figures of the literary world. Though some had respected her wish to remain incognita, others—such as her earlier correspondent Thackeray—were apparently incapable of keeping her secret. After meeting Charlotte at her publisher's house, he had gone straight round to his gentlemen's club and announced to the gathered members, "Boys! I have been dining with 'Jane Eyre.'" It seems little wonder then that by the following year, literary London was rife with gossip over the identity of Currer Bell. For the wealthy Kay-Shuttleworths, the prospect of being the ones to introduce Charlotte to Elizabeth must have been simply too enticing to resist.

It was dark when Elizabeth entered the house, but the well-appointed drawing room was all adazzle. Charlotte, perhaps feeling that she and her fellow guest knew each other through their correspondence and novels, abandoned her customary shyness and directly shook hands. The two exchanged pleasantries, and then Elizabeth, who at close to forty was six years Charlotte's senior, went upstairs to lay down her things and remove her bonnet. Later, over tea, while Charlotte worked away at her embroidery, Elizabeth would take a good look at this slightly built woman, making a mental inventory of her features—details that she'd record in writing and use to beguile first her friends and, later, a far larger reading public. Elizabeth noted the light brown hair and expressive eyes of more or less the same color, the "reddish face; large mouth & many teeth gone." Less cutting in her judgment than the schoolgirl Mary's impressions, she decided, nonetheless, that Charlotte was plain. But she was taken by the sweetness of the novelist's voice and how she "rather hesitates in choosing her expressions, but when chosen they seem without an effort, *admirable* and *just* befitting the occasion."

From her hostess, Lady Janet, Elizabeth would soon receive an exaggerated version of Charlotte's life in Haworth with the supposedly crazed Reverend Brontë—a man who in fits of pique allegedly burned hearthrugs and sawed chairs into pieces. And Elizabeth lapped up suggestions that his mental instability had sent his wife to an early grave. In the years to come, Elizabeth's dealings with him would moderate her opinions, but she continued to believe that he made life a hardship for his daughters. This view would prime her to accept the image of Charlotte's sad existence that Mary would later convey.

In August 1850, the same month that Charlotte and Elizabeth met for the first time, Mary sent Charlotte her thoughts on *Shirley*. As with *Jane Eyre*, she'd had to wait a lengthy time to receive her copy, and it would be a good while longer before Charlotte received her response.

The consignment containing Charlotte's latest novel had reached Mary one Monday afternoon. She and her cousin Ellen, with whom she now lived and ran an adjoining shop, were getting ready for a small party, but had abandoned these preparations to open the box and read all the letters. Mary hadn't found the time to start reading *Shirley* that day or on Tuesday

either, since—clearly untroubled by the clumsiness she'd ex-
hibited in her Brussels classes—she and Ellen had stayed up
dancing until three or four o'clock in the morning. But on
Wednesday, Mary had begun reading the book.

Given Mary's criticism of the previous novel, Charlotte
must have looked forward to her friend's verdict with considerable apprehension. But unlike many critics, including the
once kindly George Henry Lewes—who wrote an unenthusiastic assessment for the *Edinburgh Review*—Mary concluded
that *Shirley* was superior to *Jane Eyre*.

Set against a backdrop of industrial agitation in Yorkshire
during the time of the Napoleonic Wars, the new novel dealt
more explicitly with social issues. And so it seems that Charlotte had taken Mary's criticisms of *Jane Eyre* to heart. According to Mary, *Shirley* had "so much more life & stir—that it
leaves you far more to remember than the other."

As she had done with *The Professor* and *Jane Eyre,* and
would do again with *Villette,* Charlotte had drawn inspiration
from many individuals personally known to her. In the case
of *Shirley,* this included the Taylor family, whom she reimagined as the Yorkes. Back in Gomersal, Mary's mother was furious at Charlotte's cold depiction of her. Her daughter's letter
made no comment on this, but it took issue with the portrayal
of Mr. Taylor, whom Mary said Charlotte hadn't made sufficiently honest. This seemed to be an important point for Mary,
whose admiration of her late father remained strong. It was he,
she said, who'd taught her "not to marry for money nor to tolerate any one who did." As for Rose Yorke, the character based
on her, Mary joked that Charlotte had made her "a little lump
of perfection." But it must have been a relief for Charlotte to
learn that her friend felt that she had captured the atmosphere
of the Taylor home, and that she thought highly of the book.

Mary's own novel continued to come in fits and starts. All she had to say on the subject was that she wrote "a page now & then." Typically, though, she retained her optimism, saying that whenever she found a free moment to read over what she'd produced, it looked "very interesting."

Charlotte must have picked up on some of the hidden frustrations beneath such cheerful pronouncements because she was to comment to Ellen Nussey, on receipt of this letter early in 1851, that Mary was not in the best emotional state. As the year wore on, Mary's spirits sank lower still when her cousin Ellen's health seemed to weaken. She, like Emily, and probably Branwell and Anne, had become a victim of tuberculosis. By early January 1852, even those back in Yorkshire could guess that Mary's cousin would not be long for this world. Charlotte predicted that Mary would be devastated if Ellen Taylor were to die. But parted as they were by such a great distance, the long gaps between the sending and receipt of letters meant that their conversations often ran at cross purposes. By the time that Charlotte voiced these worries to Ellen Nussey, they were out of date. Mary's cousin Ellen Taylor had passed away on December 27.

This then was how Mary began the new year—all alone in her timber house. In the early months of 1852, she sat down to write to Charlotte, telling her how life felt so quiet, so lonely, without Ellen. Now it seemed that it was her cousin who'd kept her so busy—at first with their work in the shop together and then lately with nursing duties. With Ellen dead, Mary occupied herself with cleaning a home once so chaotic that Charlotte had joked to her old headmistress Miss Wooler that, from what she'd heard, the cousins could never win the Roe Head Neatness Prize. Now Mary kept everything scrupulously tidy and pictured herself as an unoccupied old woman,

reduced to scrubbing her floors before they got dirty and pol-
ishing the outsides of all her pans. As with a previous broken-
off attempt to write this letter, her heavy sorrow stifled her
words. Tonight she wished that she and her old friend could
really speak face to face. "O for one hour's talk!"

On learning, several months later, that Ellen Taylor had
died, Charlotte began to feel that it would be best—not just
for herself but for Mary too—if her friend came home. During the same period, Charlotte continued to strengthen her
relationship with Elizabeth Gaskell, even persuading her publisher to delay the date on which they brought out her own
new novel, *Villette,* ultimately in January 1853, because it would
have clashed with the publication of Elizabeth's new book,
Ruth. Despite enjoying this closeness with a writer of comparable commercial stature, Charlotte continued to place great
importance on her bond with Mary—her first literary friend
outside the Brontë family. And in an unlikely turn of events, at
a moment when both Ellen Nussey and Elizabeth shied away,
Mary would soon send Charlotte some much-needed support,
all the way from the other side of the world.

As a woman in Victorian England, in her late thirties,
Charlotte, like her unmarried friends Ellen and Mary, assumed
that she would now never wed. In her twenties, she had received two proposals but turned them both down. To one
suitor, a clergyman brother of Ellen's, she'd said that she was
"not the serious, grave, cool-headed individual" he supposed,
and that she would not be able to make him happy. Later that
year, she'd refused another man of the cloth. Twelve years later,
in 1851, she was also the recipient of, if not a proposal exactly,
a promise of sorts from James Taylor, an editor at her publishing house. Following a visit he made to the parsonage, Charlotte had asked herself if the two would make a good match:

"Could I ever feel for him enough love to accept of him as a husband?" As with the previous offers she'd received—and taking a line similar to Mary's in matters of the heart—Charlotte, who decided she couldn't imagine loving this man romantically, turned him down.

Unknown to her, someone with whom she'd been living in close proximity for years had been growing increasingly attracted to her. The Reverend Arthur Bell Nicholls, her father's assistant curate since 1845, was not usually given to outbursts of emotion, but in December 1852 Charlotte suddenly came to understand the meaning behind "his constant looks—and strange, feverish restraint."

One evening at the parsonage, Arthur, a well-built man with dark features and uncommonly long whiskers, finally unburdened his feelings. Charlotte had withdrawn to the dining room after tea, leaving her father and his curate to their conversation. At around nine o'clock, she heard the parlor door open—a sign that Arthur must be about to leave. But rather than the expected jolt of the front door, there was a tap on the dining room door.

In a scene that could come straight out of one of her novels, this man whom Charlotte had once written off as drab and dull appeared a moment later in the dining room, suddenly much more interesting in her eyes. He was shaking with emotion. In a low voice, he told of the "sufferings he had borne for months" that "he could endure no longer." Revealing the strength of his affections was clearly a trial, and Charlotte felt moved.

"Have you spoken to Papa?" she asked.

"No," he said; he dared not.

Overwhelmed by his shockingly wan appearance, and mindful no doubt of her father's nearby presence, Charlotte urged Arthur to leave the house, promising a reply "on the morrow."

Once he was safely away, Charlotte crossed the hall to the parlor. If she hoped that her father would share her sympathy for Arthur, she was quickly corrected. As she would later confide in Ellen, "Papa worked himself into a state not to be trifled with—the veins on his temples started up like a whip-chord—and his eyes became suddenly blood-shot." Though Charlotte had never been attracted to Arthur, she felt incensed by the injustice of this reaction. Nonetheless, she quickly promised her father that she would give her refusal.

This outcome pleased Patrick Brontë, who would waste no time in letting Arthur know that he regarded the marriage proposal as an unthinkable act of subordination. He was angered not just by the man's failure to ask his permission before approaching his daughter, but also by his daring to think himself worthy of Charlotte, given his lack of financial security. Even months later, Patrick remained so furious that he would communicate with his curate only by letter. Arthur, realizing that his position had become untenable, began making arrangements to emigrate to Australia as a missionary. But in the end, being a far less adventurous character than someone like Mary, he scaled back this lofty dream and decided simply to leave Haworth.

In May 1853, not long after Arthur left the village, Charlotte, feeling exhausted and guilty for her part in his misery, developed a cold that deepened into influenza. Her father too, surely weakened by the stress of the past months, suffered a stroke, which for a time reduced his weak eyes to a state of total blindness. Charlotte, who had obeyed his wishes and rejected Arthur, was now left contemplating the prospect of a life without either of them. Thus, she decided to answer the last of the six sad letters she'd received from Arthur since his departure. Before long the two established a regular correspondence, keeping it a secret from almost all others.

Ellen was one of the few let in on developments. Apparently she viewed Charlotte's new closeness with Arthur as an act of betrayal. She felt that as a spinster like her and Mary, Charlotte should concern herself not with the possibility of happiness, but with "bearing" her current position and "enduring to the end." Ellen wrote to Mary in New Zealand, hoping to garner support for this idea. But Mary approved of partnerships not based on economic gain and, seeing marriage to Arthur as a chance for her friend to strike out in life away from the parsonage, she leapt to Charlotte's defense.

Writing in early 1854, Mary told Ellen that she talked "wonderful nonsense." "If its C's lot to be married shd n't she bear that too? or does your strange morality mean that she shd refuse to ameliorate her lot when it lies in her power." It would be August before the letter reached its disgruntled recipient, and by then Charlotte's father had at last recanted his objections to the couple's union. The far-off Mary would have been delighted.

In June 1854, they were married. Ellen, though still unhappy, traveled to Haworth to attend the wedding. Among the small party of guests was Miss Wooler, now in her sixties, who, on learning of the quarrel between the two friends, had advised them to make up. She also took on the last-minute duty of giving Charlotte away at the altar when her father suddenly refused to attend the ceremony. Although Mary was apt to overestimate the level of Patrick's control over his daughter, the saga with Arthur, culminating in his new father-in-law's pettiness on the pair's wedding day, suggests that there was some truth in her claims. Mary hoped that as a married woman, Charlotte would finally be able to acquire the happiness that Mary felt she had been lacking for so long.

Elizabeth Gaskell, by then the author of *Cranford,* had successfully combined a flourishing literary career with the duties of a minister's wife, and yet she was far less optimistic. When she had first learned about the clandestine love affair, she'd found herself swept up in the romance of it all. But since hearing more about Charlotte's fiancé, whom she had never met, she had reversed her initial optimism. In letters to a friend she confided the fear that the *"very* stern & bigoted" Arthur would seek to keep Charlotte away from those, such as Elizabeth herself—a Unitarian—who didn't share what she regarded as his "narrow" religious beliefs.

In marrying Arthur, Charlotte would not, in the end, break with her past life in the way Mary had hoped for. Charlotte had persuaded her father to relent by promising that the couple would remain at the parsonage with him. Sadly, her relationship with Elizabeth did indeed go the way of this friend's predictions, though Arthur seems not to have been the cause. Shortly after her marriage, Charlotte wrote asking her fellow author to come to stay, particularly so she and her new husband might get to know each other. But Elizabeth, wrapped up in a new friendship with Florence Nightingale—soon to be made famous by her nursing work in the Crimean War—put off the invitation. Letters, which the two authors had frequently exchanged, began to dwindle. By the beginning of January 1855, Elizabeth found herself regretting that Charlotte had apparently stopped writing to her entirely.

A fortnight later, and unbeknownst to Elizabeth, Charlotte had begun to develop the feverish symptoms often associated with tuberculosis. But in her case—and unexpectedly, at thirty-eight years of age—her first pregnancy was the cause. This fact may have initially assuaged the fears of her husband, but as the weeks passed and Charlotte's sickness did not abate, Arthur began to send letters to Ellen that hinted at his worst fears. In March 1855, Charlotte rallied a little and, as she told Ellen in a note written in a shaky pencil script, she took "some beef-tea—spoonfuls of wine & water—a mouthful of light pudding at different times." But later that same month, she slipped into partial unconsciousness. On March 30, her father, whose recent conduct had fallen so far short of exemplary, wrote a courageous and dignified letter to Ellen, preparing her for the imminent death of her beloved friend—which ended up occurring early the next morning.

He asked Ellen to inform Miss Wooler, and he contacted Elizabeth himself. Someone must have written to Mary at around this time. But, as ever, it would be several months before she received the news. Mary's sorrow on hearing that Charlotte had died can only be imagined. By then, she'd learned that Charlotte and Arthur had been living at the parsonage for the duration of their marriage, and it surely pained her further to realize that her friend had never gained a freer life. This seems to have made Mary particularly amenable to the approach of Elizabeth, who tracked her down by letter with the news that she would be writing Charlotte's biography.

Here, at last, or so it appeared to Mary, was a chance to give the public an accurate picture of her creative yet cruelly stifled friend. Elizabeth, from what Mary could tell from her letter, seemed to be a competent woman, although Mary wondered how on earth she would cope with all the differing stories about Charlotte. Still, here in Wellington, feeling that she must do something to help, Mary put together pages of recollections—a letter long delayed on its journey to Britain owing to the lack of sufficient postage, but eventually reaching a grateful Elizabeth.

The past year or so had been far from Mary's most successful. Not so very long ago, she had thought that, thanks to her various business ventures, it wouldn't be long before she'd make enough money to leave Wellington behind and return to Yorkshire with the means to live with the same independence that she enjoyed overseas. Now, though, stuck in her timber house without her cousin, despite the presence of her brother nearby, Mary felt increasingly alone. So it must have been a comfort to hope that even from a great distance, the words she had written for Elizabeth would shape the public's view of her selfless friend and the oppression she endured.

It would be another decade before Mary finally began to publish her own work, but in a sense her first foray into print came with *The Life of Charlotte Brontë*. Elizabeth quoted verbatim large parts of Mary's letters to her. Mary, who'd told Ellen Nussey that she could "never think without gloomy anger of Charlotte's sacrifices to the selfish old man," hoped that readers of Elizabeth's book would come to share her anger. The biography generated almost as much excitement and attention as Charlotte's first published novel, *Jane Eyre*. But its reception left Mary indignant. Elizabeth, mindful of the Victorian mood, had expunged any hint of scandal from the *Life*: she presented Monsieur Heger, once the focus of Charlotte's affections, as merely a tutor whose scholarly nature Charlotte admired; and she dismissed the wild writings of Charlotte's youth as curiosities, comprehensible to the "bright little minds" of the Brontë children alone.

Mary was horrified by how easily the public accepted this simplistic portrayal. Charlotte came across as merely long-suffering, the depiction of her many hardships failing to cause Mary's hoped-for public fury, or any genuine appetite for change regarding the situation of women. Instead, Elizabeth's portrait made the image of the controversial author of *Jane Eyre* more palatable. The critic George Henry Lewes felt that the biography presented "a vivid picture of a life noble and sad . . . a lesson in duty and selfreliance." Sir James Kay-Shuttleworth, who'd introduced Elizabeth to Charlotte, wrote that he hoped the widowed Arthur, who did not share his enthusiasm for the book, would "learn to rejoice that his wife will be known a Christian heroine, who could bear her cross with the firmness of a martyr saint." When Mary heard of such responses, no wonder she felt dismayed.

In July 1857, still living in Wellington, she penned a letter to Elizabeth, thanking her for sending the copy of the *Life* —the first, Mary believed, to arrive in New Zealand. Of the two reviews she'd read, Mary complained that "neither of them seems to think it a strange or wrong state of things that a woman of first-rate talents, industry, and integrity should live all her life in a walking nightmare of 'poverty and self-suppression.' I doubt whether any of them will."

She would be further demoralized when, following a slew of complaints to the publishers from, among others, the friends and family of Reverend William Carus Wilson—the headmaster of Charlotte's hated first boarding school—Elizabeth was forced to retract and rewrite several sections, and issue a public apology. Mary wrote to Ellen in January 1858 that she thought Elizabeth seemed to be a "hasty, impulsive person." "Libellous or not," she maintained, "the first edition was all true."

Mary would return to Yorkshire in 1860, when she was in her forties. Having shored up her own finances through her business ventures in New Zealand, she built herself a house,

High Royd, near to her childhood home in Gomersal. Here, she lived what neighbors regarded as an eccentric and certainly independent life. Ellen too came to regard Mary as decidedly odd—and although the pair now lived close to each other, they grew increasingly distant.

Mary continued to travel into old age and finally committed herself to the act of writing from which she'd been so distracted in her thirties. Her first published work was a series of articles for *Victoria,* a progressive magazine edited and printed by women. Later came her chapters of the travelogue *Swiss Notes by Five Ladies,* following an expedition to the Alps when Mary was fifty-seven.

Unlike Anne Sharp, who never saw an official account of Jane Austen's life, the first being sanctioned some five decades after the author's death, Mary would witness the appearance of various works of biography over the coming years. Ellen Nussey published her "Reminiscences of Charlotte Brontë" in *Scribner's* magazine in 1871. Casting herself as the custodian of Charlotte's memory, she would go on to cooperate with several future Brontë biographers. Mary, on the other hand, obliging though she could be on occasion, became increasingly unwilling to talk to researchers as time went by. Sadly, her reticence allowed a more socially acceptable mythology to build up around Charlotte's female relationships, which excluded the kind of politicized friendship that she had enjoyed with Mary.

Mary published her own novel, *Miss Miles,* much later, in 1890. Owing to her long period of adventuring, it took her four decades to complete, and appeared just three years before her own death at the age of seventy-six. Though largely ignored by the reading public, its exploration of the lives of working women was ahead of its time. Mary's book stands as a testament to all that she held most dear. Her plot celebrates the

enduring power of female friendship—with the personal relationship between Mary and Charlotte refracted and reflected
many times over in its interlocking stories. Its characters include the outwardly placid Maria Bell, a schoolteacher who
grows up in a moorland parsonage, and the Sarah Miles of the
title, someone who believes passionately in the power of education as a means to independence. Mary's message in *Miss
Miles* is reminiscent of her youthful debates with Charlotte.
There exists an alternative path in life for women, she insists, at
least for those willing to reject the expectations of society and
fight instead for their own happiness.

GEORGE ELIOT
&
HARRIET
BEECHER STOWE

*a hand stretched forth in the dark passage of life
to see if there is another hand to meet it*

HARRIET BEECHER STOWE TO GEORGE ELIOT

MAY 25, 1869

7

The Stuff of Legend

A WONDERFUL SURPRISE lay in wait for George Eliot as she drew up outside her north London villa in May 1869. The weary forty-nine-year-old, who'd been writing for over a decade under this masculine nom de plume, had spent an exhausting spring in continental Europe. She'd been traveling with the philosopher and critic George Henry Lewes. Controversially, the couple lived together as husband and wife, though they were not legally wed. Marian—or Mrs. Lewes, as she was known off the page—had gone in search of new sights, the rekindling of memories from previous trips abroad, and the much-longed-for warmer weather that always did wonders for her health. But unusually cold winds and rain had plagued the couple's travels. Added to this were worries about her sick stepson, currently making his way back from his South African home, and Lewes's mother, now in her eighties, also in poor health.

It was in a relieved frame of mind that Marian returned to her house, the Priory, in the elegant neighborhood of Regent's Park. As the carriage reached the end of the drive, she glimpsed the tiled roof and large chimney stacks emerging above its high surrounding wall. It had been fifteen years since she and Lewes began "living in sin"—an act that led London's polite society to shun her. Some female writers who might otherwise have befriended Marian felt it wise to steer clear, and even her own siblings followed suit. But such strains were surely far from her mind as she and Lewes stepped down from the carriage footplate. In the property's neatly kept garden, a path surrounded by plentiful rosebushes led to the inner sanctuary of home.

Though situated close to the park's zoological gardens, the newly opened London Underground, and the busy local canal, the Priory's grounds and walled fortifications shielded it from the capital's hustle and bustle. After all the journeying of the past two months, Marian could note the quiet with pleasure. Their temperamental maidservants, sisters Amelia and Grace Lee, were waiting inside with the customary greetings, ready to unburden their master and mistress of the cloaks, hats, and gloves that they'd worn for the carriage ride.

There was much to cheer Marian after nine weeks spent in the homes of friends and foreign hotel rooms: familiar leather spines of books on shelves, the grand piano—even with its somewhat plodding sound, and her favorites among the many framed pictures all fitted onto backdrops of wallpaper custom-made especially for her and Lewes. The handsome returns from Marian's writing had allowed them to buy the Priory for a costly sum and to engage a fashionable designer to redecorate it. But though she was the main breadwinner, Marian, who wished the world to regard her as conventionally married, seemed content for Lewes to remain ostensibly in charge of the household finances—an arrangement that freed up more time for her writing and reading.

Needless to say, now that she had returned to Britain, she had many tasks to fulfill: appointments to keep, domestic orders to deal with, her journal—abandoned for the entire trip —to bring up to date. But in the drawing room, the sweetness from the customary vases of flowers could uplift her, as could the happy memories of their regular Sunday gatherings, in the company of fellow intellectuals. Little did Marian know that among the stacked correspondence accumulated during her travels was an item that, when she slit open its seal, would do even more to raise her mood.

The letter, which she must have all but given up hope of ever receiving, had begun its long voyage across the Atlantic three weeks before. It had been sent by another novelist whom she'd never met, but whose bestselling fame surpassed even her own.

Harriet Beecher Stowe, eight years her senior and close to sixty, was an international celebrity and someone Marian had long admired from afar. Harriet's antislavery novel, *Uncle Tom's Cabin,* remained the publishing sensation of the age, its fictional characters having become so well known that their images appeared on everything from handkerchiefs to ceramics, while unauthorized Uncle Tom shows flooded the vaudeville stage. Some even regarded the book as a cause of the American Civil War, ended just four years earlier. Legend has it that during a visit Harriet made to the White House, President Abraham Lincoln greeted the author, who was short of stature, with the words "Is this the little woman who made this great war?" Her critics were vocal and numerous, but Harriet had fans aplenty too. In 1851–52, when *Uncle Tom's Cabin* appeared in its original form, as a newspaper serialization, readers bombarded the editor with enthusiastic letters. When Harriet went on to tour the land of Marian's birth, twelve months later, crowds turned up in droves to catch a sight of her, and she was wined and dined by London's high society. At one such dinner, hosted by the Lord Mayor, Harriet was seated opposite Charles Dickens, who had mixed feelings about her work. Queen Victoria, on the other hand, was an all-out fan of the novel. On Harriet's return to Britain in 1856, the queen was keen to meet her. Advised against publicly associating with the controversial author, she had the palace arrange a supposedly chance rendezvous on a restricted platform area of King's Cross railway station.

Now, almost thirteen years on, Harriet had decided to make contact with another author much admired by the monarch—the great George Eliot. In 1869, Marian had yet to write *Middlemarch,* her most famous work, but she was already one of the Western world's most well known and respected literary figures. Exercising even greater caution than she had with Harriet, the queen would always make sure that she never came face to face with the unmarried Marian. Nonetheless, greatly taken by her first novel, *Adam Bede,* the queen had commissioned the artist Edward Henry Corbould to paint watercolor images of scenes from the book.

While Marian's sales figures paled in comparison with those of her American counterpart, in 1862 she sold the exclusive serial rights for her novel *Romola* for a staggering seven thousand pounds. This was over three times the price of her impressive home, the Priory, which she and Lewes bought the following year.

Decades later, long after her death, Marian's preeminent biographer, Gordon S. Haight, would claim that Harriet's first letter to Marian was unexpected. But a careful perusal of Harriet's words, written in April 1869, reveals that they had not come entirely unbidden. A year earlier, Marian had hosted a visit from a mutual friend, the American writer Annie Adams Fields. Annie was married to James T. Fields, the editor of the

Atlantic Monthly and a partner of the publishing firm Ticknor and Fields. Marian had given Annie a kindly message for Harriet, which she in turn had passed on.

A woman more conventional than Harriet might have kept her distance. The novelist and minister's wife Elizabeth Gaskell, for instance—who'd been keen to get to know Charlotte Brontë and had also sought out Harriet's company during her first British tour—would remain perpetually perturbed by Marian's being unwed and what Elizabeth regarded as Lewes's "soiled" morals. Though she'd written to Marian a decade earlier to express admiration for her fiction, the future author of *The Life of Charlotte Brontë* had steered clear of pursuing a friendship. And she had not been able to keep herself from lamenting to Marian, "I wish you *were* Mrs. Lewes." The couple had been in what they regarded as a marriage since 1854, when they were both in their mid-thirties, but had never officially tied the knot. For Lewes was already wed to another woman—the mother of his children—whom he continued to support. As the success of Lewes and Marian's regular Sunday gatherings show, by 1869 the social frost that she, in particular, had suffered was now somewhat thawed. Nonetheless, much prejudice endured.

Harriet, despite her ardent Christianity, didn't much bother herself with the couple's unusual domestic arrangements. And yet, although she had intended initially to write at once, she'd ended up leaving it all these months. Intriguingly, she had found it necessary to embark beforehand on a literary marathon, carefully rereading six of Marian's seven books to prepare for putting pen to paper. Especially given the heavy demands of her own writing schedule, and her tendency to be rather slapdash in the projects she undertook, the amount of energy Harriet put into this task was extraordinary—and her dedication points to a hidden motive for seeking out a relationship with Marian at this time.

A date three weeks prior to Marian's arrival back in London marks the moment at which Harriet reached out in friendship across the waves. Four thousand miles away, she was staying at her Florida winter home, which was surrounded by orange groves. In this idyllic spot in the rural community of Mandarin, the blue St. Johns River flowed by the front of her house—and future tourists would pay to take the steamer for a promised glimpse of the famous author sitting on her open porch.

Harriet dipped her pen into its inkwell. This letter would need just the right greeting. "Dear Mrs. Lewes" would be one possibility, as would the warmer "My Dear Mrs. Lewes." But disregarding the British author's reputation for high-minded reserve, Harriet tossed aside any initial hesitancy and wrote the words "My Dear Friend." She had already sidestepped the awkward issue of Marian's marital status by deciding to refer to Lewes as Marian's husband, therefore thinking of her as a wife, like herself.

Over the following pages, in a more sloped hand than the upright lettering that flowed from Marian's nib, Harriet would launch into a review of Marian's published works. She'd even dare to make a candid appraisal of her recipient's *"thoroughly English"* personality, which Harriet felt she knew intimately through the page. Explaining that she had *"studied"* these books *"more* than read them," Harriet praised Marian's originality and moral perception. Nonetheless, she went on to make several criticisms. Some of the strongest aspects of Marian's early stories, she wrote, had never been fully achieved in her novels. And she even dared to suggest that *The Spanish*

Gypsy, a hit with the literary establishment of its day, would have been rendered better in prose than verse.

Harriet's considerable preparation faded into the background as she moved deeper into the letter. Gathering pace, she began to drop punctuation and leave sentences unfinished. She signed off by promising to send Marian a copy of her next book and inviting the British author to come and stay at her winter home in Florida, before also jotting down her permanent Connecticut address. Now, with her missive ready to seal up and send on its way, Harriet could only hope that Marian would be ready to look upon its sender with generosity.

Harriet's letter had alluded to the heavy burden of writing *Oldtown Folks*—her new novel, due to be published in exactly a month's time. Work on this book, she said, was her reason for not making contact sooner. She didn't directly say that the decision to write to Marian now was motivated by nerves over its impending release, though this concern can be inferred from her first two letters.

Harriet had high hopes but also fears for *Oldtown Folks,* a novel over which, unusually for her, she had labored for several years. She had put her "heart soul & life blood" into it, she'd say in her next letter to Marian, adding that it "cost me more to write than anything I ever wrote." Worried that delivering her story in installments could dilute the impact of a book she regarded as her tour de force, she had insisted to her editor that serialization in the *Atlantic Monthly* was not an option and that *Oldtown Folks* should appear from the beginning in book form. Harriet's tale chronicled the Massachusetts town of Natick and was inspired by the boyhood of her husband, who had experienced visions from a young age of what she called "spiritualistic phenomena." She'd begun the endeavor with all her usual enthusiasm, but now that the American and British publication dates drew near, Harriet fretted that her huge overseas audience would struggle to engage with a work "so intensely American" in character.

Finding an appreciative reader in someone with as high a profile as George Eliot could be a tremendous help and, given Harriet's sudden decision to get in touch at this time, it certainly seems that this had occurred to her. Little did she know that, by the time the early copy of the novel she'd promised arrived with her new friend, she would be looking to Marian for support on a rather more volatile matter.

Sensing nothing of this brewing storm, Marian simply rejoiced to receive that first letter. Three days after her return from her European travels, she wrote a response, addressing Harriet in kind as "My dear Friend."

Although Marian's tone was markedly more measured, she too wrote with a startling level of candor. Even in this initial reply she alluded to her frequent bouts of depression and talked—surprisingly to the modern reader aware of her enduring reputation—of her uncertainty about the quality of her literary work. Harriet's letter, she said, made her "almost wish" that her correspondent could have a fleeting sense of the "paralyzing despondency in which many days of my writing life have been past," so that she might truly see "the good I find in such sympathy as yours—in such an assurance as you give me that my work has been worth doing." The Marian who appears in the pages of this letter reaches out for Harriet's extended hand, recognizing her correspondent for what she is—a "fellow-labourer" and a woman with whom she has something unique in common. Despite marked differences in their temperaments—Harriet being the livelier and more impulsive of the two—their experiences as the most celebrated living female authors on either side of the Atlantic immediately drew them close. That the pair shared this extraordinary status makes it all the more surprising that their friendship has not gone down in history.

The act of sitting down to write to Harriet would turn out to be the high point of a distressing weekend for Marian. Later that Saturday, her stepson, Thornie, dramatically and un-expectedly returned home. The twenty-five-year-old had been in South Africa for close to five years, hunting big game and seeking his fortune in farming, but his attempts had proved unsuccessful. Not long before Marian and Lewes departed for their European trip, he'd written a pitiful letter to his fa-ther complaining of debilitating pains in his back and request-ing funds to cover the return journey to London. Lewes had obliged at once, but with the health of his elderly mother to worry about too, and aware of Thornie's tendency to play fast and loose with the truth, neither he nor Marian seemed to rec-ognize the extent of his son's ailments.

When, that day, the couple returned from paying a call on Lewes's frail mother, they were astonished to discover that Thornie had completed his voyage back to Britain weeks ear-lier than anyone thought possible. The spinal disease from which he was suffering now had such a grip on him that he had lost more than fifty pounds in weight. His once strapping physique had wasted away, leaving him weak and gaunt. Still, he valiantly attempted to reassure his father and Marian that all was not as bad as it seemed. Later, he would sit down with the couple, giving the impression of pleasure as he listened to Marian play the piano. This was enough, for the moment at least, to convince Lewes to record in his diary that his son was in good spirits.

The next day, Thornie was far worse. The Priory was

thrown into such disarray by his deterioration that Marian
and Lewes scarcely had time to remember that Sunday afternoons were usually reserved for their popular gatherings. And
so, hours later, and for the second time within a matter of days,
an American author would make an unexpected appearance
into the life of Mrs. Marian Lewes.

The young Henry James, on his first overseas trip as an
adult, had been persuaded to tag along with two American
friends who'd previously visited in January. By this time, Sunday afternoons at the Priory had become so successful that
— as Henry was to note in a subsequent letter to his father
— to go accompanied with a "received friend" was the only
way for a stranger to gain entry, so "hedged about with sanc-
tity" had Marian become. Henry's female companions had perhaps already painted a picture of the Priory's artfully decorated
drawing room, the theatrical sweeping curtains across its central archway, and the armchairs carefully arranged by Lewes and
Marian in the hope that no one present should be seated less
comfortably than anyone else.

Many famous personalities were said to have made ap-
pearances—over the years, Robert Browning, Lord Tennyson,
and Charles Dickens would be among them. And so the young
man must have arrived that day with more than a little trepidation. Little known though he was at this early stage of his career, Henry had written three reviews of Marian's work so far,
both praising and criticizing her writing. His verdict on *The
Spanish Gypsy* agreed with Harriet's assessment that poetry was
not quite Marian's forte. If Henry fretted about such matters
as he approached the house that Sunday, he would soon learn
that he had no need to worry. The three friends were about to
enter a moment in the life of George Eliot when her career

and literary reputation could not have been further from her thoughts.

Inside the walls of the Priory that afternoon, there was much commotion. Thornie's back had begun to pain him so badly that, although he had dressed and come downstairs, he could do nothing but writhe in agony on the floor. His frantic father—usually a gregarious presence at these Sunday gatherings—had gone out on a quest to purchase morphine, leaving Marian to tend to her stepson. The jangling gate bell, heralding the arrival of Henry and his friends, was a distraction certainly, though hardly a welcome one.

Perhaps a kind of crisis-induced numbness encouraged Marian to allow her three American visitors into the house while her stepson still thrashed and groaned on the floor. Almost five decades later, when he wrote of the afternoon's drama in his memoirs, Henry would recall that even in these extreme circumstances, Marian kept up polite conversation. If his word is to be believed, it seems that she felt compelled to go through the motions despite her distress, thereby rewarding the trio with the kind of learned talk they expected.

During the gap in years between the day's experience and the writing of it, Henry certainly added layers of varnish to his story. He embellished the cause of Thornie's suffering, for instance, by suggesting that his injuries stemmed from a past encounter with an angry bull. As an old man, Henry remembered his hostess's very human agitation, but her "*illustratively* great" demeanor, her black silk dress, and the lace mantilla covering her hair remained at least as strong in his mind. Even in a letter to his father, written the day after his visit in 1869, his chief impression, it seems, was that—despite the most taxing of circumstances—Marian remained a beguiling hostess.

What neither Henry nor his friends, nor perhaps even Marian and Lewes grasped at this point, was the irreparable nature of Thornie's condition. His torments that Sunday merely marked the beginning of his decline. That evening, Queen Victoria's celebrated surgeon James Paget visited the house, and Lewes rose four times in the night to give morphine to his son. Marian too would soon be devoting much of her energy to caring for Thornie, who continued to suffer excruciating bouts of pain.

Under these heart-wrenching circumstances, she took some much-needed cheer from Harriet's second letter, of late May. Having previously confided doubts about her own literary endeavors, Marian would have appreciated Harriet's description of writing a book as "*a hand* stretched forth in the dark passage of life to see if there is another hand to meet it." Harriet's copies of Marian's books were full of annotations, she told her. If Marian could only see them, she would find "how often the hand has met the kindred hand."

While Thornie's health was steadily worsening in London, on the other side of the Atlantic Harriet had become embroiled in troubles of a very different nature. In the six-week gap between her first and second letters to her new friend, Harriet's thoughts had turned from *Oldtown Folks* to the prospect of writing another, shorter work—one that would soon eclipse public interest in the novel and mark a turning point in her literary reputation.

Within months, Marian would know all about this risky venture, but this second letter from America gave only the merest hint of what was to come. Harriet wrote that she had returned from Canada, where she had gone to establish copyright on *Oldtown Folks* for the lucrative British market. On her journey there, stopping at a Boston bookshop, she'd happened on a much anticipated, newly translated title, just out in America. Harriet bought a copy of *My Recollections of Lord Byron,* written by the poet's last mistress, Countess Guiccioli, and read it on her Canadian trip. What she found within its pages astounded her, and she'd returned to her home in Hartford, Connecticut, burning with a sense of injustice.

During her first tour of Britain in 1853, Harriet had become close friends with the late poet's widow, Lady Anne Isabella Byron—a woman she believed to have shown a great capacity for love, charity, and forgiveness. On her return trip, in 1856, Lady Byron had confided in Harriet a long-held secret and asked the American author whether she thought that this was the right moment to break her vow of silence. Lord Byron, his widow claimed, was guilty of an incestuous relationship with his half sister. Though Harriet didn't doubt her friend's word, so scandalous was the accusation that she had urged Lady Byron to keep her "sacred veil of silence" tightly drawn. But now, over a decade later, with the publication of the countess's book, Harriet was beginning to rethink the advice she had given.

Countess Guiccioli's memoir of the dead poet painted Lady Byron, now also deceased, as a cool, unfeeling woman, while Lord Byron came across as very much the wronged hero. Harriet, who had long harbored a deep resentment for her late friend's husband, was incensed by the thought that the British and American public, upon reading this work, could come to regard the pair's marriage thus. Harriet knew that the rumor of incest gave a figure as influential as her a potent weapon with which to answer the countess's claims. But she also knew that airing such matters in public could lead to her own censure.

Not long after her letter to Marian, Harriet began work on her rebuttal to the countess's book. Over three weeks in

June, she toiled furiously on "The True Story of Lady Byron's Life," an article that would in time be published in the *Atlantic Monthly*. Her correspondence with another, long-established friend, the famous author and physician Oliver Wendell Holmes, hints that the unease Harriet felt about her endeavor was growing day by day. But given what she saw as unjust attacks on the memory of her friend, she still felt impelled to act. As she made clear in her letter to the doctor, she wanted his advice "*not* . . . as to whether the main facts shall be told, for on this point I am so resolved that I frankly say advice would do me no good." Harriet hoped instead that he could take a look at the draft of her article in order to help her tell her story "as wisely and well" as this sort of story could be told. Seeking this critique before she sent the manuscript to the *Atlantic*'s Boston offices was a good decision, for when the doctor returned it, Harriet discovered that he had corrected many errors —some grammatical, others reflecting her tendency to exaggerate. Holmes predicted that her claims were bound to ignite an explosion of controversy unlike any seen before. Yet he also let her know that he admired the substance of the article.

Harriet must have hoped that her British friend would be equally enthusiastic. Marian by now had received her copy of *Oldtown Folks* and, despite Harriet's fears expressed in her first letter that readers abroad wouldn't understand it, Marian had written back to let her know how much she'd enjoyed it. Given the frequency with which Marian herself wrote of past generations, it is no surprise that she had been drawn to the novel's evocation of an "old-fashioned provincial life." And as someone who had given up the ardent faith of her youth but remained deeply interested in religion, she'd warmed to the "insight & true tolerance" with which the book's author had presented her Calvinist characters—especially since Marian knew that Harriet did not quite share their religious convictions. She did not feel excluded as a non-American reader; instead she appreciated Harriet's willingness to tackle the subject—"rare even among writers" and one missed "altogether in English drawing-room talk." On reading these words, Harriet perhaps dared to dream that Marian would also look favorably on the article about Lady Byron and speak of it with equal admiration among the intellectual company within her own drawing room.

In August 1869, with the piece soon to be published simultaneously in the *Atlantic Monthly* in America and *Macmillan's* magazine in Britain, Harriet sat down once again to write to Marian. This letter, like her second missive, of May 1869, is among that portion of the pair's correspondence that remains unpublished. To read it, researchers must gain access to the locked archive of the Henry W. and Albert A. Berg Collection at the New York Public Library, where we called up these neglected manuscripts. The 150-year-old sheets of cream-colored paper hold Harriet's words of sympathy for Marian and her sick stepson. Her letter goes on to share with Marian her own sadness about her eldest living son. The twenty-nine-year-old, "wounded and shattered" during the American Civil War, had been suffering physically and mentally for years—his afflictions including an alcohol addiction that preceded his army career, although Harriet didn't mention this. Knowing all about the emotional strain of constant caregiving, Harriet cautioned her friend to guard her own health.

Given Marian's circumstances, it would not do to make too much of the Lady Byron article, and yet Harriet could not quite let the opportunity pass. And so she casually threw in the admission that she was enclosing two items that "I thought might interest you": a sermon written by her preacher brother and her as-yet-unpublished piece for the *Atlantic Monthly*. In the letter's closing paragraph, she told Marian that she should not rush to answer this missive, adding the perhaps not entirely honest wish that her words should simply drop on Marian "like a snow flake—melt & be gone."

As Harriet guessed, the continuous upheaval of life at the Priory could not have made it easy for Marian to keep up with the daily ritual of dealing with the post. Thornie was growing ever weaker and suffering from attacks of paraplegia. The family had engaged the services of a nurse, but their growing sense of helplessness at the march of the disease had taken a toll on each one of them.

When Marian received Harriet's letter, the look of its first page must have been unexpected; her friend's writing appeared faint and frail. Unbeknownst to her, Harriet too had been suffering in body of late, her fears about the possible public reaction to her Lady Byron article having apparently brought on a physical collapse during which she temporarily lost the full use of her arms and legs. As Marian continued to read, though, she would have witnessed Harriet's script growing visibly stronger as she hit her stride. Then, halfway through the letter, came the brief mention of the Lady Byron piece.

This likely made little impact at first. But it must have come as a shock when, having finished the letter, she began to read this accompanying article.

Marian could not have expected what followed. In contrast to the lively flow of Harriet's correspondence and, indeed, the greater part of her published prose, the voice of "The True Story of Lady Byron's Life" was trimmed of its author's emotion. Nonetheless, Marian balked at the rumor about incest that Harriet was on the verge of making known to a far wider reading public.

Marian was no fan of Lord Byron. As it happened, she had recently reread a significant number of his poems to confirm that she was being fair in her views, and had concluded that his writing was indeed repugnant. Be that as it may, Harriet's literary endeavor appalled her too. She understood that Harriet wanted to defend her late friend but felt certain that such a course of action could only make matters worse.

Another jolt was yet to come. Two thirds of the way through the article, Marian discovered what must at first have seemed a random mention of the author of "the novel of 'Romola'"—a reference to Marian herself. Owing to her own socially precarious unmarried status, Marian typically went out of her way to disassociate herself from any further notoriety. So how disconcerting it must have been to find that Harriet had evoked the tragic relationship between two of the book's central characters to demonstrate "the whole history of the conflict of a woman like Lady Byron with a nature like that of her husband." This unexpected mention of such supposed similarities may have had an additional purpose. Given Harriet's anxieties about the public's potential response to the article, and its description of Marian as "one of the first of living writers," these lines come across as a pointed and only thinly disguised request for endorsement.

Had Marian felt herself capable of publicly supporting her friend, their relationship could perhaps have made it into literary legend. But the notion of defending Harriet's article was quite unthinkable to Marian, who even felt at a loss as to how she should answer this private letter. Against a backdrop of household anguish, she would keep mulling over its contents in the weeks to come, mentioning the piece when she wrote to other close friends and noting how much it had unsettled her. Nothing could outweigh "the heavy social injury of familiarizing young minds with the desecration of family ties."

Coincidentally, Marian had recently been working on eleven sonnets, together titled "Brother and Sister." The sequence was inspired by her early closeness with her own brother, from whom she'd been estranged for the past two decades—ever since he learned of her relationship with Lewes. Though the poems, which portrayed the breakdown of their sibling relationship, were now finished, Marian would delay their publication for almost five years. Looking back on the writing of the sonnets some time later, she would recall in a letter to her publisher that "this was always one of my best loved subjects. And I was proportionally enraged about that execrable discussion raised in relation to Byron"—the implication being that Harriet's decision to write of such unsavory things and drag Marian's name into it could have led readers to misconstrue Marian's own work.

The British author was far from alone in her distaste for the article; the press on either side of the Atlantic would roundly condemn it. Despite her own misgivings, however, Marian worried about Harriet. But with Thornie's health worsening by the day, she could not find a moment to pen what would be a difficult reply. And so, with the weeks passing, she could only trust that when at last she was able to send off such a letter, any hurt feelings on Harriet's part would not loosen the clasped hands of their bond.

A watercolor by Cassandra Austen of her twelve-year-old niece, Fanny, painted during Anne Sharp's two-year tenure as the girl's governess (*Jane Austen's House Museum*)

Godmersham Park in Kent, the home of Jane Austen's brother, where Anne was a member of the household staff (*© TopFoto / The Image Works*)

A portrait included in the Friendship Book of court librarian James Stanier Clarke, which some claim he painted of Jane following her visit to the royal library at Carlton House in 1815 *(Permission granted by Simon Wheeler)*

Above: Jane in her mid-thirties, drawn by her sister Cassandra in about 1810 *(World History Archive / Alamy Stock Photo)*

Left: The posthumous and romanticized portrait, based on Cassandra's sketch, commissioned to create the frontispiece to *A Memoir of Jane Austen* *(Heritage Image Partnership Ltd / Alamy Stock Photo)*

Portrait of Ellen Nussey as a schoolgirl, believed by some to be the work of Charlotte Brontë *(© The Brontë Society)*

Charlotte's caricature of herself waving goodbye to Ellen Nussey across the sea, included in a letter Charlotte sent from Brussels after returning there in 1843 *(© The Brontë Society)*

Mary Taylor regarded George Richmond's 1850 portrait of Charlotte as overly flattering, and questioned the decision to include a copy in Elizabeth Gaskell's *Life of Charlotte Brontë*. *(World History Archive / Alamy Stock Photo)*

Mary Taylor (far left) on an alpine expedition in Switzerland in 1874, when she was aged fifty-seven *(Kirklees Museums & Galleries)*

Earliest known photograph of Mary Ann Evans, as George Eliot was then known, taken in the 1840s *(Image courtesy of Coventry Archives and Research Centre)*

The drawing room at the Priory—the scene of the regular Sunday gatherings Marian hosted with her partner George Henry Lewes *(Chronicle / Alamy Stock Photo)*

Harriet Beecher Stowe in the late 1870s, during the period of her friendship with Marian *(Alpha Historica / Alamy Stock Photo)*

Harriet with her husband Calvin Ellis Stowe (both far right) on the porch of their idyllic Florida home *(Hulton Archive / Getty Images)*

Katherine Mansfield at Garsington Manor in Oxfordshire, around 1916, the year when she became friends with Virginia Woolf (© *National Portrait Gallery, London*)

Society hostess Ottoline Morrell (far left) in the gardens at Garsington, 1915, with Virginia's sister Vanessa Bell (far right) and Virginia's friend Lytton Strachey (seated on chair), who introduced her to Katherine (© *National Portrait Gallery, London*)

Virginia in her mid-thirties, at Garsington Manor,
where she first met Katherine (© *National Portrait
Gallery, London*)

❧ 8 ❧

The Specter of Scandal

AS THE SUMMER of 1869 drew to a close, in a world unknown to George Eliot's reading public, Marian Lewes of the Priory, Regent's Park, girded herself for the worst. Within her north London villa, the forty-nine-year-old's sick stepson showed few signs of recovery. In fact, since his unexpected return in May, his symptoms had only gotten worse. In July, a glandular disorder, which the doctor feared might be tubercular, had added to the young man's sufferings. By mid-September, Marian was recording in her journal that her stepson looked "distressingly haggard." Once a lively personality, he had all but lost his zest for life. Well-meant gifts of flowers from family friends brought him little pleasure, and even conversation with his nearest and dearest often proved too great an effort.

Within this much subdued household, the scents of sickness and increasing desperation lent a sourness to the air. Though the new nurse was on hand, Thornie's father and stepmother frequently took their turns at the young man's bedside. On at least one afternoon his mother came to visit, but Marian was the more frequent companion, sitting among medicine bottles inscribed with Latin names, quietly reading a book.

Her daily life bore almost no comparison to the hopeful

new year she'd planned. Back on January 1, she had cheerfully noted in her diary that she and her partner were well
and that the "many tasks" she'd set herself for 1869 included
"A Novel called Middlemarch." Now, though, as the browning leaves beyond the window heralded the arrival of autumn,
Thornie remained in grave danger, Marian's own health continued to suffer, and progress on this new book was arduously
slow. Recently, the thought had come to her that "I do not feel
very confident that I can make anything satisfactory of Middlemarch." Under normal circumstances, she might have written sooner to her American friend. But the pair's epistolary
conversation had been on hold for the month since the British
author received her copy of the Lady Byron article, and Marian
would put off replying for several weeks more.

In mid-October, she recorded in her journal that her
stepson was declining fast. He would soon lapse into partial
consciousness, and on the early evening of the nineteenth, with
his nurse and Marian at his side, he took his final breaths. Afterward, Marian could at least console herself that his death had
been peaceful. In the past, she had sometimes felt frustrated by
Thornie's lack of self-discipline and few worldly accomplish-
ments, but the past months had brought them closer, and her
bereavement was as genuine as his grieving father's. In a journal
entry for that date, when she was almost fifty years of age, she
wrote that "this death seems to me the beginning of our own."

While the Priory fell into deep mourning, across the
ocean, the life of Marian's friend had been turned upside down
following the publication of the piece she'd written for the *Atlantic Monthly*. As the author of *Uncle Tom's Cabin*—a book that
remained controversial, particularly in the American South—
Harriet had made the decision to publish "The True Story of
Lady Byron's Life" with some understanding of the risks in-

volved. Indeed, based on past experience, the fifty-eight-year-old author anticipated that her revelations could ruffle feathers, so she had done her best to avoid public outrage. She wrote in a style more restrained than usual and sought the support of important cultural influencers like Oliver Wendell Holmes and, so it would seem, Marian herself.

But the sheer scale of the scandal unleashed by the magazine article had taken Harriet by surprise. After the story came out in the summer of 1869, the press attacked the accuracy of her account, questioning the credibility of her source, the late Lady Byron. What's more, Harriet's critics pronounced that— even if the allegations against Lord Byron were true—they were so obscene that Harriet should not have revealed them. A few voices, including that of Elizabeth Cady Stanton, came to Harriet's defense. As one of America's foremost campaigners for female suffrage, she believed that the case of Lady Byron illuminated the powerlessness of *all* women. But the majority of journalists, governed by Victorian ideas about decency, were indignant that a subject as shocking as sibling incest should have been made public under any circumstances.

A fighter by nature, Harriet refused to be cowed by her critics, setting her mind instead to turning her article into a book. She had adopted such a strategy in the past, with mixed results. When some readers had accused Harriet of vastly exaggerating the horrors of slavery depicted in *Uncle Tom's Cabin,* she'd written a work of nonfiction that provided documented proof of the underlying truths of her most famous novel. *A Key to Uncle Tom's Cabin*—a bestseller, like the work that preceded it—had its vocal supporters. Nonetheless, it had done little to change the minds of Harriet's most vehement opponents. Her critics accused her of cherry-picking the worst examples, claiming that the experience of most slaves at the hands of their masters was far better than Harriet would have it. Others attempted to shift the terms of the debate, putting forward the view that even if her claims had merit, Harriet was as guilty as the perpetrators of such violence for bringing indelicate matters into the open—a shameful premise by any standards. Those who deplored the article in the *Atlantic Monthly* forcefully repeated a similar argument now. Harriet, fueled by the criticism, threw herself into writing this new book. If the varied responses to *A Key to Uncle Tom's Cabin* raised any doubts within her, she swept them aside, remarking to her publisher that this was "*war* to the knife."

Whereas Marian had applauded the power of *Uncle Tom's Cabin,* she too raised objections about Harriet's piece on Lady Byron, albeit privately and in a gentler manner. During the winter of 1869, while Harriet was so deeply embroiled in her work, across the ocean in London a bereaved Marian finally gathered the strength to respond to her friend's last letter. On December 10, 1869, she began with the usual heartfelt greeting, "My dear Friend," then outlined Thornie's final months. "I am recovering now from a very shattered state of health," she told Harriet, but added that "I cannot feel at ease without writing you a brief letter, first to tell you how my silence has been occupied . . . and next to thank you for all the helpful words that you sent me." Marian knew from Harriet's letter of May that her friend had lost a son of her own—a nineteen-year-old who'd drowned accidentally in the Connecticut River twelve years earlier, and whom she'd described as her "silent blue eyed golden haired boy—who never gave me any sorrow but his death." Knowing of Harriet's troubles with her surviving veteran son too, still suffering from the aftereffects of war, Marian would have expected her recipient to understand the depth of her grief. On the tricky subject of the Lady Byron article, Marian tactfully wrote that, although she "should have preferred that the 'Byron question' should not have been brought before the public," she felt sure that Harriet had been "impelled by pure, generous feeling." Marian was careful to make it clear that she hadn't written to express a judgment and that she was anxious only to convey to Harriet a sense of "sympathy and confidence, such as a kiss and a pressure of a hand would give, if I were near you."

Sealing up the letter, Marian could only wait to see how Harriet would respond. It was likely, of course, that Harriet might have felt some disappointment at the lukewarm response to her *Atlantic Monthly* article. But bearing in mind all that they had in common, Harriet was exceptionally well positioned to offer a unique kind of solace.

Marian would have sent her letter to her friend's main address in Hartford, Connecticut, unaware that Harriet was not there. Since deciding that autumn to devote herself to the research and writing of *Lady Byron Vindicated,* she had taken herself off to the New York City clinic of George Taylor, well known among the wealthy for his Swedish Movement Cure. This urban version of the better-known water cures of the era relied on a regimen of massage and repetitive exercise instead of bathing rituals.

Boarding at Dr. Taylor's facilities, Harriet had now established a regular daily routine. In the morning, she worked ceaselessly on her manuscript, putting additional pressure on a mind already strained by the writing and reception of the *Atlantic Monthly* article. Confined to her private room, she could at least be buoyed by the thought—as she would tell her daughters—that Lady Byron's voice would soon rise from beyond the grave, "clear as the sun fair as the moon, & terrible as an army with banners." Mindful of the need to keep up

her strength, Harriet relieved her anxiety with a regular afternoon ride or walk in Central Park—a newly established oasis
of calm within the bustling metropolis.

Here she cut a diminutive figure, making her way along
the sculpted paths around the lake or by the sheep grazing on
the Green. Passing the shadow outlines of bare winter trees, her
small frame cloaked against the cold, she must have found that
her thoughts kept returning to her struggles to restore Lady
Byron's reputation. If only the great George Eliot had joined
the few individuals who had praised her *Atlantic Monthly* article. But Harriet was not the type to accept defeat easily, pre-
ferring instead to soldier on, focusing her energies on defending her cause.

Once the time for walking drew to a close, she could turn
her mind to her daily four o'clock appointment in Dr. Taylor's
Movement Room. There, she would be called on to perform a
series of exercises using the clinic's gymnasium equipment. As
Harriet had described it to her daughters, under the watchful
gaze of the staff, she could expect to be "ribbed & stretched &
otherwise operated on" until at last a sense of inner calm returned.

Dr. Taylor's clinic was, in fact, not entirely unfamiliar to
her British friend. In the same letter in which Harriet had enclosed the copy of "The True Story of Lady Byron's Life," she'd
mentioned that her older sister, Catherine, had been successfully treated by the doctor for a "paralysis of the sciatic nerve
which had crippled her for twenty years." Knowing how Marian had also been suffering physically from the strain of caring for poor Thornie, Harriet had explained that she was mentioning this "philosophic system of exercising" in the hope that
"possibly in that way some avenue of relief may open to you."

With the household now in mourning, Marian—still

struggling to muster enthusiasm for *Middlemarch*—prepared to spend a sad and lonely Christmas in London. As she'd told Harriet when she wrote to her in December, even in the midst of her own misery these past months, she had often thought of what Harriet must be enduring, fearing that "you were undergoing considerable trial from harsh and unfair judgements, partly the fruit of hostility glad to find an opportunity of venting itself, and partly of that unthinking cruelty which belongs to hasty anonymous journalism."

There was a confidence to Marian's belief in her fellow writer's integrity, suggesting that, from the eight months of their correspondence, she trusted she had a good measure of Harriet as a woman. In truth, even before the start of this epistolary friendship, Marian had formed a warm impression of the author of *Uncle Tom's Cabin* based on, of course Harriet's hugely popular publications, but also on a private though widely circulated letter that found its way into Marian's hands.

A decade and a half earlier, back in March 1853, Harriet's bestselling antislavery novel had already made her enormously famous. Marian Evans, on the other hand—though anonymously established as an assistant editor of the radical *Westminster Review*—remained largely unknown. An acquaintance of Marian's, the American abolitionist and author Eliza Lee Cabot Follen, on an extended trip to Britain, had written to Harriet Beecher Stowe, asking the lauded author to turn her pen to an account of herself. Harriet had obliged with a long letter, and Eliza had enjoyed sharing its contents with her guests.

When the then thirty-three-year-old Marian called one morning, she was treated, just like Eliza's other visitors, to a reading of the letter by her hostess. Seated on a drawing room chair, her skirts arranged neatly about her, Marian thrilled to the deeply personal voice of this author she so greatly admired.

As she would remark at a future date, when the two had become friends, Marian thought how generous Harriet must
have been to put aside the busy demands of her successful life
to write at great length to this woman whom she didn't personally know. The Harriet that emerged from the pages of the
letter was, in many ways, much the same as the one who would
make contact with Marian sixteen years later—her tone serious and amusing by turns, her words brimming with emotion
for the things that mattered the most to her. The jovial portrait she painted of her husband Calvin Ellis Stowe—"a man
rich in Greek & Hebrew, Latin & Arabic, & alas! rich in nothing else"—would still reflect her feelings about her marriage
in later life. She talked with passion of the faith in God that
had burned so fiercely from the pages of *Uncle Tom's Cabin* and
would continue to blaze throughout the years to come. Playing down the professional zeal that, in 1869, would lead her to
Dr. Taylor's clinic in order that she might preserve her strength
for work, Harriet modestly presented herself as someone who
became a famed author merely by chance.

A career in writing was all but forced upon her, she
claimed, by economic circumstances and the expectations of
a public clamoring for more stories. The thought of a pro-
posed tour of England and Scotland raised this comment: "It
seems to me so odd & dream-like, that so many people want
to see me—and I can't help thinking, that they will think that
God hath 'chosen the weak things of the world' when they
do." Harriet dwelt also on the death of one of her seven children—not Henry, yet to drown as a young man of nineteen,
but little Charley, who had died of cholera as a baby in 1849.
Looking back on scenes of sitting beside his bed or standing
mournfully at his grave, she drew a lesson. The experience of
losing this little one, she felt, had taught her the pain a slave

mother must feel when forcibly separated from her children—a theme that remains one of the most powerful of *Uncle Tom's Cabin*.

Marian, who had read the groundbreaking novel when it came out in 1852, was interested, no doubt, in this hint at one of the seeds of its plot. In the letter sent to Eliza, Harriet mentioned the nonfiction follow-up, which she was already writing. She described being deeply affected by the shocking true stories that her research had uncovered—many even worse than those featured in *Uncle Tom's Cabin*. "It may truly be said I write with *heart's blood!*" she exclaimed.

What seemed to make the greatest impact on Marian, though, was the physical description that Harriet gave of herself. When Eliza reached the end of her reading, Marian asked if she might make a copy of something from the first page. "I am a little bit of a woman," Marian penned, "rather more than forty, as withered and dry as a pinch of snuff—never very well worth looking at in my best days, and now a decidedly used up article." Marian savored these words. Why, she thought to herself, it "makes one love her."

Something in this description particularly appealed to Marian. Though Harriet's prose was typically merry, this careful British reader thousands of miles away was able to peer behind its façade. And Harriet's comic portrayal of her own plain looks must have chimed with Marian, leading her to feel that she and the American writer, eight years her senior, shared a deeply personal affinity.

Born in rural Warwickshire in 1819, Marian's physical appearance had been a matter of family concern from her earliest years. Her father, fearing that his daughter stood little chance of securing a husband, had taken an approach similar to that of Reverend Brontë in the same period. He hedged his bets by investing in an unusually extensive education for a girl of the early nineteenth century. He sent Mary Ann—as she was known, before renaming herself Marian on her arrival in London in 1851—to a series of local schools. After the death of her mother when Mary Ann was sixteen, he allowed the young woman to continue her studies independently, engaging tutors to teach her German and Italian, Greek and Latin. This way, at least, Robert Evans—an estate manager for a local landowner—must have reasoned that his clever young daughter would be equipped to support herself if his worries about her marital prospects were borne out.

On the other side of the Atlantic, and close to a decade before, the plain looks and bookish eccentricities of Harriet Beecher had led her family to predict that she'd end up an old maid. Growing up in liberal Connecticut, she, like Mary Ann, had benefited from progressive schooling. In 1824, when Harriet was thirteen years old, she enrolled at the Hartford Female Seminary, founded by her older sister Catherine. After a successful career as a student, Harriet would later become one of the seminary's teachers. Unlike the constantly frustrated Charlotte Brontë, Harriet found her job as a schoolmistress stimulating. Living among a group of other forward-thinking female tutors suited her, and in her lessons, teaching rhetoric and composition, she tended to have a good relationship with her students. The school was also perhaps a companionable environment for someone who, by her early twenties, seemed set never to wed.

Unlike Harriet, who distracted herself from the lack of romance in her own life by helping one of her brothers through his turbulent courtship, Mary Ann felt humiliated by her likely destiny of remaining unmarried. Nonetheless, she was not prepared to wed just anyone.

In 1845, at the age of twenty-five, Mary Ann accepted a proposal from a local picture restorer. But she swiftly broke off the engagement, deciding that she could neither love nor respect him—his profession, considered lowly, seemed to influence her decision. It wasn't only snobbery, though. She apparently felt that marrying such a man might hinder her ambitions; a friend of hers at the time claimed that Mary Ann had felt it would prove "too great a sacrifice of her mind and pursuits."

When Mary Ann *did* fall for someone's charms, however, she could behave in ways that challenged accepted social norms and caused great consternation. Though she would later claim never to have felt anything for him—and to have been laughing at him up her sleeve all the while—a year or so earlier, when she was almost twenty-four, she had become friendly with the father of an acquaintance, the sixty-two-year-old Dr. Robert Brabant. Mary Ann, who initially considered the doctor quite as learned as he did himself, went to stay with him and his wife. During her month-long visit, she spent hours reading to him in German—on occasion continuing for so long that she began to feel faint and had to lie down. He showed her his library, told her to consider it her own, and talked of the great philosophical work over which he had been toiling for years—one he would never finish. At the time, the young woman exclaimed that she was "in a little heaven here, Dr. Brabant being its archangel," but this was a paradise from which she would soon be cast out—ordered to leave by the doctor's wife, who grew suspicious of the pair's relationship.

In later years, she suffered two even more serious humiliations, inflicted by men she had grown close to. John Chapman, the owner of the *Westminster Review,* whose family Marian had boarded with when she first moved to London, toyed with her feelings by visiting her room, holding her hand, and quite possibly having a short-lived affair with her. Mysterious symbols in his diary, similar to those he used when recording erotic encounters with other women, certainly suggest this. But with a watchful wife and jealous mistress—officially employed as the children's governess—also living under the same roof, he likely felt that he already had enough domestic drama to cope with and drew the line at pledging himself to Marian in any more meaningful way. Having rebuffed her, he then assured her that he "felt great affection for her," in contrast to his stronger feelings for his wife and mistress. His words caused her to break down in tears.

When working on *The Life of Charlotte Brontë* in the mid-1850s, Elizabeth Gaskell had felt the need to shield her deceased friend's true feelings for her married Belgian tutor from a respectable Victorian readership. Early biographers of George Eliot, writing soon after her death, would be equally keen to gloss over the exact arrangements of Marian's stay in the Chapmans' home. The shocking revelation that she had allowed the man of the house to visit her private sleeping quarters would not be made known until the publication of his diaries, six decades after her death.

Having gotten over this rejection, Marian found her hopes raised once again, this time by the philosopher and sociologist Herbert Spencer, a regular correspondent for the *Westminster Review*. He took her out to the theater and the opera, leading many to assume that he was all set to propose. But in an extraordinary show of courage and vulnerability that flouted the social conventions of the day, she was the one who eventually declared the depth of her true feelings to him. Holidaying alone in the seaside town of Broadstairs, Marian wrote to confess that her whole life had begun to revolve around her love for him, although she knew that he did not feel the same way. If he would only have patience, she implored, he would find that she could be "satisfied with very little." The entreaty did nothing to sway him and can have served only to reinforce her self-image as someone unworthy of romantic love.

As with Charlotte Brontë—characterized as "very ugly" by her school friend Mary Taylor—Marian's deep embarrassment at her appearance would last a lifetime. Two decades after this romantic rejection, when Harriet enclosed a photograph of herself with one of her letters, Marian would let her know that she'd treasure it, but claimed she could not reciprocate. Unable to bear having her own likeness captured in this way, she said she had no such pictures of herself.

But in fact, Marian *had* sat for a few studio sessions—deeply unsettling experiences for her. As a young woman, she'd seen the results of what was likely the first ever photographic image taken of her. Though its exact date remains unknown, a friend's more flattering pencil drawing of 1849, which looks as if it is a copy of the photograph, suggests that Marian is under thirty. By this age, she would have been well aware of society's harsh judgment of her appearance. But it would have been one thing to have heard of her supposed lack of beauty, quite another to see herself for the first time shot from this unfortunate side-on angle. The cruel artificial light accentuated the hooked nose and pointed chin of a woman seemingly much older than her years. Metaphorically, and perhaps also literally, Marian would soon place the black-and-white picture out of her sight.

By the time Marian and Harriet became friends, contrary to the expectations of their families, each woman had long been in a partnership with a man who loved her. Calvin Ellis Stowe—characterized so amusingly by Harriet in her letter of 1852 to Eliza Lee Cabot Follen—had first declared his affection for the twenty-three-year-old Harriet Beecher back in 1835, just months after the passing of his first wife, who had died of cholera. An earnest biblical scholar, though not without a sense of fun, Calvin, then in his mid-thirties, had gotten to know Harriet through the Semi-Colon Club, the literary society to which the two belonged. The Semi-Colons met at regular Monday evening gatherings, for readings and discussion, dancing and sandwiches, and Harriet and Calvin began to attend these occasions together. Their courtship culminated a year or so later in their marriage at the beginning of 1836.

When, soon after, Harriet learned she was expecting a child, her family, still unaccustomed to the notion that this highly educated, rather odd young woman might be marriage material, wondered exactly how she would cope with her new home life. Matters weren't helped by the fact that shortly after she became pregnant, her groom, still grieving his first wife, Eliza, departed on an eight-month trip to Europe. There he planned to study the Prussian school system and buy books for the seminary where he lectured. It could hardly have brought the intended cheer when Harriet received these words by post shortly before his departure from America: "I think all the time of you and Eliza, and hardly know which I want to see the most." During his long absence, she dutifully followed his instructions to visit the grave of the first Mrs. Stowe at times set by Calvin and synchronized with the time zones through which he traveled. On giving birth, she also honored his wish to name the baby Eliza. Unexpectedly, the labor didn't stop there, and the child was followed by a twin sister. When the news finally reached her husband after his two-month return crossing to New York, he insisted that his two daughters should be the namesakes of each of his wives and that she must therefore call the second child Harriet.

Another woman also haunted the relationship between Marian and George Henry Lewes, and her presence loomed larger still—Agnes Lewes, the legal wife of Marian's partner. Lewes had married Agnes in 1840, when he was in his early twenties. Some years into their union, she had begun an affair with his close friend, the journalist Thornton Leigh Hunt, after whom Thornie had been named. After his birth and that of two other legitimate sons, Agnes had gone on to bear at least two, probably four, children by her lover—though it was Lewes's name that appeared on the birth certificate each time. Although he apparently knew that he was not the real father, Lewes did not wish to tar his wife and her offspring with any disgraceful brush of adultery.

It was Marian's former flame, John Chapman, who had introduced her to Lewes in 1851—the same year as the publisher's own dalliance with his boarder. Both Lewes and Marian were in their early thirties, and Lewes had moved out of the home he'd shared with Agnes. But the former couple would never make their separation legal and, consequently, Marian had to risk social exclusion if she wanted to share her life with Lewes.

In 1854, they "eloped" to Germany, for a six-week "honeymoon," followed by several more months of study and work, leaving behind concerned friends who were aghast at the rumors. On their return to London, Marian and Lewes would announce their decision to live together. Such a departure from recognized Victorian norms caused outrage. Even some of Marian's closest liberal confidantes showed initial hostility, and so, demoralized by this, she put off sharing the news with her more conservative family. When a long time later, in 1857, she eventually wrote to her brother to tell him, he swiftly disowned her and also persuaded their sister to cut off contact. Marian found herself barred from polite society and

—especially in the early years of their relationship—when Lewes was invited to dine at the homes of his friends, the invitation was often not extended to her.

Seeking a legal end to his marriage with Agnes would have been just about possible for Lewes. To do so, he would have to petition Agnes on the grounds of her adultery—something that in the past he had chosen to cover up. Neither he nor Agnes would have welcomed the publicity that such a claim inevitably would have stirred up. For Marian, by the time a change to the divorce laws in 1857 had made this possibility more viable, her first stories were being published—initially anonymously and later as "George Eliot"—in *Blackwood's* magazine. Now that she had found success as an author and a romantic partnership, the prospect of a public shaming must have filled Marian with dismay.

Thanks to Harriet's willingness to ignore Marian's unsanctioned relationship—geographical distance perhaps making this easier—the pair could share on the page the kind of friendship that might have been trickier if they had resided in the same country. The thousands of miles that separated them may, in fact, have encouraged their intimacy. Unlike Arthur Bell Nicholls, the husband of Charlotte Brontë, who worried about the candor of letters she exchanged even with her mild-mannered friend Ellen Nussey, the menfolk of both Harriet and Marian positively encouraged the correspondence between them. Lewes and Calvin—a man Harriet called her "Rabbi" on account of his long white beard and hair and the skullcap that covered his bald spot—frequently appear in the women's correspondence. In fact, Calvin sometimes entered the conversation directly by sending his own notes to Marian.

The first of these dates from the spring of 1869, less than

a month after Harriet's first letter to Marian. With a twinkling sense of humor, Calvin wrote: "Since Mrs. Stowe has spoken to you so freely about her reticent, introspective husband, I feel moved to say a word or two on my own account." Harriet was apt to remark on his near illegible hand, but on this occasion, when writing to the great British author, Calvin made a special effort. When his wife had the chance to read this missive, she would find herself tickled not just by the sixty-seven-year-old's amusing self-description, but also the level of care he had taken with his usual scrawl. "My Rabbi," she'd tell Marian in an appending note, "has been moved to write to you the enclosed in his very best improved Arabic English characters," mischievously adding that since she knew Marian was a linguist, perhaps she would be able to decipher it.

In neat, forward-sloping black lettering, avoiding the looped flourishes that characterized Harriet's script, Calvin declared that he was an admirer of both Marian's and Lewes's work. Of all her fictional characters, he said, the female preacher in *Adam Bede* was the one that moved him the most, and he related that he had once believed Marian to be a preacher. In order not to stumble into difficult territory, Calvin would always keep the steadfast thought in his mind that — though his wife's friend might controversially have turned her back on the church — she was a Christian at heart. As he would write to her on a future occasion, no one could conceive of a character like the Methodist Dinah Morris without "a *Christ in dwelling.*"

In this first letter of May 1869, he talked of the strength of his own religious faith and his scholarly interest in the works of the German writer Johann Wolfgang von Goethe, something he knew he shared with Lewes. Calvin also mentioned the visions of ghostly phenomena that he had been experiencing since he was a boy—a subject his wife had explored in her recently completed novel *Oldtown Folks*, described in a separate letter to Marian just five days before.

Spiritualism—the belief that the dead have the ability to communicate with the living, which grew rapidly in Victorian times—was a topic of great interest to Harriet. Her attraction to Dr. Taylor's Swedish Movement Cure cannot be disentangled from her fascination with the practitioner's enthusiasm for spiritualism. While at his clinic, she would take part in several séances, which were not her first. Unlike her husband, who was naturally inclined to see visions since his boyhood, Harriet required help to summon the dead. As she had already claimed to Marian in her second letter, written in May 1869, she had been experimenting in this area for some time and had even managed to contact the ghost of a famed female author.

Made unusually reticent perhaps by the newness of their friendship, or by Marian's reputation for rationality, Harriet initially brought up a particular incident without going into great detail. But even from two short paragraphs, Marian would have gained quite a sense of this curious episode.

Harriet's words painted a picture of a darkened room, where she sat with another woman. Beside them lay a planchette, a small heart-shaped plank-on-castors, with a pencil held in a hole at its tip. The spirit medium handled the wooden apparatus to channel the spirit of none other than Charlotte Brontë.

Harriet, like Marian, greatly admired the late author of *Jane Eyre,* and she had many things she wanted to know. For the next two hours, in the half-light of the séance, Harriet articulated her questions. And as she'd tell Marian in a later letter, via the moving pencil of the planchette, Charlotte answered her.

Harriet asked where Charlotte was residing now.

"Not heaven," came the reply, "but its antechamber."

Charlotte described this as a place of "Peace Calm—improvement. order usefulness.—the mistakes of life gradually being corrected the errors & frailties of life passing away." Her fellow writer, William Makepeace Thackeray, was there too: "The 'slight savageness' is all passed away—he is perfectly lovely now."

Charlotte talked also of her sister Emily, and her husband, Arthur, and a lingering sense of hurt because literary critics had characterized her work as *"coarse"*—a sentiment that Harriet knew all too well. With the wealth of evidence delivered through the planchette—the personal details of Charlotte's life, the French words and *"wild* & Bronteish" language, Harriet felt certain that she and Charlotte had really been talking together. It stood to reason that no trickery had been involved, since the medium was a "cool headed clear minded woman," and neither a French scholar nor poet. Later, though, to make absolutely certain, she verified the details transcribed by the planchette by reading *The Life of Charlotte Brontë* by Elizabeth Gaskell—the author who had sought out Harriet's company on her first trip to Britain in 1853.

Prior to Elizabeth's death in 1865, she had met with Harriet twice more and the two had kept up a letter-writing friendship for several years. It must have gratified Harriet to read in the *Life* that Charlotte had been interested in hearing about the author of *Uncle Tom's Cabin*. It had also perhaps amused her that, on asking of Harriet's appearance, Charlotte was pleased to learn that—like her—Harriet was small in stature.

On that first occasion, in May 1869, when Harriet mentioned her encounter with the dead British author, Marian felt skeptical. But using the method that Harriet adopted to deal with Marian's unwed status, she tactfully chose to ignore these references to Charlotte Brontë. On the other hand, bound by politeness and probably some genuine interest too, Marian could not completely disregard the many paragraphs Harriet had devoted to talk of spiritualism. Both she and Lewes, she told Harriet in July 1869, were "deeply interested" in Calvin's "peculiar psychological experience," and would "feel it a great privilege to learn much more of it from his lips." In this letter, Marian stated that she wondered whether the fervor for spiritualism in her friend's home country—so recently ravaged by civil war—could be regarded as a kind of outpouring of grief "towards the invisible existence of the loved ones." Perhaps also recalling that Harriet had suffered the death of two sons, Marian let her know that she found such an interpretation "deeply affecting." Nonetheless, while carefully avoiding speaking directly of Harriet's communing with Charlotte Brontë, Marian remained resolute in the strength of her opinion that—at least from her own experience on the other side of the Atlantic—"spirit communications by rapping, guidance of the pencil etc." had always appeared to her as "degrading folly, imbecile in the estimate of evidence, or else as impudent posture." But concerned that Harriet might take offense, she assured her correspondent that "my deep respect for you" compelled her to be truthful, and that she would still gladly read anything that Harriet sent her on the subject.

Walking this tightrope between blistering honesty and lukewarm encouragement seemed to do the trick. In her next letter, Harriet would leave the theme of spiritualism alone. At a later date, though, she brought up the Charlotte Brontë episode again, furnishing her friend with many more details about what had happened. On this occasion, Marian was firmer still, letting Harriet know that "whether rightly or not," the story struck her as "enormously improbable."

Marian, then, could at times be sternly frank with Harriet. But in her closing communication of 1869—that letter of December 10, which told of the passing of her stepson—she would open herself up with great intimacy.

Death had been a stranger to her for two decades, she told Harriet, ever since—as an already motherless young woman of twenty-nine—she'd lost her father. Talking of the great privilege of ministering "comfort through love and care," Marian was quick to acknowledge that Harriet's experience in this area was far greater than hers. And so, she surely assumed that Harriet would soon send a sympathetic response.

During the last weeks of the year, Marian and Lewes prepared for a sad Christmas in London; on December 25, they would walk to Highgate Cemetery to spend some time by Thornie's grave. Little kindnesses, recorded in their letters and journals, brought some cheer to the dark days of their bereavement: a basket of gifts from a friend of Marian's, which brightened a foggy winter's morning; Christmas dinner with two of Lewes's children; the prospect of a possible trip to Germany if Lewes's mother's health held out.

As the clinging winter frost eventually made way for the spring flowers of a new decade, it also heralded the approaching first anniversary of Marian's literary alliance with Harriet. Through their regular and affectionate exchange of post, the pair had steered each other through their mutual experience of fame and notoriety as well as sharing intimate reflections on their private lives. But now it looked as if their friendship was not so secure: Marian's last letter had specifically requested some contact from her "sister woman," and yet the weeks continued to go by and by and still there came no response.

❧ 9 ❧

An Act of Betrayal

MORE THAN TWO YEARS would pass before Marian Lewes at last received an explanation, of sorts, for the silence of her faraway friend. During the many months since she had poured out her grief on paper, sharing her deep feelings of loss over the death of her stepson, she had not forgotten Harriet Beecher Stowe. Now at last, in early 1872, a letter arrived at the Priory. But when Marian sat down to read, its contents would fall far short of her hopes.

In the chill of her north London home, Marian surveyed the day's post laid out before her. As was his usual habit, the man she called her husband, George Henry Lewes, had already vetted her correspondence. Having effectively taken on the role of Marian's literary manager, for some years now he had been weeding out anything that he deemed unworthy of her attention, to deal with it himself—an intrusive, though well-intentioned, act meant to save Marian the pain of seeing upsetting reviews of her work. A noncritical letter from a literary friend such as Harriet would have made the cut, but if Lewes lingered over the American woman's words, he too may have wondered at what she said to Marian.

"Dear Friend" the first line read, the familiar greeting offering cold comfort, for it was followed by Harriet's paltry excuses for her failure to write. Her letter claimed that she would have been in touch sooner if only "two years of constant and severe work" had not "made it impossible to give a drop to any thing beyond the needs of the hour." As Marian read on she found no belated condolences; not even a mention of her bereavement; no acknowledgment of that plea in her own last missive when she'd reached out across the waves in her anguish. In December 1869, Marian had written that she would not "be so unreasonable as to expect a long letter," but that "some brief news of you and yours will be especially welcome just now." And yet even this simple request had remained unanswered by Harriet.

Now, at last there *was* news from her, but it could hardly have brought Marian much cheer. The pages she grasped in her fifty-two-year-old hands were largely taken up by a long commentary on the work of several spiritualists known personally to her friend. Harriet talked of George Taylor, the doctor who held séances by night, and at whose New York clinic she'd been residing while working on her book about Lady Byron. She also mentioned the social reformer and author Robert Dale Owen and lavished great praise on his books, *Footfalls on the Boundary of Another World* and *The Debatable Land Between This World and the Next*. Harriet said he was a great admirer of Marian's and planned to send her some of his writing in order to seek her opinion.

As Marian continued to leaf through the paper sheets, embossed with Harriet's personal seal—a creeping-branch *S* for *Stowe*, sprouting leaves from its bark—how could she not lose heart? A single moment was the letter's saving grace. Marian would mention it in the opening paragraph of her own otherwise understandably curt reply, sent off promptly within days despite her own demanding schedule. Harriet, who had written from her winter home in Florida, had painted a picture of her surroundings, so ripe and vivid that—in spite of everything—Marian could briefly leave behind the wallpapered rooms of the Priory, fires burning in the grates at this time of year, and go out into the sunshine of this rural idyll.

Following the trail laid by her friend's words, Marian could breathe the fragrant air of the distant orange orchard. Within the wooded land surrounding Harriet's house on the banks of the St. Johns River, she could take in the sight of the glittering water, and, as Harriet had described them to her, "the waving of the live oaks with their long, gray mosses over head & the bright gold of oranges looking thro dusky leaves around." Here, Marian felt she could "bathe in that quietude." Within this landscape of creeping vines and flowers, Harriet had told her that the pressures of the world receded. Here, there was "no winter" and it was warm enough to spend one's days outside in a tent: writing letters, reading books, and "spinning ideal webs" for stories as yet unwritten.

Harriet's letter had also mentioned that she'd ordered copies of *Harpers Weekly,* the American magazine in which *Middlemarch* was now being serialized. This continued literary engagement must surely have appealed to Marian despite the sense of having been badly let down by her friend.

In the two years since December 1869, when the pair had stopped corresponding, Marian's attitude toward the manuscript of what would become her best-known novel had moved from a state of utter despair to one of hopefulness and eventually great activity. In December 1870, many months since she started the book, she'd recorded in her journal the seemingly unconnected entry that she was now experimenting with a different story, which she had first begun "without any very serious intention of carrying it out lengthily." This was to be "Miss Brooke"—the imaginary account of a passionate, deeply pious young woman—strikingly similar to the young Marian —who becomes the wife of a fusty, petty-minded clergyman. This tale of the undermining and eventual triumph of Dorothea Brooke would ultimately break through the constraints of the short story originally envisioned by Marian. In time, she would stitch Dorothea's tale into the fabric of *Middlemarch,* where it would become, for many readers, the most memorable part of the book.

At the beginning of December 1871, the novel's first substantial volume (of a planned eight) was published in Britain, followed swiftly by its release in weekly installments in America, much to the chagrin of Marian's British publisher, who feared that "bits will be published right and left in this country in spite of our teeth." By the time that Harriet wrote in February 1872 to let Marian know that she had "sent north" for copies of *Harper's Weekly,* she was already several issues behind. But being able to receive post only once or twice a week in her remote home in Florida, she could at least claim honestly that arranging for the magazines to be sent was no straightforward matter.

As usual, Harriet had traveled down to Mandarin in November, to avoid the coldest months in Connecticut. More than ever this winter she must have felt that she needed this annual escape. In February 1871, her troubled son Fred, whose alcoholism had already caused her so much heartache, had announced his intention to go away to sea. His parents would learn that he made it as far as San Francisco, but on disembarking there he disappeared, never to be heard from again. With no body, and no final communication from him, Harriet still held on to the hope that Fred might be found alive. Though in the past, she had opened up about some of her son's troubles to Marian, she could not bring herself to mention him at all in this letter, perhaps mindful of her own neglect during her friend's time of need.

The year preceding Fred's disappearance had also been one of stress, this time of a professional nature. Harriet's book *Lady Byron Vindicated,* over which she'd been laboring so madly when Marian last wrote, had been rushed out, just a month later, in January 1870. Rather than restore the reputation of either its author or its aristocratic subject, so badly shredded in the response to Harriet's *Atlantic Monthly* piece, this longer work did more harm than good. *The Nation* criticized Harriet for failing to supply the reader with any substantial new evidence and damningly likened her account of the Byrons' marriage to that of a "drawing-room scandal." The *Charleston Daily News,* and several other southern papers, gleefully reprinted the words of the *New York Sun,* which had called the book a "weak and trashy production." Similarly, the Virginia-based *Richmond Dispatch* decried Harriet's intended vindication of Lady Byron as "a turning over again of the offensive mass of scandal, whose exhalations can have no effect but that which is bad."

Marian's last letter of two years earlier, mostly filled with her palpable sadness over the death of Thornie, had also summarized her disapproval of Harriet's article on Lady Byron. Unfortunately, this criticism would have arrived as Harriet faced the sorry aftermath of her new book's publication. This meant that the timing of Marian's words, measured though they were, would have sharpened their impact.

Though this catalog of sorrows and disappointments cannot excuse Harriet's failure to write earlier, they do at least offer an explanation for her delay. What's more, Marian's grief perhaps brought back memories of Harriet's own son—the nineteen-year-old who, well over a decade earlier, had drowned in the Connecticut River. Rather than making her well-placed to empathize, as Marian might reasonably have assumed, this sad news could have brought up buried sorrows, which Harriet, as a twice—possibly thrice—bereaved mother herself was still not ready to face.

Marian's decision to forgive, if not forget, cannot have been easy—something more than hinted at in her response of March 1872, written while she was still only about half-way through the labor of producing the eight volumes of *Middlemarch* promised to her publisher. With a frostiness new to her correspondence with Harriet, her letter began: "I can understand very easily that the last two years have been full for you of other & more imperative work than the writing of letters not absolutely demanded by charity or business." As to her friend's lengthy discourse on spiritualism, although Marian told her that she would "certainly read Mr. Owen's books if he is good enough to send them to me," she was unequivocal in her view that, in terms of what she had seen for herself, "spirit-intercourse" seemed to her to be "the lowest form of charlatanerie." She signed off by saying, pointedly, that she wrote "very imperfectly, for my letters are always written in shreds of time." Nonetheless, she added that she was, and would always be, "Yours with sincere affection and gratitude."

This initial reply was notably shorter than usual, but over the coming months the pair swiftly steered their relationship back on course. Other women, though perhaps more reliable, could not share personal insight into both literary challenges and the experience of fame and notoriety. The ostracism that Marian had faced may have made her generous. Having been shunned herself, she understood the suffering that Harriet had endured at the hands of the press during her period of silence.

Marian's swift reply prompted another letter from Harriet, this time sent within a couple of months. Treading carefully for now, Harriet began by offering another vivid description of her Florida home: an entrancing place of labyrinthine creepers, swinging draperies of moss and yellow jessamine climbing "into & over every thing with fragrant golden bells & buds." Despite Harriet's continued entreaties that her British friend should come and stay, Marian did not feel that traveling such a distance from London was a possibility. Lewes's health had suffered terribly following the death of his son, and Marian's constitution remained as easily upset as ever. So she must have particularly appreciated Harriet's efforts to sketch out the scene in such detail, offering her the opportunity to visit "in spirit if not personally." If Marian were here with her, Harriet wrote, she would take her "in heart & house & you should have a little room in our little cottage." They would go out gathering flowers and, for the length of her enchanted stay, they could forget the worries of the world.

After the warmth of the letter's beginning, it might even have amused as well as exasperated Marian that the following pages were stuffed, once again, with Harriet's usual outpourings about ghostly phenomena. But her following letter, written in September 1872, would present something else entirely.

Since the revival of their correspondence in the spring, it had seemed to Harriet that she'd been involved in two distinct conversations with her British friend: one within the pages of their letters, and another in the installments she had seen of *Middlemarch*. After leaving sunlit Mandarin behind, she had been away for much of the summer, first staying at a resort in New Hampshire — escaping the heat this time — and then giving a series of readings in cities around New England. As a consequence, she'd been able to read *Harper's Weekly* only on and off, but moments from the novel had kept playing, reimagined, in her mind. And now, today, though she was presumably still mid-tour, she found herself suddenly overcome with an urge to write Marian another letter.

There was a line she believed to be spoken in the book by Dorothea's suitor, "Ladislaw or whatever his name is." Being away from her papers, Harriet was unable to look it up, although this may hardly have been the best way to put it to the meticulous Marian. According to Harriet, the young man said something to the effect of "whatever is honestly & purely attempted for good becomes part of the great force that is moving for good thro the universe." This struck her as such a wonderful notion that she declared it "one article of my creed."

The worlds of their published works and their personal letters provided a space in which these literary legends could come together. But the ocean that parted them could also exacerbate misunderstandings. The unintended friction soon to follow could perhaps have been avoided had the pair been able to sit together, sharing confidences on the veranda of Harriet's Florida home.

Presumably not realizing that Lewes vetted at least some of Marian's post, Harriet wrote, "My darling I confess to being very much amused & sympathetic with Dorothea's trials with a literary husband." And then, "Now, dont show this to Mr. Lewes, but I know from my own experiences with my Rabbi that you learned how to write some of those things by *experience*. Don't these men go on forever getting ready to begin — absorbing learning like sponges — planning sublime literary enterprises which never have a *now* to them."

Like Mr. Casaubon, the husband of Dorothea in Marian's novel — forever buried in his *Key to All Mythologies* — Calvin Ellis Stowe, had made a lifelong habit of researching ad infinitum without completing several of the ambitious books he planned to write. What's more, Harriet seems to have sensed that her well-meaning attempts to chivvy him along had often served only to slow his progress. By sharing this part of her own marriage, Harriet was offering Marian the chance to take their friendship to a new level of closeness. But, removed as Harriet was from Marian's life in London, she hadn't allowed for the reality that her friend—who remained controversially unmarried to Lewes—would never have felt able to engage with this line of conversation.

Resolute to steer clear of scandal and present her "marriage" as an entirely unblemished union, Marian would write back, telling Harriet in no uncertain terms that it was "impossible to conceive any creature less like Mr. Casaubon than my warm, enthusiastic husband." In fact, when he failed to get down to work, Lewes himself joked that the "shadow of old Casaubon" hung over him. Nonetheless, he hardly resembled Harriet's characterization. Even now, when his management of Marian's career took up so much of his days, he continued to publish books. In his time, he'd turned his hand to subjects as varied as the theater, philosophy, and the natural world. His sociability too made him a very different personality from the cold, mean-spirited Mr. Casaubon.

But Harriet—who, in any case, had been focusing on only the tarrying side of Mr. Casaubon's nature—was talking of her own partner as much as Marian's and had seemed keen to admit as much to her friend. Even if Lewes did not entirely fit the bill, there were figures in Marian's past—most notably the overbearing Dr. Brabant of her youth—who likely did mix with her rich imagination to help create Mr. Casaubon. The pair might indeed have been able to discuss such former associations if Marian hadn't felt bound by then to present such a chaste version of herself. But since Marian remained reluctant to divulge such details, she rejected the opportunity to deepen her bond with Harriet.

To make matters worse, Harriet unwisely fired off another missive to her friend even before she'd received Marian's strongly worded response. The fact that both letters must have arrived at the Priory in quick succession can only have worsened the damage.

On receipt of this second letter, Marian learned that Harriet was staying at the home of the author Annie Adams Fields —the thirty-eight-year-old wife of Harriet's publisher James T. Fields, and the woman who had first put them in touch. Usually, such news would have brought Marian pleasure. But when Harriet told her that the by-now precarious subject of Mr. Casaubon had dominated recent conversation with Annie too, her happiness must have soured somewhat.

Harriet's letter invited Marian to envisage the two women huddled together in the dove-like Annie's "sweetest little nest" of a house, where the sound of the sea could be heard from the back rooms and the sights of a busy Boston street seen through the front windows. Framed pictures crowded the walls of Annie's elegant parlor and, as could be expected for a literary home such as this, there were shelves of neatly bound books. In light of the recent comparisons Harriet had made between Casaubon and Lewes, Marian surely felt alarmed when Harriet declared the younger Annie and herself both "out of our senses with mingled pity & indignation at that dreadful stick of a Casaubon—& think of poor Dorothea dashing like a warm sunny wave against so cold & repulsive a rock."

To add insult to injury, though Harriet remained gripped by *Middlemarch,* she had already—part way through the serialized novel—come to some conclusions about where its author was going wrong. And she didn't hold back on telling Marian where the issue lay—namely, the story's lack of "jollitude." Harriet claimed that "you write & live on so high a plane—it is all self abnegation—we want to get you over here, & into this house where with closed doors we sometimes make the rafters ring with fun—& say any thing & and every thing no matter what & won't be any properer than we's a mind to be."

In Marian's prompt reply, she was firm in her guarantees that her partner was nothing like Mr. Casaubon, but when it came to this appraisal of her lack of fun, she fell back to the technique of simply ignoring the words in question. Harriet, for her part, held off on answering for several months and eventually wrote back with the insistent assurance that there had been a misunderstanding: "Dear Love, did you think for one moment that I fancied a resemblance between Mr. Lewes & Casaubon?—Oh thou of little faith!"

Despite Harriet's feelings about the lack of "jollitude" that she perceived in *Middlemarch,* Marian would remain keen to explore her work with her friend. Over three years later, in 1876, Marian's eagerness to discuss her next novel with Harriet shows the premium she placed on her fellow writer's opinions.

Unlike *Middlemarch,* set in the era surrounding the Great Reform Act of 1832—the political event that had so excited the young Charlotte Brontë and Mary Taylor a generation before—*Daniel Deronda* would take place in contemporary times. This was unusual for Marian, whose fiction tended to focus on the recent past. What's more, this new work would take a further unexpected turn when, partway through the novel, its titular protagonist turns out to be Jewish. Within the context of the English literary world of the time, this felt revolutionary indeed.

Since her early days as an editor and writer for the *West-*

minster Review, Marian had rated the creator of *Uncle Tom's Cabin* as an author of "rare genius." She admired Harriet's ability to weave a story that could hold her audience in thrall, while also raising important social issues. Just as Harriet's best-known novel had sought to open the eyes of her readers to the evils of slavery, Marian now hoped to encourage her audience to ask themselves difficult questions about their own deeply ingrained prejudices against Jewish people. Her praise for Harriet's talents was not without limits — she disliked what she termed the "feeble" travelogue *Sunny Memories of Foreign Lands* and, more recently of course, she had expressed her disapproval of Harriet's writings on Lady Byron. Overall, though, she felt that her friend's best work assured her a place "in that highest rank of novelists." Regarding Harriet — discomfitingly for a modern reader — as someone who had "*invented* the Negro novel," she understandably desired her friend's thoughts on the subject of racism in her own new book.

When *Daniel Deronda* came out in America in 1876, Harriet and her husband read it faithfully in serial form each month — with Calvin, now in his seventies, staying up well past his usual eight o'clock bedtime in order to finish the latest installment. Harriet, fatigued with the literary world due to her public battering in recent years, found herself stimulated, right from the start, by this new tale from Marian.

In Florida, it was orange blossom time once again. Bees were roaming about the white-flowered branches, filling the air with their humming. In the fruit tree, just beyond the window where Harriet sat, a red cardinal was singing with such sweetness that she almost broke off midflow. Glancing out at the sunny scene, pen and paper before her, Harriet wrote of her wish to really send some of this southern winter weather to the British recipient of her letter. But, as ever, she had to rely on her words to do the job, transporting rays of light and warmth across the waves.

She could tell Marian, for instance, all about this "easy undress, picnic kind of life, far from the world & its cares," where, now that she had reached her mid-sixties, her twin daughters, aged almost forty, relieved her entirely of former domestic chores. It was as well, really, for—though she could not describe it with any more clarity than this—a strange feeling had been coming over Harriet recently. It was, she confided in the privacy of her correspondence with Marian, as if she had "been playing and picnicing on the shores of life" and now woken with a start from an afternoon's dream to find almost all of her companions gone and the few that remained "packing their trunks & waiting for the boat to come & take them."

But their later years nonetheless offered Harriet and her husband some pleasures. They continued to read the installments of *Daniel Deronda,* and Harriet would ultimately proclaim it "a splendid success." Literary critics of the day, however, would be more divided in their opinions, particularly regarding what Marian termed "the Jewish element" of the novel. Even before publication, her editor had expressed concern that the Jewish characters were the least well drawn of her cast. Later, in the pages of the *Atlantic Monthly,* Henry James—no longer the relatively inexperienced writer who'd made his way to Marian's front door, but now a published novelist himself—complained that neither the hero, Deronda, nor his love, Mirah, was remotely convincing. According to Henry, they had "no existence outside of the author's study." On the other hand, Marian was pleased to receive a letter from a London rabbi, who—writing within an age of pervading anti-Semitism on both sides of the ocean—let her know of his "warm appreciation of the fidelity with which some of the best traits of the Jewish character" were illustrated in her novel.

Yet some of Marian's subconscious prejudices—the stereotyped Cohen family, with its oily-skinned pawnbroker patriarch and his vulgar-looking mother, whom the hero supposes sleeps in her jewelry—are troubling to today's reader. By contrast, the object of Deronda's affections, Mirah, also Jewish, embodies a saintliness so all-encompassing that it is hard to credit. Such a criticism can also be leveled against Harriet's creation, the pious and long-suffering Uncle Tom, whose story had so profoundly moved and influenced Marian.

In late 1878, Harriet sent her friend the gift of a new edition of her most famous book. This time, it would be Marian who delayed responding, since the package arrived in the middle of a difficult period. She and Lewes had bought a second home in the Surrey countryside two years earlier, and were still deep in renovations. As they had with the Priory, they spent considerable money doing the place up, overhauling the plumbing, the poky butler's pantry, and the kitchen. Here, they were planning to spend many more happy summers together.

Sadly, this was not to be. By 1878, Lewes was suffering so greatly with his health that a friend of Henry James had recently remarked unkindly that it looked as if Lewes "had been gnawed by the rats—and left." In November of that year, the couple returned to London and, while their servants hurried ahead to open up the Priory, they went to stay at a hotel. Lewes had been complaining for about a week of what he believed were hemorrhoids. But when James Paget, the family's long-serving doctor, was summoned, he pronounced the condition considerably more serious, describing it ominously but mysteriously as "a thickening of the mucous membrane." On the thirtieth of that month Lewes died at home at the Priory, plunging Marian into a period of deep mourning.

Separated as they were by the Atlantic Ocean, it must have been some time before Harriet learned of Marian's sorrow. For a week, the grieving woman did not leave her room. Below stairs, the servants could hear her anguished cries, which rang throughout the house. It would be several months before Marian replied to Harriet to acknowledge the gift of *Uncle Tom's Cabin*. And so, this new edition of the book would have been Marian's main way of communing with Harriet for the time being. Attired in mourning clothes, turning the pages of the novel, Marian must have found the lively voice of its narrator a touching reminder that its story was her first introduction to this dear literary friend.

When, in April 1879, Marian at last wrote to tell Harriet of her loss, there would be another significant gap—of a year—before Harriet answered. This certainly firms up the impression created in the aftermath of Thornie's death: when confronted by events that mirrored her own worst fears, Harriet responded by retreating within herself. This time, though, her letter—which, unknown to either woman, was to be the last between them—acknowledged the real reason behind her lack of action. Marian's missive, she said, was "so deeply hopelessly sad" that it had made her feel "a sort of despair." Unable to find the right words, she had delayed replying, reassuring herself that she would write when her orange trees blossomed again, "but the time came & passed." She was always busy now, she continued, caring for her elderly husband. Calvin was aging fast, and although his mind remained "yet as clear as ever," his physical strength was ebbing away, so that Harriet could no longer hide from the fact that their time of "earthly companionship" was "drawing to a close."

Given the warmth of Marian's and Harriet's enduring feelings for each other and their hard-won capacity to face difficult truths, it seems strange that neither woman took the opportunity to speak publicly about their relationship — a silence that Harriet would maintain, even when their correspondence came to an abrupt end.

At the close of 1880, eleven years after they first began writing to each other, the sixty-one-year-old Marian fell unexpectedly ill. Sitting in the audience of a Greek-language performance of *Agamemnon,* she'd felt the stirrings of a sore throat. By the next day, her condition had grown drastically worse, much to the distress of her new partner, John Walter Cross, whom she had married earlier in the year — in fact, on the same May date of Harriet's letter. His age, at two decades her junior, had set people gossiping about her once more. But at least this man — who'd seemingly been a confirmed bachelor — was someone she could legally wed. When her husband sought medical assistance for her, a first doctor suspected laryngitis, but Marian was eventually diagnosed with heart problems brought on by kidney failure. She declined quickly, and three days before Christmas, she slipped away from life.

Not long after, a sad Harriet spoke with the publisher husband of Annie Adams Fields about the possibility of bringing out an article, in the *Atlantic Monthly* again, commemorating her friend. Her collection of letters from Marian, she wrote, showed her to be "so fine and noble." Harriet's only hesitation was "one of delicacy." Although Marian had been able to officially call herself Mrs. Cross in that last year of her life, any biographical piece would have to acknowledge her longer romantic partnership, which had lasted until Lewes's death. Harriet feared that even the American public, less bound by formal conventions than the British, would find Marian's conduct anything but "fine and noble" in a woman. Harriet asked whether James T. Fields knew if "any marriage ceremony of *any* kind" had taken place between Marian and Lewes. As neither he nor his wife was able to give such a reassurance, Harriet quietly let the subject drop.

Just as Harriet's own epistolary boldness had once given Marian permission to express herself candidly, so Harriet in turn seems to have learned from Marian when it was better to keep quiet. In doing so she honored the spirit of her friend. But in remaining silent, Harriet would leave their relationship at the mercy of biographers.

Unlike the family of Jane Austen, the male relatives of Marian and Harriet felt no compulsion to hide the women's alliance. In his three-volume work, *George Eliot's Life,* Marian's widowed husband included several of her letters to Harriet. And one of Harriet's sons published a memoir of his mother. He wrote it during her twilight years, when her mind became increasingly confused—moments of lucidity, as his sister put it, coming and going "like falling stars." Charles Edward Stowe devoted a whole chapter of his book to the women's bond, calling it one of the "most delightful" experiences of his mother's life. But—perhaps because of the eventual disparity in the authors' reputations—later researchers would show little interest in the friendship or its historical importance, leaving it to become all but forgotten.

KATHERINE MANSFIELD
&
VIRGINIA WOOLF

the queerest sense of echo coming back to me
from her mind the second after I've spoken

VIRGINIA WOOLF
DIARY, AUGUST 25, 1920

10

Friends or Foes?

VIRGINIA WOOLF stepped out of her Richmond townhouse one April afternoon in 1917, embarking on her mission without feeling assured of success. The thirty-five-year-old author of just one novel so far was on her way to see Katherine Mansfield—a writer who, despite being six years younger, had carved out rather more of a literary name for herself. Although Virginia tentatively considered Katherine a friend, she still regarded the charismatic New Zealander as an "utterly unscrupulous character." Despite this ambivalence, Virginia knew that the proposal she intended to put to Katherine would have the power to draw them into a close alliance.

The unlikely pair had first met the previous year, introduced by Virginia's flamboyant friend, the bearded and bespectacled Lytton Strachey. He had come across Katherine at Garsington Manor in Oxfordshire, where the literati flocked to salons hosted by the aristocratic Ottoline Morrell. During this time, Lytton was hard at work on *Eminent Victorians*—the biography that would make his name. But Katherine's attention was on *The Voyage Out*, Virginia's recently published first novel, and she told Lytton that she wanted to get to know its author more than just about anyone else. He promptly wrote to Virginia, suggesting that she consider meeting this young woman whom he found so intriguing. But with a cattiness characteristic of the writers who congregated at Garsington, he sniped that Katherine had "an ugly impassive mask of a face—cut in wood, with brown hair and brown eyes very far apart; and a sharp and slightly vulgarly-fanciful intellect sitting behind it."

As was her wont, Virginia had attempted to match his gossipy tone in her response: "Katherine Mansfield has dogged my steps for three years," she claimed. Yet this haughty reply was contradicted by her evident keenness to get to know this woman, who had brought out dozens of short stories in magazines as well as a book-length collection.

Through Lytton, the pair arranged to meet at Garsington, where a poker-faced Katherine would sit ramrod straight at the very edge of the sofa, regaling her fellow guests with witty tales. Her talk transported Virginia to worlds so different from her milieu among the London intelligentsia: a far-flung childhood in colonial New Zealand; tours in Scotland with a traveling light opera company; early employment as an entertainer at private parties, offering mimicry, recitation, and music.

Nine months later, Virginia had read Katherine's writing, admiring its extraordinary evocation of the sensory world. Although it had been two years since the New Zealander had published any significant new work, Virginia's esteem for these stories had prompted her mission today.

Her walk from her elegant Georgian home took her along the edge of the squash courts on Paradise Road, where balls rifle-cracked against rackets, and next past the public house at the corner—a male refuge of smoke and warm beer. The uphill climb to the railway station gave Virginia the chance to stretch her limbs for the first time in days. Since the delivery of her new printing press earlier that week, she had been happily

ensconced in her dining room, setting up the machine. Virginia
and her husband, Leonard, had purchased the hand-operated
press in the hope that an involving physical occupation would
alleviate the stresses of his work with the Women's Co-operative Guild. More important still, Leonard believed that the
press might ward off the debilitating bouts of depression and
mania from which his wife had suffered intermittently since
adolescence. After the arrival of the machine, Virginia's attention had certainly been absorbed in separating the blocks of
type by letter and font before storing them in the correct com-
partments—a time-consuming job made more laborious by
her failure to distinguish between the *h*'s and the *n*'s.

The task complete, and her health currently on an even
keel, Virginia was ready to venture from this sleepy, outlying
suburb of Richmond to London's bohemian quarter of Chelsea. Here, she would visit Katherine—whom she'd first met
while emerging from her most recent and protracted mental
breakdown. Four years earlier, when Virginia was finishing *The
Voyage Out,* she had begun to experience headaches, insomnia,
and a revulsion to food—all symptoms of an impending cri-
sis. Sure enough, from 1913 to 1915, she had endured a series of
deep depressions interspersed with spells of violent hallucina-
tion. Up to four live-in nurses treated her with a regimen of
enforced bed rest and overfeeding, and she was banned from
writing fiction or journalism, which were considered dangerously stimulating. During the following months and years
of recuperation, Virginia was once more making her creative
work central to her life.

As the train trundled east, she left behind leafy Richmond, whose tranquility Leonard insisted was essential for his
wife's continued well-being. Her journey took her from the
royal parkland and military hospital of her own locale toward

the artists' clubs and colleges of Katherine's home in Chelsea. Along the way, she passed close to streets that had been devastated by the previous year's Zeppelin raids. Although the ongoing war with Germany had inevitably caused Virginia much anguish—the air-raid sirens frequently sending her from her bed to seek shelter down in the cellar—she had not lost a close relative in the bloodshed. Katherine, however, hadn't escaped with such good fortune. Her beloved brother had died in the trenches two years earlier, and none of her friends who'd departed for the front had returned.

Upon arriving at Katherine's studio flat, Virginia found herself in cramped, damp-ridden quarters that could not have been more different from her own spacious residence, Hogarth House, or indeed her secluded country home on the South Downs. Despite the talk that had circulated about Katherine's relationship with the small-time magazine editor and writer John Middleton Murry, this modest space betrayed no sign that she was currently "living in sin." Murry, as he was known, was in fact residing in his own rooms nearby, for he and Katherine had recently parted ways.

If there was hardly sufficient room in this studio for a couple, there was certainly none for a live-in servant. Katherine's lifestyle may well have appeared oddly enviable to Virginia. She had fraught relations with her parlor maid, the passionate foundling Lottie Hope, and her cook, the affection-starved Nellie Boxall. Katherine would, in fact, soon squeeze a second occupant into her flat—someone whose role in her life was crucial yet unconventional. But Virginia had yet to encounter this companion.

So much here was hidden from view: a mattress stowed in the minstrels' gallery created a secret sleeping area, and a curtain drawn across the studio concealed another bedroom plus a kitchenette where Katherine kept her saucepans, nutmeg grater, and coffee mill. The unsightly makeshift furnishings were a perpetual source of frustration for Katherine, who fended for herself without the assistance of a husband. How she longed for a maid, but she could afford only a charwoman. Someone of Katherine's genteel colonial upbringing would never have expected to lug heavy buckets from the coal cellar, wash her own dishes, or empty her bedpan.

Despite drab surroundings, Katherine had long found innovative ways of entertaining company, on occasion donning a kimono and instructing guests to sit upon floor cushions while she served up tea in bowls. Her conversation could be equally surprising, frequently turning to stories of her youth: expeditions into Maori country; sailing in a cargo ship from New Zealand to Britain; playing the cello for the local factory girls during her stint at a boarding school on London's Harley Street, where she was sent at fifteen years of age. Such tales must have seemed extraordinary to Virginia, who—though given free rein in her editor father's well-stocked library—received little formal education, and whose childhood holidays were spent in the Cornish fishing town of St. Ives, just a day's journey southwest of London by rail.

Katherine had never before shared a bond with a woman she considered her intellectual equal. Despite her early publication successes, the New Zealand banker's daughter felt very much the outsider in literary London—ill-equipped to decipher its unwritten rules. On this spring day in Chelsea in 1917, Virginia steered the conversation to her new printing press, sharing her hopes of starting her own small publishing house. In so openly setting herself up as an editor, she would be overturning outdated Victorian ideals of womanhood. Even George Eliot had felt compelled initially to hide her professional identity, by working anonymously as an editor within the male coterie of the *Westminster Review*—not to mention her later adoption of a male pseudonym. The social changes of the past half century, however, had opened up chances for female writers to work together—along with the prospect of new professional rivalries. The scheme that Virginia planned to suggest to Katherine involved just such opportunities and just such risks.

Virginia hoped Katherine might consider submitting her work to the newly formed Hogarth Press. Aside from planning to bring out one short piece of her own and another by Leonard, Virginia had not sought stories from anyone else. She was pinning all her hopes on convincing her new friend to provide the imprint's very first commission.

Katherine's keen acceptance established a professional alliance between the two women and also deepened their personal relationship. Within a few months, Virginia would invite Katherine and Murry (who were back together once more) to dine with her and Leonard at Hogarth House, where they could all take a look at the new printing press.

The evening left a strong impression on both women. Their memories have been handed down through correspondence from Katherine to Virginia, and from Virginia to her artist sister, Vanessa, who called by during the evening.

Katherine recalled sitting alone, hearing the sounds of Virginia and Vanessa chatting outside in the garden. The night, thus far, had been free of the sinister gleams of airships and subsequent flashes of shells, which so frequently forced the Woolfs' household to congregate in the basement kitchen—the servants huddled on one camp bed, Virginia on another, and Leonard under the table. During these hours of peace, Katherine breathed in the scents of the coffee and strawberries that the two couples had been enjoying. The men had gone off to examine the handle and cylinder of the printing press, and so, when Vanessa left and Virginia returned inside, the two writers were free to converse undisturbed.

Falling back on one of her longstanding techniques for winning over female friends, Katherine confessed to Virginia some of her seamier personal stories, but history leaves us to guess at which ones: her marriage to an older bachelor, which lasted just one night but still prevented her from marrying the young and handsome Murry; her unwanted pregnancy, which ended in miscarriage; a regrettable liaison in a German boarding house; or the erotic encounters of her youth, more taboo still.

Such talk would have caused Virginia some distress, for her own earliest sexual experience had been intensely traumatic, occurring back in 1889 when she was a very young child. At the family's holiday home in the seaside resort of St. Ives, her eighteen-year-old half brother had lifted her onto a stone slab in the hallway. Reaching beneath her skirt, ignoring her resistance, his hands had firmly and steadily explored her body, insistently and intimately. Almost thirty years later Gerald now owned a leading publishing company, and Virginia had felt forced to rely on him to bring out her first novel and her only short story to date.

By her mid-thirties, Virginia had long since learned to hide her vulnerability behind an armor of aloofness and arch asides. And so, her friend's contrasting boldness would lead her to remark that Katherine "seems to have gone every sort of hog since she was 17, which is interesting." For all the attraction and repulsion that Virginia simultaneously felt about Katherine's sexual escapades, she couldn't help but take unalloyed pleasure in the unusually insightful literary conversation she also offered.

For her part, Katherine so badly needed a creative ally

that she gushed about this longing. "My God, I love to think of you, Virginia, as my friend," she declared in a letter of that summer of 1917. "Dont cry me an ardent creature or say, with your head a little on one side, smiling as though you knew some enchanting secret: 'Well, Katherine, we shall see' . . ."

A flurry of visits between the new friends ensued, with Virginia regularly calling on Katherine at her studio in Chelsea, and Katherine repaying the compliment by journeying out to Virginia's Richmond home. The talk between the two women would meander from literature and politics to news of their respective acquaintances. In this way, the pair managed, for a while, to nurture their fledgling friendship. Between visits, Katherine wrote to Virginia, urging her to "consider how rare is it to find someone with the same passion for writing that you have" and expressing a desire "to be scrupulously truthful with you." Had they both maintained this dedication to honesty, perhaps they could have protected themselves from the dual threats of literary rivalry and Garsington gossip. But it would only be a matter of time before their shields clashed.

The first blow was delivered later that same summer by a group of Virginia's Bloomsbury friends who had not fully welcomed Katherine into their ranks. The name for this loosely defined group harked back to their prewar Thursday-night meetings in the Bloomsbury area of London. The male-dominated crowd would gather at the home that Virginia shared with her siblings. There, over cigarettes, buns, coffee, and whiskey, they would debate questions of philosophy, religion, and art, as well as egg each other on with gossip. Virginia enjoyed such banter, wielding insults as if they were a competitive sport and sometimes expressing her affection through eye-wateringly cruel teasing.

In early August 1917, Virginia had certainly carped to one

friend about Katherine's days as a chorus girl, her overuse of makeup, and her tendency to frequent low-class teashops. But the particular incident that caused Katherine to take umbrage has been passed down only through asides in surviving diaries and letters. Pieced together, a picture begins to emerge.

Virginia's male friends congregated at Hogarth House, surrounded by the paraphernalia of the Woolfs' publishing venture—inking discs and blocks of wooden typeface. Between mouthfuls of the meager treats that Virginia's ration book could supply—plain buns, perhaps filled with sugarplums; cups of weak tea powdered with Nestlé's dried milk—the men divulged the latest gossip. There were so many salacious stories to choose from, but it appears that the Bloomsbury men accused Katherine of conducting a flirtation with the mathematician and philosopher Bertrand Russell—a feminist and philanderer who was by now accusing Katherine of being poisonous and untrustworthy, consumed with envy for other women. Among her old friends, Virginia was known to shed her aloofness and become quite the raconteur, her quick wit frequently causing the rest of the company to collapse in laughter. As the conversation progressed, it would have been in character for her to serve up salacious tidbits about Katherine's sexual encounters with traveling musicians, older bachelors, and impoverished Poles, and to succumb to snobbery, telling her friends that the New Zealander surrounded herself with unsavory characters, that she was part of a shadowy underworld.

The visitors had to head off before nightfall, when searchlights would comb the sky for German airships, and the mean-spirited talk would be replaced by the ghostly wails of sirens. At some point before they took their leave, Virginia mentioned that she and Katherine made unlikely comrades: the "Chaste & the Unchaste," she joked.

The gossip inevitably got back to Katherine through mutual acquaintances via Garsington. Some of the crowd that descended on the Elizabethan manor of literary patron Lady Ottoline Morrell were old friends of Virginia's from Bloomsbury
days. But others, like Katherine, moved in slightly less privileged circles. Here, all sorts of artists and intellectuals, shirkers
and genuine conscientious objectors escaped war-torn London for weekends of whiskey and wine, dips in the ornamental
pond, parlor games, love affairs, and endless conversation.

Windswept guests would roar on motorbikes through
Garsington's imposing gates while others arrived more se-
dately by train, all of them glad to immerse themselves in the
peaceful Oxfordshire countryside. The Battle of Passchendaele
must have seemed impossibly distant when the kitchen here
supplied plentiful provisions of ham, eggs, and scones, and the
household staff catered to each guest's every whim.

It was likely through Garsington's host herself that Katherine heard of Virginia's comments. In the summer of 1917,
Katherine returned to Ottoline's home, where she threw herself into the weekend's activities, cultivating a mysterious air in
her voluminous cloak, her face partially hidden by a small black
fan. Pacing the paths of the topiary garden by moonlight, she
paused now and then to rub between her fingers here a spike
of rosemary, there a spear of lavender. She often seemed cold
and inscrutable, but she came alive in the gardens at Garsington, enchanted by the Chinese lanterns; the still, dark ponds;
and the talcum-powder scent of stock flowers—a perfume re-
leased only at nightfall.

Katherine wandered the garden with her six-foot-tall,
flame-haired host, Ottoline, filling a basket with a potpourri
of fresh rose petals, sweet geranium, and verbena, which they'd
scatter on a sheet, ready to dry when the sun rose the next

day. Katherine's thoughts sometimes turned to Virginia, who had not joined them on this occasion. "I do like her tremendously," Katherine would tell Ottoline, following this visit. "The strange, trembling, glinting quality of her mind."

Upon Katherine's return to London, she wrote to Virginia, sharing her recollections of the gardens at Garsington. The description clearly made quite an impact, since Virginia recounted it in a letter to Ottoline on August 15: "Katherine Mansfield describes your garden, the rose leaves drying in the sun, the pool, and long conversations between people wandering up and down in the moonlight." This is the only glimpse we have of Katherine's exchange with Virginia, because Katherine's original letter has never been found. This omission is unusual, for Virginia always fastidiously cataloged her correspondence—a habit that would stand her in good stead in later years, when she had reason to believe that there might be posthumous interest in her life and work.

However, on the very same day that Virginia's pen had turned to the gardens at Garsington, Katherine also described them in her own missive to Ottoline, suggesting that the location would make an ideal setting for a piece of creative work. Given what would happen next, it seems likely that Katherine's conversation with Virginia had also turned to this idea. In *her* letter to Ottoline, Katherine began by asking herself "*who is going to write about that flower garden*"—this seemingly innocuous question would ripple beneath the surface of her friendship with Virginia for years to come.

The golden oranges and reds of the zinnias germinated in Katherine's imagination, the snapdragons and sunflowers, the pale pinks of the stocks. "It might be so wonderful, do you see *how* I mean?" Katherine went on in her letter to Ottoline, describing the approach she might take if she were to write a story inspired by Garsington's lawns and ponds. She would focus on "people walking in the garden—several *pairs* of people—their conversation their slow pacing—their glances as they pass one another—the pauses as the flowers 'come in' as it were." She failed to form full sentences as her ideas seized her more swiftly than her ink could flow. She likened the composition of such a work to that of music: a "conversation *set* to flowers." Knowing that someone ought to write about this symphony of sight and scent, she proclaimed that "it's full of possibilities" and vowed to "have a fling at it as soon as I have time."

This idea, it seems, was also blossoming in Virginia's mind. Her health was continuing to improve, and she relished the chance to return to her desk. She could not have asked for a timelier gift than the seed Katherine planted in her mind. As Virginia wrote, a new kind of rhythm made its way from her pen to the page: a fresh view of the world. She transposed the setting from Garsington to the botanical gardens at Kew, which she could see through the rear windows of Hogarth House.

Once Virginia had finished her draft of "Kew Gardens," she took steps to deepen her friendship with the woman who'd surely inspired it. Their mutual friend, Lytton Strachey, would be spending a few nights at Asheham, the Woolfs' country home in the South Downs, and Virginia hoped that Katherine might also come to stay. The invitation arrived at just the right moment for Katherine, who was feeling despondent because of the recurrence of rheumatic pain—a symptom that had intermittently flared up over the previous seven years, ever since her sexual liaison with a Polish man in a German boarding house, which had perhaps left her with gonorrhea.

The lengthy delays to Katherine's rail journey from London on August 18, 1917, could not have improved the state of her body or mind. Those who had known Katherine as a plump child would have been hard-pressed to recognize the gaunt woman whom Virginia greeted off the train at the county town of Lewes. Virginia's arms were laden with the lily roots and red-leaved plants that she'd bought while she was waiting. Over the coming days, the fine weather would allow for many pleasurable hours outdoors: strolls along the lane, the air thick with thistledown; the sighting of a caterpillar turning into a chrysalis, airplanes as well as butterflies on the wing overhead; the planting of crimson-petaled flowers in the walled garden's overgrown beds. Such pursuits were fitting, since it was during this stay that Virginia, anxious to gauge her reaction, would show Katherine her draft of "Kew Gardens."

It wouldn't have been hard for Virginia to get Katherine on her own. Leonard had various commitments in London that week, and Lytton was dividing his time between Asheham and Charleston, the home of Virginia's sister. During this visit, when Katherine read "Kew Gardens," the story apparently based on her own ideas, her behavior became guarded.

No wonder she felt aggrieved. She had already heard word of Virginia's backbiting talk, and now her friend had taken up her story plans almost wholesale: pairs of people talking in a flower garden, slowly pacing, glancing at each other as they passed—the conversation just as musical as she had envisaged it. It would be only natural for her to envy Virginia's creative industry, since the lethargy, pain, and ill temper brought on by Katherine's recurrent rheumatism frequently forced her from her desk. At some point, however, her garden idea did eventually migrate from notebook jottings to a poem titled "Night-Scented Stock." Its lines, just like Virginia's story, featured people talking in a flower garden, pacing its length, casting sidelong glances. But it would not find a publisher. After a promising start to Katherine's career, Swift & Co., which had brought out her first collection, had gone bankrupt. Most of the magazines that had run her early work had since folded, and her first champion, the editor of the *New Age,* had fallen out with her when she'd dared to sell her stories elsewhere.

Katherine's situation contrasted with that of her friend. Because Virginia co-owned the Hogarth Press, she faced fewer concerns about publication. Back at home in Chelsea, aware of this difference, Katherine mulled over both Virginia's short story and the gossip she had spread. Katherine tended to be defensive when she felt under attack, and to be spiteful when afflicted by jealousy. On this occasion, she had an arsenal of weapons at her disposal. She could pretend to brush off the rumors spread by her friend or expose this fellow writer as a filcher of ideas. She could even demand the return of her story that Virginia had commissioned for the Hogarth Press — a radical redraft of a much longer work begun in 1915.

How different life had been back then, when she'd first set to work on this narrative of colonial family life in the years preceding the First World War. Her younger brother, Leslie Heron Beauchamp, had not yet left for the front, and Katherine too had seemed invincible, her work almost guaranteed publication. Less than a year later, Leslie's death had made her keener still to "make our undiscovered country leap into the eyes of the old world."

After returning from Virginia's country home in late August 1917, Katherine decided that it would be far more important to her future as a writer to maintain the friendship than to become distracted by literary possessiveness or embroiled in Garsington affairs. But the situation continued to irk her.

Sitting down to write Virginia a letter, Katherine noticed the gladioli in her studio, which she considered "very proud &

defiant, like indian braves"—qualities that could just as easily describe Katherine's behavior. Pausing for just one moment to admire what she would call the "green gage light on the tree outside," she reminded her friend of their literary ties. But she couldn't help wryly alluding to the similarities in their work, remarking that it was curious they "should both quite apart from each other, be after so very nearly the same thing. We are you know; there's no denying it."

In this letter, Katherine found it in herself to be magnanimous indeed—a strategy that would prove tough to maintain—praising "Kew Gardens" and noting her particular fascination with the "still, quivering, changing light over it all and a sense of those couples dissolving in the bright air."

Thinking of the gossip that had gotten back to her, Katherine let her pen race ahead, unhampered by punctuation: "But dont let THEM ever persuade you that I spend any of my precious time swapping hats or committing adultery—I'm far too arrogant & proud."

When Virginia received this indignant plea, she wrote up her version of events in a letter—justifying the hurtful words she had spoken among her Bloomsbury friends. But she hesitated before posting her missive, wondering whether such a strategy might do more harm than good. And she wasn't quite sure what to make of Katherine's proud denial. After all, her impetuous friend had already confided her history of sexual affairs, and given that Katherine was still legally married to someone else, even her relationship with Murry officially counted as adultery. But mostly, Virginia felt keenly aware of what she stood to lose. She would shield this friendship from the Bloomsbury men in the future. Surely the women's bond was strong enough to withstand this current difficulty. And so Virginia tore up her note and penned an invitation instead, asking Katherine to come over to dinner when, as she would confide in her diary, she knew that "many delicate things fall to be discussed." In the meantime, she devoted her afternoons to setting the type for the first page of *Prelude,* Katherine's story for the Hogarth Press—the idea that its author might hold a grudge against her for writing the flowerbed story hardly likely to have crossed her mind.

By the time the date of the meal came around, the path to Virginia's home was scattered with acorns and there was sufficient bite in the air to warrant a fire in the grate. But though it was October, the leaves had not yet yellowed or fallen, and Virginia clung to the hope that her friendship with Katherine might likewise outlast a chill.

When the host and her guest sat down together in the paneled dining room, the tension was surely palpable. As well as the issue of the gossip, Katherine felt anxious about Virginia's opinion of *Prelude.* In such situations, Katherine tended to protect herself with a show of impassivity.

The Woolfs were known among friends for the paltry refreshments they served to guests, but the success of the evening wouldn't so much rely on the quality of the meal as on the women's capacity to chew the fat. With the fire spitting from the range, Virginia expressed her genuine admiration for the sensory richness of *Prelude,* which she considered to have "the living power, the detached existence of a work of art." Katherine especially appreciated Virginia's praise, since the story had become for her a way to resurrect her brother and their prewar idyll. The new title, changed from "The Aloe" to *Prelude* as suggested by Murry, would subtly remind readers that the world of the story would soon change irrevocably, for war lurked on the horizon. Astounded by the depth and sincerity of Virginia's words, Katherine couldn't help but feel gratified, later telling a friend that she imagined these accolades being served up to her in a golden bowl.

As the evening unwound, both women began to relax, their conversation turning to their shared opinions on the ponderousness of the work of Henry James, who had recently died at the age of seventy-two. And as the hours passed, Virginia eventually acknowledged that she had played a part in the unkind gossip. But she was quick to claim that it had all been wildly exaggerated, that she absolutely, categorically, did not say *quite* what she was alleged to have said: something about the "Chaste & the Unchaste."

According to Virginia's diary entry, at the end of the evening a woman showed up to accompany Katherine home. This was Ida Constance Baker—the friend who had moved into Katherine's cramped studio in Chelsea at around the time that Virginia had called in to commission a story. Katherine had first met Ida, a fellow daughter of Empire (having lived in Burma and later Rhodesia, as they were then called), back when they were both adolescent students at Queen's College boarding school, and they had grown unhealthily dependent on each other over the years. Unlike the self-absorbed Murry, Ida couldn't bear the thought of Katherine alone in her studio, racked with pain and afflicted by night terrors during the pitch-dark hours. But when Ida moved in, Katherine, who often found Ida infuriating, forbade her from returning before nine o'clock in the evening. Should she be around when Katherine was receiving a guest, Ida had to conceal herself by lying in her makeshift bed up in the minstrels' gallery, still and silent. Her presence didn't always go undetected, however. The author Aldous Huxley, for instance, was rather taken aback when, halfway through a visit, he heard someone coughing from behind the curtained-off mezzanine.

On this autumn evening in 1917, Virginia, falling back on her habitual snobbery, treated the cheery Ida with condescension, writing her off as lower-class and coarse. The privileged author merely noted the sallowness of Ida's complexion and her war work at a munitions factory.

Virginia would soon tell Ottoline that the falling-out was "formally buried." Unbeknownst to her, however, Katherine had not quite laid it to rest. Over a month after their supposed rapprochement, in mid-November 1917, Katherine wrote to one of Ottoline's guests, saying: "I am sorry the Wolves are at Garsington. There will be a rare bone dragged into the light before they are gone—." Yet deep down, Katherine knew that she could be just as indiscreet as Virginia, that as fiction writers, they were both natural gossips of a sort—trading in stories passed back and forth. For all their suppressed hostility and half-truths, the pair did manage to negotiate an uneasy truce.

During the rain-sodden summer of the following year, 1918, Virginia devoted her mornings to completing her second novel, *Night and Day,* and her afternoons to working on the publication of Katherine's *Prelude.* While hailstones the size of pigeon eggs hammered against the windowpanes, Virginia laboriously set the type for her friend's lengthy story, placing each and every letter on a composing stick, face-up and upside-down, then tightly packing each line with blocks of spacing.

Once all sixty-eight pages were produced, the Woolfs were ready to bind them within covers. But herein lay a potential pitfall. Katherine was a friend of the Scottish artist John Duncan Fergusson, who had designed a linocut for the cover. It featured a simple outline of a woman's head surrounded by aloe flowers, like those in *Prelude,* which bloom just once every hundred years. Virginia took an instant and intense dislike to

the design, and although she included it on the first few copies, she couldn't help but tell Katherine that she did not care
for it. Her preference, she explained, would be to feature only
the story's title and the author's name on Persian blue covers.

Fortunately for Virginia, Katherine was gracious indeed,
backing down straightaway and bowing to her friend and publisher's apparent better judgment. She did let herself vent about
it to Murry, though, exclaiming: "To Hell with other people's
presses!"

The matter of the design apparently settled without ran-
cor, Virginia holed herself away for days on end, turning down
tempting invitations from the likes of Ottoline. Behind the
closed doors of Hogarth House, Virginia filled her days with
folding, stapling, and gluing sheet upon sheet of her friend's
words, binding them within the plain blue covers that she considered so stylish. Pleased with the professional appearance of
the work—despite misnaming the title on several pages—the
couple then readied themselves to parcel up each of the three
hundred books.

The more immersed Virginia had become in typesetting
the story, the more sisterly she had felt toward its author. Virginia and Leonard harbored high hopes for this book, which
had cost them such time and effort to produce. Buoyed by
their enthusiasm for the work, they committed to a print run
of about three hundred copies—at least double the amount of
their first publication, which had contained two of their own
stories. And yet, in the run-up to publication, they had managed to secure only six or seven orders. When Virginia admitted this, Katherine had felt understandably mortified. "I shall
have to come back & persuade you & L. to let me sell it on a
barrow," she wrote in response, "customers to bring their own
wrappings."

When the story finally winged its way into the world in July 1918—three years after Katherine began writing it and fifteen months since Virginia first commissioned it—both women eagerly anticipated its reception. The Woolfs sent copies for review to several magazines and newspapers, and then waited to see what the critics would make of it—a wait that was largely in vain. Only two publications considered it worthy of review, and even they pronounced it unremarkable.

Virginia continued to champion Katherine's story, undeterred by the scarcity of critical attention and its lack of popularity among some of her friends. She defended *Prelude* when one of the original Bloomsbury gossips sneered that it "doesn't set the Thames on fire," and assured another that "Katherine is the very best of women writers—always of course passing over one fine but very modest example." Buried in Virginia's droll aside was the knowledge that shared artistic aspirations could easily descend into dangerous envy. And yet for now, Virginia and Katherine had managed to rise above their feelings of envy to support each other's literary careers. At their best, both women recognized that when "afflicted with jealousy," as Virginia would put it, "the only thing is to confess it." This lesson allowed these two ambitious women to benefit from their creative competition, the process proving as valuable for them as it did for duos of male writers more positively mythologized. But history has resisted weaving Katherine and Virginia's rivalry into the fabric of their relationship, too often misrepresenting these literary friends only as bitter foes.

11

Cat-and-Mouse

DESPITE WORKING SO CLOSELY with Katherine Mansfield to bring *Prelude* to press, Virginia Woolf still found her fellow writer fascinatingly "marmoreal." But she felt that the two had come to "an oddly complete understanding" based on their shared love of literature. At the beginning of 1918, back when Virginia was embarking on typesetting the first pages of Katherine's story, its author had headed off to the south of France. This trip, taken on medical recommendation, must have appeared as only a minor interruption in their relationship. Since Katherine behaved as if she were simply keen to catch some winter sun, Virginia could hardly be blamed for failing to appreciate the precarious state of her friend's health and well-being.

In fact, Katherine felt lonely and frightened. The War Office had forbidden her on-off partner John Middleton Murry to accompany her to the Côte d'Azur on account of his new post as chief censor. Nor could Katherine's live-in friend Ida Constance Baker get permission to leave her job as a tool setter at a West London airplane factory.

On January 7, Murry and Ida waved off Katherine as she staggered onto the boat train alone. She was suffering from a spell of pleurisy in addition to the rheumatism that intermittently plagued her, and the three-day journey weakened her further still. Neither food nor hot drinks were served on board the French locomotives, and Katherine had to sit for hours on end beside a broken window, which let icy air into the carriage, snowflakes soon covering the fur muff that Ida had insisted she wear.

The test of Katherine's endurance didn't end there. On arrival in war-weary Bandol, she found a destroyer anchored in the harbor, the patisserie closed down, the shops bare of tobacco and short on meat. The Hôtel Beau Rivage, where Katherine had booked a room, stood almost empty, a cold wind blowing through its halls. Here, under these inauspicious conditions, Katherine would write the ironically titled "Bliss"—a story that would later cause Virginia much distress.

By the time Katherine began to work on this piece, however, she was no longer alone. Ida, concerned by Katherine's despairing letters, had wept before a government official, who relented and belatedly granted her request for leave.

"What *have* you come for?" Katherine asked incredulously, when the exhausted woman showed up beneath the mimosa trees that lined the courtyard of the hotel.

What a welcome for poor Ida, whose journey had hardly been less grueling than Katherine's. But both women knew deep down that she would be grudgingly allowed to stay. For Katherine planned to write intensively, and for this, she relied on Ida's ministrations.

Ever since their boarding school days, Ida had willingly taken on Katherine's chores, thus freeing the writer to pursue her creative endeavors. Falling back into their well-established routine, Katherine soon enjoyed a sustained *"state of work,"* as she put it in a letter to Murry: "dead quiet and spinning away."

While working on "Bliss," she tended to rest in bed throughout the morning, lunch with Ida, write industriously each afternoon, and then take supper with fellow guests in the hotel's
salon. Sometimes Katherine's dependency on her old friend
could turn into a swollen sense of hatred. When a sugar-starved
Ida dared to delight in Bandol's plentiful supply of bananas
and Medjool dates, for instance, Katherine could not disguise
her revulsion. But egged on by Murry, who recommended she
treat Ida as an "abject slave," Katherine stomached her loathing—which was always combined with a contrarian kind of
love. Claiming to "use her as a walking stick," Katherine produced reams of writing, leaving her companion to build the
fire in the grate, buy supplies from the local stores, and liaise
with the doctor.

Katherine may have been making great progress with her
writing while Virginia was delivering *Prelude* into the world,
but she was still confined to the literary wilderness. As far as
either woman knew, the Hogarth Press could well prove little more than an enthusiastically pursued hobby, and, regardless, there was no guarantee that Virginia and Leonard would
seek more of Katherine's work. She wrote in Bandol without
any guarantee of publication, while Virginia, at home in Richmond, could at least bring out her stories through her household printing press.

Anxious for Katherine's literary future, not to mention
his own, Murry hatched a plan to set up a rival press. Before
Katherine had completed the enjoyable toil of drafting "Bliss,"
Murry was already negotiating with his brother about the joint
purchase of a hand-press, imagining the sensation of sheets of
paper bright and clean between his palms. Just over a week after first mentioning the idea to Katherine, Murry wrote again,
insisting that his ambition to establish their own publishing

house was not just a passing phase. This time he tried to convince her of its good sense by sending financial projections. He had published a thinly disguised autobiographical novel with Constable & Co. two years earlier, which had been a critical and commercial failure. He had come around to the idea that he could not hope to profit from publishing in the conventional manner. The same, he suggested, might well be true of Katherine. By following the subscription method the Woolfs had instituted—whereby customers could pay in regular installments to receive each title that the Hogarth Press brought out—he and Katherine could anticipate an annual profit of 300 pounds. She didn't take much persuading. This was hardly a sum to sniff at, given that she managed largely on an allowance from her father of just over 150 pounds per year—sufficient to live on, but only with frugality. "It's the soberest sense I'm talking," Murry insisted. "I haven't got a bee in my bonnet or a maggot in my brain. It's a chance of real salvation." They would surely have no problem producing beautiful books, he assured Katherine. "Think of that *tripe* of the Woolves!"

While Katherine was beginning to share in Murry's dreams of setting up a press, her chest was causing her increasing pain, and she yearned for his company. Such privations would cause her to feel increasingly envious of the Woolfs. It was no wonder that Virginia could write so freely, Katherine later exclaimed in a letter to her partner: "her roof over her—her own possessions round her—and her man somewhere within call." On the other side of the English Channel, Virginia was indeed enjoying a much-needed period of wellbeing, while in France, Katherine's health was about to take a turn for the worse.

Insisting that a spot of exercise would do her no harm, Katherine tramped with Ida through feathery fronds of undergrowth, leading the way through the slate-blue olive groves that lined the heat-soaked hillsides. Nestled among banks of blue violets, she spotted an empty house, its stones a yellowish shade of pink, white hyacinths growing in the cracks of its veranda. She let herself imagine making a home there with Murry, just as Virginia and Leonard had their creative haven at Asheham. But the impossibility of her dream soon crashed over her, and before long, Katherine felt too weak to continue the steep climb. Despite taking a shortcut back, she returned to the hotel physically exhausted and emotionally drained.

On waking the next morning, she got up to open the shutters, admiring the plumpness of the rising sun. Her situation brought to mind a line from Shakespeare, which she felt compelled to recite aloud: "Lo! here the gentle lark, weary of rest."

For lack of a sofa or an armchair, Katherine bounded back onto her bed. But the energetic leap brought on a coughing.fit. Her saliva tasted strange, and as the coughs continued to rack through her thin frame, she spat into a handkerchief. When she looked down, she saw that the cotton was stained with blood.

Although it would be a few months before her tuberculosis was officially diagnosed, the possible seriousness of her condition had already struck home. She was overcome with anxiety that she might die, leaving just snippets of work—her best as yet unwritten.

She already regarded "Bliss" as representing a new direction, and she longed for the chance to write more in this vein. Katherine was not the only one to hold this story in high regard. For five years she had failed to secure significant publication by anyone other than Virginia, but now "Bliss" was picked up by the *English Review*—a prestigious magazine, which offered to run it in the August 1918 issue, alongside a poem by William Butler Yeats.

Its readers would be treated to the story of naive thirty-year-old Bertha Young and her husband, who "got on together splendidly and were really good pals." The passionless yet jovial couple can afford an "absolutely satisfactory house and garden," entertaining "modern, thrilling friends" and employing a new cook who "made the most superb omelettes." The authorial irony is tinged with longing for elements of such a life—sentimentally so, as Virginia would soon have it.

The story is set on the day of a dinner party thrown by the Youngs. They have invited a guest named Pearl Fulton, and Bertha has "fallen in love" with this striking and enigmatic character, just "as she always did fall in love with beautiful women who had something strange about them." Pearl's arrival fans within Bertha a "fire of bliss." Although she herself does not fully comprehend her own erotic stirrings, she senses that they are silently shared by her guest. In the dark of the garden, beneath the blossoming boughs of the pear tree, Bertha feels in perfect communion with Pearl, both of them containing "all this blissful treasure that burned in their bosoms."

This moment of silent desire is interrupted by the voice of Bertha's husband—a scene curiously similar to one that Virginia would include in *Mrs. Dalloway* several years later. In Katherine's story, when Bertha joins her husband back inside, the feelings she has experienced for Pearl begin to transfer toward him. "For the first time in her life," the reader learns, "Bertha Young desired her husband." But no sooner does she long for the dark warmth of her marital bed than she spies her husband following Pearl into the hallway. Thinking himself unobserved, he holds their guest in his arms, whispering plans for an assignation the following day.

The August 1918 issue of the *English Review* containing this new story would come out at around the same time as a scheduled visit from Katherine to the Woolfs' country home. Now that she had returned to Britain for the warmer months, Virginia and Leonard had invited her and Murry to come to stay at Asheham. There were multiple reasons for celebration. Not only had the Hogarth Press published *Prelude,* but Katherine's divorce had finally come through, dissolving her short-lived first marriage and allowing her and Murry to wed. Virginia, whose partnership with Leonard formed the bedrock of her existence, knew that Katherine made out that "marriage is of no more importance than engaging a charwoman." But she put Katherine's nonchalance down to "the obligation she is under to say absurd things."

Here, on the South Downs, Virginia envisaged the two going off for walks along the windswept cliffs, inhaling the salty air, and invigorating their minds with free-roaming conversation. During this time together, Virginia had good reason to assume that she would, as usual, "get down to what is true rock" in her friend.

A few days ahead of their guests, the Woolfs had traveled by rail from suburban Richmond—finding it almost miraculous that the trains they took left and arrived on time. The sharing of tea and sandwiches in the carriage created the feeling of a family outing. The motley crew consisted of a Jewish businessman, who took charge; an injured soldier, whose kneecap and foot arch had been fashioned of nickel; and a gaggle of children with their mother, who steadied her nerves with sips of whiskey.

On arrival, and with much assistance from their two servants, Lottie Hope and Nellie Boxall, Leonard and Virginia set about opening up Asheham for their guests. They aired the rooms, unlocking the latticed windows to let in the summer breeze, and they rid the place of the small frogs and black beetles that had found their way in from the neighboring field. On the table, Virginia set a vase of carnations that she'd brought from a recent trip to Garsington Manor, their petals still pleasingly bright, and Leonard harvested beans from the overgrown garden, the smoke from the nearby farm settling in a haze on the meadows beyond.

But the warm spell failed to hold, succeeded by mornings of black skies and torrential rain. This downpour augured ill for the much-anticipated visit, and Virginia predicted that the Murrys might not manage the tortuous excursion by train. Her fears proved well founded. As Katherine explained to her would-be host, she had been beset by a "beastly attack" of rheumatism. "The sofa leg has got me & I cant move from it," she wrote in her short, apologetic letter. "My right wing is playing up, too," she said, referring to her lung, "so that altogether the machine is a thoroughly unsound machine and wont stand a journey."

On this occasion, Virginia did not stew over possible unvoiced reasons for the last-minute cancellation. She was well placed to sympathize with the Murrys' predicament since she knew all too well the privations of ill health. When Katherine played down her ailments by exclaiming, "Its the devil of a blow —but there you are!" and sent them up by signing off "Yours funereally," she did not fool Virginia. Recognizing the falsity of the cheer and darkness of the comedy, Virginia guessed that her friend "may be rather hopelessly ill." But she naturally believed Katherine's claim to feel "horribly disappointed" that the pair couldn't walk together by the sea "with sudden immense waves of conversation scattering us, or flinging us together."

But on the same day that Katherine wrote this message to

Virginia, she also penned a note to their mutual friend, the literary hostess Ottoline Morrell. And here she put a rather different slant on her decision. "We are supposed to have fought our way over to Asheham today—hung with our own meat and butter," she complained, "but I couldn't face it." Virginia's request that the Murrys bring along their own provisions must have seemed stingy indeed to Katherine, who coveted the unattainable comfort her friend enjoyed. Katherine was currently staying in Murry's rented bed-sit in Chelsea, and Ida, who had returned to work at the airplane factory, was living in one of its hostels. Katherine positively relished the seediness of Murry's building and its inhabitants, enjoying the everyday pleasures of boiling her own egg or running her own bath. But it was so much easier for Virginia to keep producing high-quality creative work with a maid and cook on hand.

Virginia had no inkling of Katherine's growing resentment, and she would have felt aghast to know of her friend's peevish complaint. As Virginia would admit to one of her houseguests, her weekly pat of rationed butter "merely greases the top of one's toast at breakfast, and leaves one to dry bread at tea." True, Virginia's inheritance yielded about four times Katherine's yearly allowance. But the Woolfs' annual expenditure in 1918 came to double Virginia's income, and like Murry, Leonard was not of moneyed stock. The couple kept careful accounts to ensure that they could afford to remain warm, fed, and watered. Especially during the threadbare war years, they labored to maintain their enviable way of life, which Leonard considered necessary for Virginia's health. Plus, they had to keep a contingency fund for her costly and unpredictable medical expenses. Unlike Katherine, who hardly received a penny from Murry despite his well-paid job at the War Office, Virginia had insisted on a joint budgeting system with Leonard, pooling most of their income for shared costs and keeping some aside for individual treats. The Woolfs worked hard to earn their required additional four hundred to five hundred pounds per year, both of them toiling at the hand-press and each aiming to write 1,250 words per day—an ambitious and unremitting output. As with Katherine and Murry, much of their time and intellectual energy went into journalism, which, in the early decades of their marriage, brought in far more money than their books.

In August 1918, it did not occur to Virginia that Katherine might have reasons other than ill health for choosing to cancel her visit. Deprived of literary debate and lively company, Virginia indulged instead in a quiet weekend, foraging for mushrooms, spotting the first ripe blackberry of the season, and enjoying the sight of a hare loping through the long grass. The tranquility was interrupted only by a Silver Queen from the nearby airship station, which floated in the blue skies above.

But an intrusion a few days later would truly unsettle Virginia. As she would recount in her diary and letters during the days, weeks, months, and even years to come, Katherine, toward whom she had been feeling so fond, was the source of her disquiet.

The return of her servants, Nellie and Lottie, from the nearby town seemed at first a cause for celebration, since they carried with them a stack of political books for Leonard and a copy of the *English Review* for Virginia. After days hidden away in her secluded home, with little more to note than the price of eggs or the squashing of a caterpillar, the prospect of a new work by her friend offered Virginia a diversion. She wasted no time in settling down and opening the teal covers of the magazine containing "Bliss," Katherine's story of female desire and betrayal.

As Virginia began to read, her friend's words gradually disturbed the peacefulness of the summer evening. The further she immersed herself in the pages, the more violently she reacted. Virginia recoiled from this fictional world, unable to judge "Bliss" purely on its literary merit. Katherine herself kept springing into Virginia's mind. This story, she felt, unmasked its author's "callousness & hardness as a human being."

When Virginia reached the final line, she threw down the magazine. "She's done for!" she exclaimed out loud. The mind of such a writer, Virginia would conclude in her diary the next day, "is a very thin soil, laid an inch or two deep upon very barren rock."

In the moment, Virginia felt compelled to rinse her own mind by soaking herself in the words of a very different type of author. She rushed to the bookcase, scouring the spines of her books, which were rotting in the damp. First she searched for one of the plays of William Shakespeare, next a novel by Joseph Conrad, even her own book *The Voyage Out*. But her gaze ended up alighting on her copy of Lord Byron's *Don Juan*. Given the infamously erotic nature of the poem, this choice of reading material could hardly be more ironic. But it did the trick, and she soon found herself musing on the surprising ease with which she could imagine the effect that the lothario Byron must have had on women.

Virginia had yet to acknowledge what she would come to call her "Sapphic" desires, but "Bliss" had clearly touched a raw nerve, vivifying something that she could not yet name. It was hardly surprising that she should take the story personally, since the character of Pearl Fulton shared some of her own most prominent qualities.

Back when Katherine had first shared a draft of the story with Murry, she'd admitted to basing some of the characters on people they both knew, warning him that he would recognize them as "fish out of the Garsington pond." She had insisted, however, perhaps protesting too much, that Pearl Fulton was her "own invention." And yet Pearl and Virginia were, in fact, strikingly similar, sharing the quality of icy aloofness. Like Pearl, Virginia was one of those pale, slender, "beautiful women who had something strange about them," capable "up to a certain point" of rare and wonderful candor, though "the certain point was there, and beyond that she would not go." Even Pearl's way of smiling and holding her head "a little on one side" is reminiscent of Katherine's earlier depiction of Virginia in one of her letters to her friend, her head "a little on one side, smiling as though you knew some enchanting secret."

Virginia would remark in a note to her sister that she felt "a little disturbed" by Katherine's story. Just like Pearl, though, Virginia could not bring herself to open up further. "Its"—she wrote, before clamming up—"well I wont say."

Such silences had never deceived Katherine. Reading between the lines of Virginia's appearance and behavior, the younger writer had revealed to Ottoline in 1917 that she put Virginia's fragility down to her being "one of those Dostoievsky women whose 'innocence' has been hurt." Such an insight was astute. Not only had the very young Virginia endured the molestations of her half brother Gerald, but she had later also been abused by her other half brother, George. It would take Virginia until 1921 to admit this to fellow members of the Bloomsbury Memoir Club. As Virginia would explain to her memoirist friends, the death of her mother had precipitated her first mental breakdown. During this time, when she was thirteen and George was twenty-seven, he had taken advantage of her grief-stricken vulnerability. A period of almost a decade was tainted for her by his habitual tapping on her door in the dead of night. He would then fling himself onto her bed, "cuddling and kissing and otherwise embracing" her.

No wonder, then, that the pleasures of the Woolfs' marriage appear to have been more gentle than rambunctious. As Virginia confided in her diary, their deep tenderness found expression in private everyday rituals such as "sitting on the green smoking, taking the letters out of the box," or "making an ice, opening a letter, sitting down after dinner, side by side, & saying, 'Are you in your stall, brother?'" Not so very long into their marriage, they stopped sharing a bed, but their unwavering love for each other found expression in their pet names ("Mandril" for Virginia and "Mongoose" for Leonard), intimate games (alone, they'd talk of indulging in something they called "airing the marmots"), and, during uninterrupted spells, they enjoyed the "space & quiet thats rather favourable to private fun."

Some in their circle wrote off Virginia as frigid; her own sister told the newlywed Leonard that her sibling "never had understood or sympathised with sexual passion in men," and Virginia's brother-in-law maliciously claimed in 1919 that her husband "fucks her once a week" and "it gives her very little pleasure." Katherine, however, had never turned her cruel tongue to criticizing the Woolfs' marital relations. And so it must have felt appalling for Virginia to read her friend's fictional depiction of a couple whose private life resembled the one she shared with Leonard. Like Bertha, Virginia had once told her husband that she loved him deeply but that she did not desire him; and, like Bertha, she had understood that he felt differently.

Despite the erotic adventures of Katherine's youth, she was better placed to empathize than Virginia could have realized. Following her daring early encounters, she had chosen in

Murry a man who was sexually naive. Leading a rather less liberated private life than the gossips at Garsington and Bloomsbury had assumed, Katherine compared her marital interactions to the joshing of two young boys. Such a characterization fails to convey the pain she must have felt at Murry's aversion to touching her, for fear of contracting tuberculosis. In his memoirs, which he would publish in 1935, Murry claimed that the couple's intimate relations had always been inadequate, admitting that throughout his long partnership with Katherine, he never truly "made love to her."

During her unwed years with Murry, Katherine had longed to be married, for all her disdain of bourgeois domesticity. Knowing that same-sex relationships disturbed him, she had hidden from Murry the experiences she'd enjoyed with women—more intimate than any she ever shared with men. Her infatuation with Maata Mahupuku, a Maori princess, was more than simply a schoolgirl crush, and Katherine had continued to explore this side of her sexuality.

Back in 1907, when she was nineteen and reluctantly living once more in New Zealand, she'd befriended the twenty-seven-year-old artist Edith Bendall and confessed in her journal to feeling "more powerfully all those so termed sexual impulses with her than I have with any men." She'd invited Edith to join her at a seaside bungalow on the far side of Wellington Harbor in Day's Bay, away from her family's prying eyes. Here, as Katherine continued to record in her journal, she lay with her head on Edith's breast, "clinging to her hands, her face against mine," feeling like a "child, woman, and more than half man."

But of all Katherine's formative relations with women, her ties with Ida would prove the most complex and enduring. During their youth, the pair had caused such consternation that, in the summer of 1909, Katherine's mother had separated them to prevent the development of what she regarded as their unwise friendship. Years later, Katherine's first husband had even cited a supposed lesbian affair with Ida as his reason for finally seeking a divorce. Poor Ida Constance Baker claimed to have no idea what was meant by a lesbian affair, but she had proved a constant friend indeed. If Katherine did harbor any secret sexual longing for the woman whose friendship would become for her "every bit as sacred and eternal as marriage," it was masked by her intense loathing of her own dependency on this devoted companion.

The two authors ganged up on Ida by referring to her as "the Monster" and excluding her from their conversations. Half a century later, Ida wrote up a detailed account of what she remembered as her only visit to Virginia's home. Her recollection differs significantly from Virginia's report of this day in her diary entry of autumn 1917. Here, Virginia wrote of Ida fetching Katherine. But Ida described a much fuller visit.

She recalled waiting for Virginia in the Woolfs' sitting room, Katherine whispering that their host was a famed beauty. A stray handkerchief, which they spotted stuffed into the edge of the armchair's seat, diverted their attention. Katherine, who was fastidiously tidy, remarked with some amusement that "if Virginia was carrying a jelly to the supper table and had dropped half of it, I can see her picking it up and dreamily putting it back on the dish as she went on into the room."

When Virginia eventually made an appearance, Ida found her as enchanting as she'd been led to expect. This tall, slender woman, her face long and fine-featured "as in a nineteenth-century portrait," greeted both guests but then immediately swept Katherine off to the study, where they could talk undisturbed.

Katherine's embittered reliance on Ida continued to in

crease even when the Murrys experienced a dramatic improvement in their fortunes. After the War Office awarded Murry a pay raise, the couple took out a lease on a spacious villa in leafy Hampstead and employed two maids and a cook. Deep down, Katherine knew that she could not survive without Ida, and so she persuaded her reluctant companion to give up her much-loved job at the factory and leave her dear friends at the hostel to join the new household. Feeling disempowered by illness, Katherine admitted that she would find it difficult to share her home with Ida, regarding it as her entire world and wanting to make it *"mine beyond words*—to express myself all I can in the small circle remaining." For her part, Ida felt utterly unequipped for her new paid role as housekeeper. She knew nothing of cooking, cleaning, shopping, or management of domestic staff. Despite her reservations, however, she never seriously considered going against Katherine's wishes. And so, by autumn 1918, Katherine, Murry, and Ida established their unconventional living arrangement at 2 Portland Villas, the house boasting views across Hampstead Heath to the city spread below.

Virginia could not stay away from Katherine's new residence, despite her continuing disgust whenever she thought of "Bliss." As for Katherine, now that her domestic setup rivaled Virginia's, she warmly greeted her friend's offer to make the long trip across London—a distance far greater than the old trek from Richmond to the studio in Chelsea. But Katherine was not motivated simply by a desire to show off. Virginia's letter had found Katherine bedridden, although she explained in her reply that she tried to behave as if she "were there for pleasure & not from necessity." Since the highlight of her day currently involved listening to the wind whistling up the chimney, the roar of the fire, and the rustle of the beech leaves tied to her bedpost, she especially welcomed the chance to talk over "a power of things."

When Virginia paid her first visit, Katherine was lying on the sofa, a glass of milk and a medicine bottle beside her. At the sound of her friend's voice, Katherine drew herself up, her movements like those of some suffering animal. But over the coming hours, the literary conversation distracted her from the worst of her pain. And by November 11, 1918, when the armistice was forged across the Channel, the two authors had already brokered their own kind of peace.

It was a fragile sort of harmony, though, requiring continuing work on both sides, and within only a month, it would be put to the test. On December 10, 1918, Virginia sensed a tense atmosphere within the Murrys' gray-painted drawing room. Murry had not gone to the office, and he sat with the two women, brooding and silent.

Virginia tried to inject some cheer by rustling up stories as bright as the greens and oranges of the curtains. She put Murry's stiff attitude down to his shyness, perhaps assuming that the couple's tempestuous marriage contributed to the ominous mood.

Murry finally admitted that he had a confession to make, directing his words at Virginia. He then went on to explain that he had bought his own hand-operated press, which he'd installed in the basement. Making out that it was really his brother's project, he talked about producing beautiful volumes inspired by the Arts and Crafts movement. Murry told her that they were intending to bring out some of his own poetry with Heron Press, which they had named after Katherine's late brother, Leslie Heron Beauchamp. But he was quick to reassure Virginia that she and Leonard might still do as they pleased with a long poem of his that he had recently submitted.

Virginia had already agreed to publish it, despite secretly finding his work laborious and crass.

Virginia took Murry's revelation in her stride. Everyone seemed to be setting up presses these days, and she prided herself on having been one of the first. She was not convinced that Murry and his brother had the skills required to produce artful printing, but by all means, let them try.

For all her mixed feelings about Katherine's work, Virginia was coming around to the idea that it was absurd to be afflicted by jealousy. Literary competitors were entirely different from romantic rivals, she told herself, though the two kinds of relationships had become entwined in her mind. In the realms of art, she decided, "there's room for everyone, unlike love"—a thought to which she would keep returning as her feelings for Katherine grew stronger and more complex.

While Katherine had put aside her desires for other women by this stage, Virginia had yet to embrace hers. This, then, was a space in time when both were repressing the element of their identities that would prove especially fascinating to later biographers. Virginia's subsequent friendship with the popular novelist Vita Sackville-West—which included a short period of physical intimacy—has become integral to the mythology that has grown up around her. This has overshadowed Virginia's more physically inhibited relations with Katherine, her literary equal.

Throughout the winter of 1918, Virginia called on her friend once a week, and in the years to come she would often reflect on these visits, which merged in her memory.

Upon arrival at the imposingly tall house in Hampstead, Virginia would be ushered inside by a nervous Ida, who'd direct the guest up to the study. On days when Katherine's health allowed, Virginia would find her friend working away at a yellow-painted table, her feet in a muff to keep them warm. Katherine loved to write up here, admiring the afternoon light, which she likened to the color of "a pale shell."

On seeing her visitor, she would fling down her pen and plunge into a literary discussion, dismissing Ida out of hand. Katherine and Virginia enjoyed literary debate, each woman fighting her corner at times, and at others backing down, both speaking with animation and ease about their work.

When Ida returned with a tray of tea, or to check that the room was sufficiently warm, the conversation between the other two women would become stilted. Ida assumed that their tartness was nothing to take personally. But there was likely rather more to their reaction. Ida's wifely role in Katherine's life, and the rumors that had circulated about a lesbian attachment, seemed to inform their discomfort. Now that Katherine had married Murry, Virginia regarded Ida as a woman spurned. Whenever she came in, it seemed to Virginia that the room became infected by Ida's "lacerated feelings." Since both writers were, at this stage, repressing their desires for women, Virginia apparently felt that Ida's supposed wounds bled into her own confusing bond with Katherine.

But Ida carried on her household chores in oblivion, hardly assuming that she was excluded from a chat between friends: Katherine and Virginia were just meeting as writers, their talk formal and erudite. But Ida could not have been more wrong.

Behind closed doors, Virginia and Katherine came to trust each other more and more, their conversation drifting beyond literature toward their own lives. Virginia would later recall being fixed by her friend's gaze, as Katherine insisted that she cared for her. Virginia would never forget those words or that lingering look, recording in her diary years later her memory of those "beautiful eyes—rather doglike, brown, very wide apart," looking as if she'd "like always to be faithful." Virginia would long treasure the sensation of Katherine's kiss: a gesture of warmth that perhaps contained a frisson of her friend's abandoned past and her own unanticipated future.

12

Life and Death

THE YEAR 1918 culminated for Virginia Woolf in a delightful balance of seclusion and festivity. Especially pleasurable, she
and Leonard had Asheham House to themselves for a week
while their domestic help took a well-earned break. During
this time, Virginia read through the manuscript of her second
novel, *Night and Day,* to work out her approach to the next
draft. This delicious solitude was followed by a period of grati-
fying social activity. Upon the birth of her niece on Christmas
Day, Virginia gladly helped her sister, Vanessa Bell, by taking in
her sons for a fortnight. The boys celebrated with the Woolfs
at their home on the South Downs, with a few old Bloomsbury friends joining the gathering for tea. Amid all this activity,
Katherine Mansfield continued to occupy Virginia's thoughts.

Both women took the time to pick out cheerful presents
for each other, parceling them up and carefully timing their arrival for December 25. Virginia also sent warm and lengthy letters to the Murrys' villa in Hampstead, which arrived, along
with her package, to scenes of wine-fueled fun: the wearing of
red and yellow paper hats and the exchange of stockings under
a decorated tree, along with dressing up in makeshift costumes,
playing charades, and eating pudding, crackers and cheese.

No record remains of the exact presents the pair exchanged. Katherine regularly destroyed great stacks of her correspondence, and so Virginia's letters accompanying her gifts have not survived. What's more, on this occasion, Katherine sent no word of thanks. Virginia received neither a reply to her inquiries after Katherine's health, nor a response to any of her offers to visit. By mid-February 1919, this wintry silence had left Virginia feeling hurt and confused. But, unwilling to extricate herself from their habitual game of cat-and-mouse, she eventually resorted to contacting Katherine's husband, John Middleton Murry, who insisted that his wife would love to see her.

And so, on February 17, Virginia readied herself to meet her friend again. At about eleven o'clock on the morning of her planned visit, the telephone rang through Hogarth House. The voice of Ida Constance Baker, Katherine's loyal companion, crackled over the line to Virginia. Katherine's health was not up to a visit, Ida explained, without going into detail or suggesting an alternative time.

Unlike Virginia's reaction to the postponement of the Murrys' trip to Asheham the previous summer, this time she disbelieved the excuse. After all, she too had been bedridden for the first weeks of the year—in her case, with toothache and headaches.

Knowing that Katherine and Murry now owned Heron Press, and that he had just been offered the prestigious editorship of *The Athenaeum*—a position once held by Virginia's father—she must have wondered whether her friend had simply used her as a means to publication. Later, in her diary, Virginia asked herself whether their relationship had been built on nothing more than "quicksands," and, to her sister, she accused Katherine of being "brittle as barley sugar."

While Virginia was getting feverish about the abandonment, it turned out that Katherine was suffering from actual fevers. Desperate to try any new treatment for her tuberculosis, she had agreed to a course of injections that brought on a high temperature for forty-eight hours each time. Several days after canceling on Virginia, she sent a letter explaining that "alas — I have just had another inoculation and by tea time tomorrow I shall be sailing on tropic seas—." She extended an invitation for the following week and even told Virginia that Murry would love her to write for *The Athenaeum,* leaving Virginia feeling rather foolish for assuming that her friend had set out to hurt her.

The weekly visits to Hampstead reinstated, Virginia would often arrive at the front door, her arms laden with gifts: a freshly baked loaf; Hogarth Press books typeset by her own hand; sprays of flowers to brighten the mantelpiece; a columbine plant, its deep purple petals aflame. The pair plunged right back into their literary conversations and more intimate discussions. Katherine was especially keen to hear Virginia's views on Dorothy Richardson, whose pioneering stream-of-consciousness technique would end up profoundly influencing them both. Virginia soon learned that her friend had pulled together enough new stories to fill a collection. Heron Press was still too small to cope with a book of this length, and even Hogarth had yet to bring out anything so ambitious. Besides, Katherine had set her sights on William Heinemann, the British publisher of Joseph Conrad and Fyodor Dostoyevsky — two writers she much admired. She was also keeping busy as the new fiction reviewer at *The Athenaeum,* hired by her own husband to critique as many as four books per week.

Still not entirely trusting the resurrected friendship, Virginia hoped that Katherine would not review her own novel when it was eventually ready for publication. Virginia was dividing her time between redrafting *Night and Day* and preparing an essay to mark the centenary of George Eliot's birth. Over the coming months, she would read every work by and about the great author, starting with one of the first biographies, by the novelist's later-life husband, John Walter Cross. In a letter to a friend, Virginia claimed "that no one else has ever known her as I know her," wishing that the novelist had lived and loved in the early twentieth century, when she could have "been saved all that nonsense" surrounding her unmarried life with George Henry Lewes. After all, Virginia had witnessed firsthand the experience of Katherine, who during the early years of their friendship had lived unwed with Murry. While cutting a bohemian figure and enduring the disapproval of her family, Katherine had never been subjected to the level of ostracism suffered by this literary forebear.

Through their discussions about writers such as Eliot, Virginia rediscovered the rare quality in Katherine that she had long admired: "a sense of ease & interest," stemming from "her caring so genuinely if so differently from the way I care, about our precious art." Virginia grew to enjoy Katherine's inscrutability, her lack of "apologies, or sense of apologies due," and began to wonder whether "its I who live in the suburbs & think it necessary to answer letters."

By Easter Monday, 1919, the two writers and their husbands were strolling together in the sunshine across Hampstead Heath. Although Katherine was more heavily made up than Virginia and had more outlandish taste in clothes, it was the older woman who tended to attract the attention of passersby. It wasn't so much Virginia's widely admired beauty that drew stares, but something odd and otherworldly about her movements. Strangers often found her appearance faintly ridiculous, reducing them to awkward laughter and leaving poor Virginia in great distress. Distancing themselves from the crowd, the two couples sat on a hillock, watching the far-off children play on canary-colored swings and a pair of dancers performing to a barrel organ's repeating song.

Both women professed a snobbish disgust at the throngs of people on the grass, and Virginia's repulsion was directed toward Katherine too. In her diary, a few days later, she couldn't resist making barbed remarks about the commonness of Katherine's prose, and her "haggard & powdered" appearance. And yet throughout the entire summer of 1919, the strength of the two women's friendship helped them to keep their demons at bay: Virginia's haughtiness; Katherine's capriciousness; their mutual literary envy.

During this period of apparent calm, an incident occurred that should have raised alarm bells for Virginia. Just weeks after that bank holiday walk up Hampstead Heath, she had eventually self-published *Kew Gardens*—the story that was so strikingly similar to Katherine's own idea. Assuming that it would not attract many readers, the Hogarth Press printed little more than half the three hundred copies they had produced of Katherine's *Prelude*. At first, their caution appeared to be wise. During the month after its release, they sold fewer than fifty copies.

On June 3, however, when Virginia and Leonard returned to Hogarth House from a stay at Asheham, they found the hall floor carpeted in postcards, the table stacked high with letters, the sofa strewn with envelopes—all containing orders from booksellers and individuals the length and breadth of Britain. This surge in interest had resulted from a review that the *Times Literary Supplement* had run a few days earlier, as Virginia and Leonard had been whiling away some unusually drowsy days surrounded by the buttercup-gilded fields of their country home. The critic's description of the story as "a thing of original and therefore strange beauty" had produced this towering pile of book orders, which the Woolfs opened over dinner. The couple hardly paused to celebrate. That evening they set about trimming covers, printing additional pages, gluing backs, and packaging the books for immediate dispatch. As they worked, they wondered how they could possibly make up and send out so many books in good time. Their growing awareness of the magnitude of their task made them anxious, and they began to bicker.

Such intense activity was not sustainable, they soon realized. They simply could not hope to meet such demand themselves. Taking on the services of a professional firm, they ran a second print run of five hundred copies. These sold at such a rate that the Hogarth Press's net profit on *Kew Gardens* ended up almost doubling that of *Prelude.*

Katherine could be forgiven for sensing that her friend was receiving recognition that rightly belonged to her. While the *Times Literary Supplement* lauded Virginia for taking the short story form in a pioneering new direction, its editor had not deemed *Prelude* worthy of review, and "Night-Scented Stock"—Katherine's flowerbed poem, likely of the same germination as *Kew Gardens*—remained in hibernation within the covers of her notebook. What's more, Katherine had recently heard back from William Heinemann, who rejected her new collection, *Bliss and Other Stories.*

On the day following the deluge of book orders, Virginia received a letter from Katherine. As fiction reviewer for *The Athenaeum,* Katherine had written a piece on *Kew Gardens* and wished to apologize to Virginia in advance. "You must forgive the review—I cant hope to please you—tho' I wanted to—," she protested. "For one thing I hadn't enough space."

Wrapped up in the unexpected success of her story, Virginia focused on negotiations with London-based printers about its second edition. Among this flurry of excitement and industry, she thought only of the possibility that the prospective review in *The Athenaeum* might further increase her sales. And she hardly allowed herself to feel the apprehension that Katherine's note should perhaps have inspired.

When the piece came out almost ten days later, Virginia was still so fixated on her triumph in the *Times Literary Supplement* that she failed to notice anything untoward. Although Katherine had bemoaned the lack of space afforded to her in *The Athenaeum*'s review pages, she had used up almost half of her not ungenerous allowance of over one thousand words on exploring a matter seemingly unrelated to her friend's story: the tendency of the era's writers to satisfy themselves with notebook jottings instead of refining their prose into works of art. "The note-books of young writers are their laurels," she complained: "they prefer to rest on them." She knew she should heed her own advice; her own journal was full of self-chastisement for failing to maintain a strict writing routine.

The author of *Kew Gardens,* Katherine opined, set an example for all dilettante notebook scribblers: here was a writer with the stamina to draft and redraft. This praise was highly charged, but Virginia failed to spot its undertones of resentment. "She begins where the others leave off," Katherine claimed; her work was infused with a sense of "leisure" and "poise." Virginia's privileged lifestyle had afforded her the luxury to lift ideas high above the level of the notebook. Although Katherine had managed to write sufficient stories to fill a new volume, she still struggled to match Virginia's productivity. Katherine's writing was hampered by the draining effects of persistent ill health, and she did not have the support of a steadfast husband like Leonard.

Far from picking up on the backhanded nature of the review's compliments, Virginia blithely continued her visits to Hampstead. She called in on the Murrys on June 14, 1919, just the day after the publication of Katherine's article, and two days after the *Times Literary Supplement* ran a biting critique of Murry's book-length poem, which the Woolfs had reluctantly brought out with the Hogarth Press.

Virginia entered a depressing scene at 2 Portland Villas. An emaciated Katherine was irritable, and defensive about her own writing, and, as Virginia would note in her diary, Murry behaved like a schoolchild who insisted that his recent caning hadn't hurt. Tellingly, Virginia took away an abiding image of the Murrys, with "nothing seeming to grow or flourish round them; leafless trees." That night, Virginia confessed in her diary to feeling "gorged & florid with my comparative success." But she ignored Katherine's frustration at her own peril.

Throughout the rest of the summer, Virginia continued to make the long journey across London to her ailing friend without picking up on any latent resentment. These visits were terminated only when Katherine, following her doctor's advice, headed off to the Italian Riviera in September 1919. Virginia found the time to write to her friend in between working on *Night and Day*'s final tranche of edits. But Katherine retreated once more into silence, leaving Virginia to agonize over what had gone wrong this time. The talk in literary London was that the balmy Mediterranean air had been beneficial to Katherine's physical health, so this time Virginia suspected a psychological motivation for her friend's sudden remoteness. Had Virginia unwittingly offended her, or could Katherine have felt jealous about the progress of *Night and Day*?

During the autumn of 1919, though, Virginia had other

things to distract her from Katherine's abandonment: both members of her domestic staff resigned; she and Leonard were considering purchasing Hogarth House from their landlady; American publishers made offers on both of Virginia's novels; and the British publication of *Night and Day* elicited a surge of letters, phone calls, invitations, and reviews. When, in the midst of this especially busy period, her November 1919 issue of *The Athenaeum* arrived, Virginia discovered between its covers an article that partially explained her friend's withdrawal. Without letting Virginia know in advance, Katherine had now reviewed her novel, *Night and Day*. This tale, while more conventional in form than Virginia's later work, explored the lives of modern women: Katharine Hilbery, an aspiring mathematician, and Mary Datchet, a campaigner for women's suffrage.

The review of this, her second full-length book, would affect Virginia's work for years to come. Surrounded by piles of typeface letters—which, just a year and a half earlier, she had arranged into each word of *Prelude*—she came across Katherine's criticism of her novel. It read like "Miss Austen up-to-date," Katherine had claimed. She, like Virginia, was a huge admirer of Jane Austen. When reading the work of her forebear, she especially cherished the sensation of becoming the novelist's "secret friend." But her review went on to explain that "whereas Miss Austen's spell is as strong upon us as ever when the novel is finished and laid by," in *Night and Day*, "Mrs Woolf's loses something of its potency." Ultimately, Katherine claimed, it "makes us feel old and chill." Virginia closed the covers of *The Athenaeum*, feeling desolate and confused by the spitefulness she detected in Katherine's words.

In the immediate aftermath of this experience, Virginia rashly issued Murry an invitation. As both the magazine's editor and Katherine's husband, she expected him to offer an explanation. What she didn't know, of course, was that Murry had encouraged his wife to be as scathing as she liked about *Night and Day,* reminding her that "we have no right to require truth from others if we don't exact it from our friends." And he did indeed class Virginia as a friend, telling Katherine that he considered her the woman with whom they had the most in common, admiring "something hard & definite & self-contained" about her.

Only a week after the review's publication, Virginia and Murry sat down to dinner in the high-ceilinged dining room of Hogarth House. The occasion fell during a brief lapse in Virginia's diary entries, but Murry would write up his account the following day in his letter to Katherine, who was still in Italy.

Just as he had predicted she would, Virginia mustered the courage to ask what Katherine had really made of her novel.

"She thinks that you make an abstraction from life, that you left one important element completely out of account, or rather withered it," he explained, referring obliquely to *Night and Day's* omission of the First World War.

Hardly reassured by his reply, and still none the wiser, Virginia comforted herself by telling him that "Katherine's review shows that she's not interested in novels." With this dismissive statement, she swept aside the difficult subject of the article, asking instead what was happening with Katherine's collection. Just seven months earlier, the pair had been on such good terms that Katherine had confided in Virginia about William Heinemann's rejection. Now Virginia asked Murry whether she might read the manuscript, for — despite her disgust at "Bliss" — Virginia remained interested in publishing her friend's work. But in the days and weeks that followed, she also kept turning the review over in her mind, wondering about the source of Katherine's apparent malice.

Certainly, Katherine bore a grudge against Virginia, considering *Night and Day* full of intellectual snobbery. "Virginia's cry that she is the flower, the fair flower of the age — that Shakespeare & his peers died that she might be saved that she is the result of God knows *how* many hours in a library," Katherine complained to Murry, "is becoming a mania with her."

What's more, Katherine despised *Night and Day*'s failure to acknowledge the changes wrought on the world by the war. In her article, she had compared the novel to a ship returning from "a perilous voyage" with a curious "absence of any scars." Privately to Murry, she described the novel as "a lie in the soul." Writers are under an obligation, she continued, to incorporate the new world order into their work, finding "new expressions new moulds for our new thoughts & feelings."

Virginia also appeared to emerge from the war unscathed, while the battlegrounds of Europe had affected Katherine so deeply. During a reckless visit to the front in 1915 for a tryst with a lover, she had seen the casualties firsthand: French soldiers with bandaged limbs; trainloads of German prisoners of war, one with a torn ear, another with blackened hands; cemeteries filled with line upon line of young men's graves. And, of course, her own brother had died in the trenches that year.

Over the next six months, Katherine did not send a single letter from the Italian Riviera to Hogarth House; nor did she receive one. Detecting anger in the reciprocal silence, tangible from across the waves, she forbade Murry from sharing her short stories with Virginia.

Back in Britain, Virginia found it crushing that Katherine's early promise to be "scrupulously truthful" had culminated in this impasse. Still immersing herself in the life and works of George Eliot, Virginia grew painfully aware of her predecessor's good sense in refusing to read reviews of her work. Virginia had often felt staid and suburban in comparison to Katherine's wilder approach to life, but the review's criticism stung her so keenly that she perceived herself as "a decorous elderly dullard." And it seems she couldn't help but wonder whether Katherine had been right about the failings of *Night and Day*.

Katherine's words continued to gnaw at Virginia long into the new year. That Easter, far from whiling away the holiday with the Murrys, she now shuddered at the high praise Katherine's writing was garnering under Murry's editorship of *The Athenaeum*. And yet, at her most self-aware, Virginia knew that the value placed on Katherine's work was not mere nepotism. And so, in May 1920, almost six months after the publication of Katherine's review, when Virginia got wind of its author's return from warmer climes, she immediately began to wonder which of them would make the first move. She vowed to wait for Katherine to initiate contact, and yet within a fortnight, Virginia, as ever, was the first to get in touch.

Katherine eventually penned a short reply to her request for a visit, agreeing to meet but failing to suggest a date. "I am grown *very* dull," she warned. Virginia, ever sensitive when it came to her friend, considered the letter stiff and formal. It seemed to Virginia that Katherine was behaving as if *she* had been the one snubbed.

But Katherine's response had, in fact, largely sprung from her continued ill health. In time, Virginia would come to understand this, well placed as she was to sympathize with bodily torment. She still suffered intermittently from headaches, insomnia, and aversion to food—symptoms related to her depression. She never seriously considered refusing to make the familiar journey from Richmond across town to Hampstead Heath.

On a cool day in late May 1920, Virginia arrived at Portland Villas to a reception from Katherine so frosty that she would later puzzle over this visit in her diary, quoting their conversation from memory.

Katherine asked after the cottage that Virginia and Leonard had purchased in Rodmell the previous summer, their tenancy of nearby Asheham House having expired. There was no pleasure in these inquiries, no excitement in Katherine's eyes.

It struck Virginia that her friend had a feline quality: "alien, composed, always solitary & observant." No sooner had this thought crossed her mind than Katherine raised the subject of solitude. Gradually, Virginia began to feel as if she were hearing her own feelings expressed as never before. Despite her initial apprehension, she was ultimately reminded of the "common certain understanding between us—a queer sense of being 'like'—not only about literature—& I think it's independent of gratified vanity. I can talk straight out to her." As their conversation began to flow more easily, it soon seemed to Virginia that "8 months were minutes." They spun gossip about their male friends and then spooled back to the subject of their literary work.

Now that the women had fallen back into step, Katherine surprised Virginia by asking whether she might commission her to write some stories for *The Athenaeum*—the very same magazine that had published Katherine's criticism of Virginia's novel.

"I don't know that I can write stories," Virginia said, voicing the sentiment that she felt Katherine had articulated in her review of *Night and Day*.

But Katherine countered: "No one else can write stories except you." *Kew Gardens,* she tellingly suggested, marked a turning point.

"But *Night and Day*?" Virginia heard herself say, although she had not meant to speak of it.

"An amazing achievement!" Katherine replied. "Why, we've not had such a thing since I don't know when—"

"But I thought you didn't like it?" asked Virginia, oblivious to the implicit criticism that her work was old-fashioned.

"I could pass an examination in it!" Katherine insisted, her tendency to dramatize taking hold.

Although Katherine had not actually disowned her original feelings about *Night and Day,* her review of the book now haunted her. Feeling that they needed to talk about the book at greater length, she invited Virginia to Portland Villas again, for lunch the following week.

It was an invitation that Virginia readily accepted. And so it was that one early June day in 1920, while high society congregated beneath a burning sun at Epsom Races, Virginia returned to Katherine's home. This time, they dived straight into talk about books.

"*Night and Day* is a first-rate novel," Katherine announced, but she knew that she could not brush off her friend so easily. "The suppression is puzzling," she admitted, obliquely alluding to the book's omission of the First World War.

Virginia found such an appraisal refreshing. "You've changed," she told her friend. "Got through something." And she savored in silence the relief that they had now progressed beyond the need for subterfuge.

Certainly, recent developments in Katherine's own career seemed to dampen her scorching resentment. A few months after her review of Virginia's novel, Katherine had eventually experienced the satisfaction of seeing *Prelude* praised in the *Times Literary Supplement* in a piece that also applauded the innovation of her latest work, *Je ne parle pas français.* The Murrys had brought out this long story themselves with Heron Press. Like "Bliss," it explored a triangular relationship, and Virginia secretly felt that it breathed "nothing but hate." Katherine had now received even better news: her collection had found a publisher. Constable & Co. would soon bring *Bliss and Other Stories* to press, finally ending the nine-year hiatus between Katherine's books.

The conversation turned toward her private life, and she admitted to Virginia that she felt badly let down by Murry, claiming that he failed to support her financially or emotionally during her illness. By the time Virginia took her leave, making her way past gardens planted with tobacco flowers and walls covered in ivy, she sensed as acutely as ever that she shared with Katherine something fundamental that even her Bloomsbury friends could not offer. Far from the backstabbing, half-truths, and downright lies that history has memorialized as the essence of the two women's relations, Virginia deeply appreciated their rare sense of communion. With her literary friend, she could talk without altering her thoughts—a level of uncensored conversation that she enjoyed with no one else but Leonard.

Virginia, in fact, owed a huge debt of gratitude to Katherine. Her friend had delved into her own intellectual reserves to work out the source of her intolerance for *Night and Day*, thereby offering Virginia one of the richest, if most unpalatable, of literary gifts. In the months following Katherine's critique of *Night and Day*'s muteness on the terrifying repercussions of worldwide combat, Virginia set to work on a war novel. *Jacob's Room*, as she eventually titled it, traces the life of young Jacob Flanders, whose surname presages his death on the Western Front.

After spending time with other writer friends, Virginia

sometimes found it difficult to re-submerge herself in the world of her novel-in-progress. By contrast, visits to Katherine stimulated her creativity. And so, over the summer of 1920, the pair enjoyed yet another rapprochement. Blessed by a reprieve from the worst ravages of illness, Katherine was even able to attend a luncheon hosted by *The Athenaeum,* where she sat opposite Virginia. But most of the time, the pair met behind the closed doors of Katherine's Hampstead home, Virginia now traveling there all the way from the South Downs.

During this period, Virginia was working on her experimental third novel and still basking in the praise heaped upon her more conventional second one. Katherine, who was anxiously awaiting the publication of *Bliss and Other Stories,* asked Virginia to consider reviewing it. Given the content of her own article on *Night and Day,* and the difficulties it had caused, her request was audacious indeed.

Virginia's immediate reaction was to refuse. Reviews detracted from the pleasure of reading, she insisted, and she could tell that Katherine had picked up on the deeper reasons buried beneath the excuse. *Bliss and Other Stories* did contain some pieces that Virginia rated highly, but others — the title story especially — aroused a vehement reaction, and she could not trust her pen.

The piece on *Night and Day* had prompted Virginia to think long and hard about the ethics of literary criticism. She acknowledged her inability to respond fairly to the work of her contemporaries — especially fiction by women — finding herself at times looking for faults, hoping even to find some. She couldn't help but wonder whether there was only so much space at the top, and yet at the same time knew it was ludicrously illogical to think that "if she's good then I'm not."

Still, Virginia wavered. In late August 1920, the thirty-eight-year-old made another trip from Sussex to Hampstead to bid farewell to her thirty-one-year-old friend, whose health had taken a turn for the worse, forcing her to cancel her planned visit to the Woolfs' new cottage in Rodmell. The wheezing of Katherine's breath and the aching of her limbs had now convinced her not simply to winter in the Mediterranean, but to stay there for a full two years. As usual, Murry would remain in London, leaving Ida to take care of his wife.

That summer afternoon, Virginia found Katherine reclining on the sofa, her sharp nose and thin lips illuminated by the summer light streaming in through the nearby window. With her thick bangs cut blunt across her forehead, she reminded Virginia of a Japanese doll, and the brightness and tidiness of the room made her feel as if they inhabited a doll's house. As usual, they talked about writing, and Virginia felt the familiar yet nonetheless odd sensation of an "echo coming back to me from her mind the second after I've spoken." In this atmosphere of camaraderie, she found herself revoking her initial refusal to write about *Bliss and Other Stories*. But even as she did so, she no longer felt certain that Katherine really wanted her to review it.

The pair continued to talk for hours, steering clear of gossip as they tried to cover as much literary ground as possible. But beneath the surface of their conversation lay the blankness of their imminent separation, the sense that so much remained to be said.

When Virginia finally took her leave—the train she'd planned to catch long since missed—both women promised not to forget each other.

"We will write," said Virginia, knowing that she would keep her word but unsure—even now—whether she could rely on Katherine to reply.

But Katherine surprised her with a pledge of greater intimacy still: "I'll send you my diary," she declared.

"Our friendship is a real thing," they assured each other, holding each other's gaze. "Whatever happens, it will always go on."

Over the coming years, the bond between the two writers would endure, but hardly in the form that they'd envisaged. As Virginia had feared, Katherine did her usual trick of retreating into silence the moment she'd left Britain's shores. Her arrival in the south of France marked a four-month period of intense productivity. During this time, Virginia did not hear anything from her, not a single letter—let alone any of the promised entries from her diaries. But word of her absent friend was everywhere: review upon review of *Bliss and Other Stories* piled on the superlatives; Katherine's own well-regarded literary articles continued to come out in *The Athenaeum* each week; and she was publishing new short stories at an impressive rate. Virginia finally decided not to add her own voice to the mix of reviews. Instead, she penned a short "insincere-sincere" note, finding that this activity excised her envy of her friend and renewed her fondness. The message, which arrived on Christmas Day, 1920, let Katherine know "how glad and indeed proud I am" of the book's success. Perhaps the four-month silence and the leagues of sea that separated them kept Virginia from asking whether, like her, Katherine ever doubted the merit of her own work—a question that she had kept circling ever since *The Athenaeum* review of *Night and Day*. But Virginia ended up saying only that it was a shame that the author of *Bliss* was not in London to enjoy her triumph.

Katherine replied swiftly, and far more honestly than she had in some of her previous correspondence—although she couldn't resist sarcastically commenting on the brevity of Virginia's letter. She cast off embarrassing talk of "triumph," admitting instead to thinking often of her friend and yearning to meet up again. Perhaps Virginia might visit her here in France? Virginia was, Katherine admitted, "the only woman with whom I long to talk *work*. There will never be another." Here in Menton they could sit on the stone terrace overlooking the garden while the cloud and light shifted in the sky above, and the breeze trembled the cups of wild orchids. Despite Virginia's loyalty over the past five years, when Katherine signed off her letter with "Farewell dear friend," she felt obliged to ask "May I call you that."

It would have been in character for Virginia to respond promptly, but it is impossible to know for sure whether she did, since Katherine continued to destroy much of her post. The next surviving letter took two months to reach her hands. Virginia wrote in February 1921, spurred on by motives very different from the congratulations of her previous note. She had been at Murry's farewell dinner in London, for he finally planned to join his wife abroad — at least for a while. The pair talked about Katherine, of course, and he ended up confiding in Virginia that he had recently strayed from his marriage. His affair with Princess Bibesco, an aristocratic contributor to *The Athenaeum*, was the talk of the town, and Katherine had already learned of it from the princess herself, who wrote to accuse the ill and absent author of cruelly refusing to relinquish her hold on Murry.

Virginia felt for Katherine, whom she knew must be suffering intense jealousy and a sense of isolation. When she returned to Hogarth House, she put pen to paper. Letting down her guard, she confessed to Katherine that, bereft of their weekly meetings, she'd resorted to jotting in her diary those things she longed to talk about with her. The missive was full of praise for the transparent quality of Katherine's work, reflections on the importance of writing by women, and even an anecdote about E. M. Forster's recent claim that Virginia and Katherine were the two leading fiction writers of their time. "Damn Katherine!" Virginia joked; "why can't I be the only woman who knows how to write?"

The peal of Richmond church bells interrupted Virginia's writing, reminding her that she and Leonard must soon crack eggs into a frying pan, it being their cook's day off. They would stand side by side at the gas stove, their rashers of bacon rippling with the heat. She had just enough time to finish up her four-page letter with a plea to stay in touch: "Please Katherine," she begged, "let us try to write to each other."

Predictably, Katherine failed to respond. Over on the continent, her health appeared to improve and she was enjoying a sense of renewal with Murry, whose empty affair with Princess Bibesco had ultimately taught him to value his marriage. Katherine was finally getting to experience some of the harmony that she had long envied in the partnership between Leonard and Virginia. Like their counterparts in Britain, the Murrys worked industriously and discussed their writing with each other. But this idyllic period would not last, as Katherine's health and marital problems inevitably reared up once more. Fearing that she was destined to die young, Katherine spent as much time as possible writing fiction: failing to mend frayed clothing, putting off visitors, feeling that she should leave letters unanswered.

This time, Katherine's abandonment pained Virginia more profoundly than ever before. Still, over the course of the year, she continued to think of things that she'd like to share with her writer friend. If she were to travel to France, as Katherine had suggested back at the cusp of the year, she predicted that their conversation would kindle within just three minutes. But she could not countenance making such a journey after "the small lies & treacheries, the perpetual playing & teasing." Besides, she too was deeply immersed in her work. Despite its more experimental structure, the drafting of *Jacob's Room* was far swifter and more pleasurable than that of her previous two novels. She nonetheless worried that it might seem to her "sterile acrobatics" by the time it came out—a fear exacerbated by the spring 1922 release of Katherine's third collection, *The Garden Party.* Virginia noted in her diary that the book "soars in the newspapers, & runs up sales skyhigh," causing her to feel so consumed with envy that she tried to persuade herself that anything so popular could hardly be much good.

By mid-August, after her two-year absence, Katherine came back to London. She stayed at the Hampstead home of a friend, Dorothy Brett, spending much of her time shut away in her room, a card hanging on her door to inform prospective visitors that she was working and did not want to be disturbed. During free hours, she attended lectures about achieving harmony between heart, body, and mind.

Although Katherine did not get in touch directly, a mutual friend let Virginia know that she was back in town, and Dorothy contacted Virginia to invite her to one of the regular Thursday evening salons she held at her house. Virginia agonized over the invitation, trying to calculate the effect of such company. It was a particularly unsettling time for her. Having now completed *Jacob's Room,* she was anxiously awaiting its launch. She identified "a certain instability" in her character (although she preferred to think of it as a "generosity of temperament"), which led her to "extremes of passion and repulsion." Right now, she felt wary of the Murrys. But if she saw them again, she knew she would warm to them once more.

Was yet another reconciliation worth the pain, and would it affect her writing?

Her latest novel would be self-published by the Hogarth Press, marking, finally, her liberation from the publisher half brother who had abused her. Virginia was now working on a new short story, "Mrs. Dalloway in Bond Street," and she was considering expanding it into a novel. After a positive start, she was now struggling—a problem Katherine was far better acquainted with. Virginia blamed intrusions from the outside world for her inefficiency, and worried that should she enter "the heart of the enemies camp" she might find herself "rasped all over, or at any rate dulled & blunted." On the other hand, she worried that surrounding herself only with old Bloomsbury pals might cause her mind to "soften and rot."

Weighing up which was the better of these two evils, Virginia decided not to visit Katherine at Dorothy's house. She simply assumed that they would meet again the following summer, when they could start afresh.

It was a choice that Virginia would live to regret. Katherine was far from cured. Her return to Britain had, in fact, been prompted by a flare-up of her lung disease. Increasingly desperate for a cure, she had come back to London for a course of new-fangled radiation treatment. And when that began to take a toll on her heart, she sought still more extreme intervention. The lectures she'd been attending in London confirmed her belief that her physical ailments stemmed from her diseased spirit—a theory that most of her nearest and dearest could not abide. But the opinions of friends and lovers were of little interest to Katherine, who had decided to break free from old relationships in order to embrace a new way of life.

At the beginning of October 1922, she returned to France, this time to join the ranks of the self-appointed guru George

Gurdjieff, a Russian of Greek and Armenian descent who'd set up a commune in Fontainebleau. Here, he was putting into practice the theories espoused in the lectures that Katherine had so recently attended. She bid farewell to both Murry and Ida, telling them that she must tread this path alone. Yet she nonetheless attempted to stage-manage their lives from afar, suggesting that the pair could set up a farm together in Ditchling—a village just across the chalk hills from the Woolfs' new cottage in Rodmell. This outlandish plan stemmed from her own eccentric regimen at the Institute for the Harmonious Development of Man. Here at Le Prieuré, pupils and patients engaged in a combination of manual labor and artistic pursuit. Katherine escaped the most punishing tasks on the institute's farm, working instead in the kitchens, scrubbing and peeling vegetables and helping with the butchery of pigs. This work was interspersed with mandatory hours spent sitting in a drafty hayloft, whose ceiling was decorated with paintings of the community's members. Here, Katherine put her faith in the dubious health benefits of inhaling the breath and aroma of cows. Come evening, she joined the vodka-fueled dances, drama, or operatics, which continued late into the night, before finally retiring to her stark, icy room.

Communication between Katherine and Virginia had become so sporadic by this stage that little had gotten back to the British writer about the New Zealander's perilous state of health. It therefore came as a great blow in January 1923 when Virginia's maid, Nellie Boxall, greeted her at breakfast with some startling news.

"Mrs Murry's dead!" Nellie informed her. "It says so in the paper!"

Katherine's obituary, which appeared in *The Times* on the twelfth of that month, announced with regret that this writer of short stories and "witty and penetrating novel reviews" had died suddenly three days earlier. Murry, to whom Katherine had issued an unexpected invitation to Fontainebleau, was with her during her final hours. That afternoon he'd found her positively glowing, but at about ten o'clock at night, when she headed upstairs to bed, she suffered a pulmonary hemorrhage, blood pouring from her mouth. Doctors soon brushed Murry to the side, although Katherine beseeched him with her eyes to come closer. She died as her husband looked on, incapable of taking her in his arms.

Katherine's death would come as a "severe shock to her friends," her obituary said, on account of the apparent improvement in her health. When Virginia heard the news, she felt overwhelmed by confusion. As the day progressed, emptiness and regret enveloped her. When she tried to embark on her usual morning routine, sitting down at her desk, she found herself unable to write. What was the point, she wondered, without her onetime friend to read it? They had shared something of deep importance; she expected never to find this in anyone else.

An image of Katherine kept intruding into her mind: the thirty-four-year-old reluctantly lifting an icy white wreath to her head before slowly turning her back on Virginia, taking her leave with dignity.

In her diary a week later, Virginia would bring herself to admit that Katherine's prose was "the only writing I have ever been jealous of." Virginia's despair at this untimely loss continued to brew. Although ink eventually flowed from her pen once more, for weeks she felt as if she wrote into a void. "There's no competitor," she lamented, feeling, as she put it, like a lonely cock of the walk: "For our friendship had so much that was writing in it."

In the mid to late 1920s, when Virginia completed two of her most lauded works, *Mrs. Dalloway* and *To the Lighthouse,* she wondered on each occasion what Katherine would have made of them. On completing the last words of *Mrs. Dalloway*—a novel about a party thrown by an upper-class woman, which is disrupted by the death of a shell-shocked man—she allowed herself to fantasize that, had her friend lived and continued to write, "people would have seen that I was the more gifted." And yet, for all of Virginia's celebratory egotism, she knew deep down that she owed a debt of gratitude to this fellow author who had pushed her to find new forms for the novel in the wake of the war. Early biographers of Woolf, though, would be reluctant to admit that a lesser-known writer like Katherine Mansfield may have deeply influenced the pioneering female modernist. But such a stance requires studious overlooking of evidence. Throughout the rest of Virginia's life, references to Katherine would litter her letters and diaries, her fiction regularly revisiting scenarios that her late friend had earlier explored.

Katherine's death abruptly ended their relationship in the midst of one of their estrangements, and so Virginia would remain haunted by her bitter opponent and beloved friend unrivaled by any other. Over the decades to come, and especially during her richly mythologized love affair with Vita Sackville-West, Virginia's thoughts would frequently turn to her complex bond with Katherine. "What odd friends I've had—you and she—" Virginia wrote in a letter to Vita in 1927, having just read the *Journal of Katherine Mansfield.*

Although Katherine was never a consistent diarist, Murry had brought together any notebook jottings he could date and published them in one volume—a laborious endeavor expressly against his late wife's wishes. He did not include entries

that explicitly referred to the Woolfs. When he later brought
out a volume of Katherine's letters, he presented his late wife
as a matchless genius who relied on no one other than him for
literary advice, leaving out several of the missives she had written to Virginia.

Murry's editorial choices, combined with the attitude
of Woolf's early biographers, resulted in a misleading and in-
complete public record of the tempestuous friendship between
these two deeply ambitious women. Virginia herself, however, did manage to forge a resolution of sorts with Katherine,
whose true feelings she had been left forever trying to read.

Eight years after Katherine's death, in the early summer
of 1931, the late author appeared to Virginia in a dream. Even
in her sleeping state, she knew that her old friend was dead,
but the words of the apparition offered her comfort nonetheless. Katherine said "something by way of explanation"—
which Virginia considered a "curious summing up" of "what
has passed since she died." And, before waking, Virginia reached
for her rival's palm one last time, responding to the hand of
friendship that Katherine had extended from beyond the grave.

Epilogue:
A Web of Literary Connections

WE BEGAN with a simple aim: to find the literary women on whom our four authors relied. But an unexpected pleasure of researching this book was the discovery of a wider web of threads linking these writers across generations and vast expanses of land, sea, and time.

Four decades after the death of Jane Austen, George Eliot read the work of her forebear before embarking on her first novel. Some seventy years later, Virginia Woolf's book-length essay *A Room of One's Own,* published in 1929, acknowledged the debt she owed, not just to Jane, but also to Charlotte and Marian. And they, in turn, she said, were indebted to the great female writers who preceded them.

Virginia wondered on the page about the sheltered existence of the women who came before her. Understandably, given the sanitized images of each author painted by their earliest biographers, she regarded Jane, Charlotte, and Marian as isolated individuals, each set apart from society. In Virginia's imagination, Charlotte languished in a moorland parsonage, "without more experience of life than could enter the house of a respectable clergyman." Marian, thanks to her frowned-upon relationship with George Henry Lewes, endured a lonely existence, tucked away in a corner of north London. Jane was a bookish spinster aunt—so shy she hid her manuscripts even from the relatives with whom she shared her tiny domestic sphere.

In the memoir of his aunt, Jane's conservative nephew naturally failed to mention the Austens' governess. His complete disregard for Anne Sharp, whose friendship Jane had placed above the loyalty she owed to her brother, represents the snapping of an important thread in the literary web that might otherwise have inspired future generations of female authors.

Long after Jane had gone to her grave, other women who forged an independent path through their writing continued to unsettle the established social order. But if it appeared that they scribbled only between household chores, their endeavors could be presented as more eccentric than subversive. Elizabeth Gaskell's portrait of Charlotte as a devoted daughter and sister hardly posed much danger. The real Charlotte, though—a woman with strong convictions of her own, who chose a friend as radical as Mary Taylor? That story would have been beyond the pale.

Far from the image of the closed community of Brontë sisters shut away in their father's parsonage, Marian is remembered as a particularly cerebral writer with little need for female company. To many critics, it has long seemed impossible that someone with such supposedly masculine qualities might have shared a sisterly bond with Harriet Beecher Stowe, whose novels are often now dismissed as overly sentimental. But—like Charlotte Brontë, born three years before her—Marian had greatly admired the antislavery novel *Uncle Tom's Cabin*. Interestingly, when she aired her affectionate feelings for its creator in a letter to a friend, back in 1853, her thoughts flitted between Harriet and Charlotte. "Villette—Villette," Marian wrote with endearing urgency, "—have you read it?"

The fascinating conversations shared between female author peers of the past continue, of course, to this day—as does communication, through the written word, across great distances or generations. Yet well into the twentieth century, the creative relationships of male writers still overshadowed those between women. Virginia Woolf may have been the high priestess of modernism, occupying her dais alongside a group of celebrated literary men, but the myth goes that there can be room at the top for just one woman. And so Katherine Mansfield was branded Virginia's enemy, and another literary thread was swept away.

Since their time, many more pairs of female writers have spun similar threads of their own. Like the two of us, Virginia's first biographer, the novelist Winifred Holtby, and the wartime chronicler Vera Brittain met when they were in their twenties. Their first encounter was, however, marked by mutual distrust.

After suffering, as she saw it, a humiliation by Winifred during a college debate in their days as undergraduates at the University of Oxford, Vera went out of her way to avoid her fellow student—a frostiness repaired only when Winifred called on Vera, who'd been fighting a cold, with the unexpected gift of a bunch of grapes. Once they'd overcome their initial wariness, they realized that—despite outward differences—they had a great deal in common. Winifred was tall, blond, and gregarious, whereas Vera was small, dark, and more reserved. But they bonded over their experiences of service during the First World War, as well as their mutual aim to become professional writers. After university, they decided to move in together, to encourage each other in their ambitions. They even lived together again in later years, when Winifred joined the family home that Vera shared with her husband and two children. During their sixteen-year friendship, the two actively supported each other's careers, and despite the soar-away success of Vera's book *Testament of Youth,* they would always regard each other as equals.

We find ourselves especially drawn to this pair, who met when they were close to the beginning of their literary journeys and — as Winifred put it — became for each other a "travelling companion," never afraid to acknowledge the depth of support they had given each other. After Winifred's early death at age thirty-seven, Vera would go on to immortalize their alliance in *Testament of Friendship* — a fitting tribute from the woman whom Winifred once described as the person who "made me."

During these interwar years, two other female authors were beginning to make their way. Long before Jean Rhys published *Wide Sargasso Sea* — her prequel to Charlotte Brontë's *Jane Eyre* — she got to know Eliot Bliss. Both women were white writers from the Caribbean, living in London at the time. During the summer of 1937, they began to see each other every fortnight for what Eliot referred to as "delightful West-Indian suppers," washed down with vast quantities of wine. Such was Jean's ability to drink that her poor friend — whose adopted pen name was inspired in part by George Eliot — always felt ill after these meals. Jean too sometimes ended up so drunk that her husband would have to put both women to bed. On such occasions, Jean would sometimes angrily accuse Eliot — the daughter of a colonial army officer — of looking down on her. But when Jean was sober, she was, according to her friend, always kind-natured and full of fun.

In the winter of that year, Eliot left for America. But the

two continued to write to each other during the decades to come, Eliot sharing her knowledge of the Sargasso Sea. Their warm and sometimes humorous letters, which Jean joked she would one day frame, challenge the common perception of her as a volatile character, unable to make friends with other women.

In Florida at about this time, a rather more unlikely friendship was being kindled between two other female writers. Zora Neale Hurston, the author of *Their Eyes Were Watching God,* grew up in an all-black town, her father a former slave. Marjorie Kinnan Rawlings, a Pulitzer Prize winner, was married to a man who owned a white-only hotel. They met at a time when their home state was a Ku Klux Klan stronghold and Jim Crow racial segregation laws were harshly enforced.

When Marjorie gave a guest lecture to Zora's students at the all-black Florida Normal and Industrial College in 1942, she was so taken with her host that, despite the many social barriers to friendship, she invited Zora to tea the next day at her husband's hotel. Prejudice and conformity ran deep, however. Marjorie, fearing the reactions of other guests, arranged for the bellboy to whisk Zora up to their private apartment to get her out of sight. Such precautions, however, would prove unnecessary. Zora, knowing that her presence would prove sensitive, entered through the kitchen and up the back stairs, allegedly dressed as a maid. Remarkably, such squalid moral compromises failed to hinder their enjoyment of each other's company. "I've never had so much fun," Marjorie told her husband. For her part, Zora, quick to realize their many similarities, would soon refer to Marjorie as a "sister."

Their mutual admiration might have been assured, but the ethical dilemmas didn't stop there. When Zora visited Marjorie's country residence, they talked, laughed, and got tipsy together on the porch. But when it became clear that Zora was in no fit state to drive, Marjorie felt she had to send her friend to sleep out in the black servants' quarters, although there were plenty of spare bedrooms in the main house.

Once again, Zora didn't seem to hold her friend's cowardice against her. But Marjorie subjected herself to tough questions about her behavior. And, on a second overnight visit, she insisted that this time Zora stay with her in the house. Marjorie went on to speak out against racial segregation, and showed solidarity with her friend by putting in a good word for her with her own esteemed editor, who had also commissioned famed literary comrades F. Scott Fitzgerald and Ernest Hemingway.

The multitalented Maya Angelou was no stranger to the sort of racial prejudices writ large in the friendship of Marjorie and Zora—something she explored in a series of memoirs. Growing up in the town of Stamps, Arkansas, the young Maya read the novels of Jane Austen and Charlotte Brontë and was entranced by the unfamiliar worlds of British nineteenth-century manners and moorland passion. Much later in life, well after the enormous success of *I Know Why the Caged Bird Sings* in 1969, Maya would find herself sharing the bill at a literary festival with fellow legend Toni Morrison. In the Welsh village of Hay-on-Wye, Maya and Toni were in strikingly similar circumstances, each far from home at a time when their mothers were ill. They were, as Maya put it, "just two Black ladies who were missing our mothers."

In the following years, they went out of their way, time and again, to show each other support. In 1993, when Toni won the Nobel Prize in Literature, Maya threw her a party because, as she would later recall, she felt it was something that the United States should have done. When Maya was honored at the National Book Awards in 2013, it was Toni who presented her award. And as Toni's tribute speech made clear, her respect for Maya went far beyond professional admiration. Having just praised her friend's culinary talents, she spoke, with clear emotion, of the sustenance she received from Maya during a particularly dark time. When Toni's son died one Christmas, Maya, she remembered, was the first person outside her family to call on the phone, "that unmistakable voice of sheer balm" offering comfort from afar.

By poignant coincidence, Toni, in her eighties by then, would find herself back at Hay-on-Wye in 2014 on the day that Maya died. Months before, when we'd heard that Toni would be speaking at the festival, we had eagerly bought tickets for the event. And so ours were among the shocked gasps that rippled through the drafty tent when Maya's death was announced. As Toni articulated her deep grief, we found ourselves saddened too. Sitting side by side, many rows back from the stage, we imagined how one of us would feel, some future day, left without her friend.

But there is so much more that we can learn from Toni and Maya, as well as the other literary pairs in this book. In stark contrast to our early fears about the threat of literary envy, the bond between Jane and Anne shows that friends can indeed overcome any friction caused by differences in worldly success. The example of Mary, whose hectoring did so much to encourage Charlotte's ambitions, suggests that the willingness to speak uncomfortable truths is sometimes the hallmark of a real confidante. Marian's forgiveness of Harriet's neglect is testament to the power of letting go of past grievances. And the friendship of Virginia and Katherine, those supposed arch foes, demonstrates that professional rivalry can actually fuel a female literary alliance.

Vera and Winifred, more recent friends who supported each other's early ambitions, will doubtless always remain a particular inspiration. And Maya and Toni reinforce our belief that it is important to celebrate the lives of those closest to us, not just in fine tributes when they are gone, but also when they are still here.

These lessons have had a special relevance to us in recent times. By 2015, we'd spent a decade and a half laboring over several books that remained unpublished. On a wintry evening, descending the escalator of a crowded London Underground station, our conversation turned to the latest writing competition that we had each entered—for "new" and unpublished authors. Neither of us felt very optimistic. Remembering that long-ago meal in a Japanese shopping mall, Emily wondered whether we'd have embarked on this literary journey at all, had we known how little ground we'd have gained professionally by now. Though equally downcast, Emma reminded us both that it wasn't the writing itself that was getting us down, but the lack of improvement in our publishing prospects.

Before the month was out, though, Emily received a message that she'd been shortlisted for that competition. She immediately thought of Emma, hopeful that she too had heard good news. But when she picked up the phone, she discovered this was not the case. And though she'd been given a ticket so that a guest could join her for the prize dinner, she wondered whether it would really be generous to offer it to her friend.

In early spring, having in fact jumped at the chance to come along, Emma sat at the judges' table alongside those on the shortlist. Despite her pride in Emily, the evening would not be without awkwardness. Over dinner conversation, Emma studiously avoided mentioning that she too had entered the prize, indeed keeping quiet about her novel altogether. This, the second she'd written, had racked up its own rejection slips. But against the banqueting-hall soundtrack of clinking cutlery and glassware, she felt grateful to be experiencing this evening with her friend.

When Emily's name was announced as the winner, it brought sheer joy to us both. The official photographer took a picture that captured the moment, a split-second later, when we threw our arms around each other in celebration.

Then, to our delighted surprise, just days later a publisher made an offer to bring out Emma's book. The upturn in fortune this time gave Emily an opportunity to toast her friend's success.

And before Emma's novel was even launched, we shared in a truly joint achievement when we sold the rights to this book. Our early fears that the success of one before the other might threaten our bond between equals had ultimately proved unfounded.

But though collaborating on *A Secret Sisterhood* brought us much happiness, it also created new stresses and strains. Leisurely conversations over coffee or glasses of wine were replaced by rushed updates snatched in library corners; we sacrificed nights out together for evenings writing at home, working into the early hours. Ultimately, though, our shared research and the experience of writing as a pair drew us closer still.

Of all the examples of literary sisterhood we discovered, the most unexpected came toward the end of writing this book. Knowing that Emma would be attending one of Margaret Atwood's public lectures, Emily persuaded her to slip the great author a handwritten note about our work. We could hardly believe it when Margaret replied, asking to read some sample chapters, and later letting us know that she'd be willing to write a foreword for this book.

Someone whose work needs no introduction, Margaret is known for her encouragement of younger writers as well as those closer to her in age. Her bond with her fellow Canadian literary star Alice Munro began in 1969 — near the beginning of their careers. Margaret recalls sleeping on Alice's floor on a visit to Victoria during that time. Looking back, the pair formulated a theory to explain why their home country had produced such a successful generation of female writers. According to them, literary endeavor was permissible for women, whereas men had to conform to rigid ideals of masculinity. Writing fiction was deemed a harmless feminine pursuit, and since most men were hardly likely to read books by women, authors such as Alice and Margaret were free to pursue their craft without interference.

When Alice won a Nobel Prize for her short stories in 2013, Margaret joined her, once again in Victoria, this time in the grander surroundings of the Empress Hotel. A heartwarming photograph, which Alice would later display on her bookcase, offers a glimpse of the pair's private celebration, their arms around each other, glasses of champagne close by.

Margaret has been prominent in voicing tributes to her longstanding friend. Female writers of the past, however, had fewer chances to publicly praise the women who helped, cajoled, and influenced them. Opportunities to converse were largely restricted to the parlor rather than amplified on the national stage. But there are other, more significant reasons why these relationships have failed to find their place in literary lore.

Again and again, such creative collaborations have been neglected, with attention being trained instead on the influence of men. Closeness with other family members has been celebrated too, while friendships women sought outside the home were regarded as a threat to the conventional roles of devoted daughter, mother and wife. Creative alliances between women, therefore, have come to be seen as subversive or a source of shame.

And so, misleading myths of isolation have long attached themselves to women who write: a cottage-dwelling spinster; an impassioned roamer of the moors; a fallen woman, shunned; a melancholic genius. Over the years, a conspiracy of silence has obscured the friendships of female authors, past and present. But now it is time to break the silence and celebrate this literary sisterhood—a glimmering web of interwoven threads that still has the power to unsettle, to challenge, to inspire.

Acknowledgments

In keeping with the theme of this book, during our years of research and writing, a great many individuals and organizations have extended the hand of friendship to us.

Margaret Atwood, so long an inspiration, took us entirely by surprise when she agreed to write the foreword for *A Secret Sisterhood*. This, at a time when we were still editing the manuscript, did so much to encourage us.

The authors and experts Lindsey Ashford, Diana Athill, Jennifer Cognard-Black, Joan D. Hedrick, Nancy Henry, Deirdre Le Faye, Rebecca Lilley, Kathleen McCormack, Laurel Ann Nattress, and Jude Piesse all gave generously of their time and vast knowledge of several of the writers in this book.

Our research was also greatly aided by the help of the following people: Morex Arai at the Huntington Library (San Marino, California); Keith Arscott and Gillian Dow at Chawton House Library; Lyndsi Barnes, Isaac Gewirtz, and Joshua McKeon at the New York Public Library's Henry W. and Albert A. Berg Collection; Sarah Baxter at the Society of Authors; Beth Burgess and staff at the Harriet Beecher Stowe Center;

John Burton of the George Eliot Fellowship; Chris Coleby and staff at Hollybank School; Rhian Dolby and Sarah Lewkin at the Hampshire Record Office; Mary Guyatt at the Jane Austen House Museum; Becky Harvey at the Nuneaton Museum & Art Gallery; Maria Isabel Molestina-Kurlat at the Morgan Library & Museum; Sarah Laycock and staff at the Brontë Parsonage Museum; Helen MacEwan and Jones Hayden of the Brussels Brontë Group; staff at the Nuneaton Heritage Centre; staff of the former Red House Museum (Gomersal); Moira Rudolf of Regency Walking Tours; Ali Wells at the Herbert Art Gallery & Museum; Stephen R. Young at Yale University Library's Beinecke Rare Book & Manuscript Library; and Helen Wicker at the Kent History and Library Centre.

We are very grateful to Jonathan G. Ouvry for granting us permission to quote from the letters and diaries of George Eliot and George Henry Lewes; to Cambridge University Press for permission to quote from *The Journals of George Eliot* edited by Margaret Harris and Judith Johnston; to Hampshire Record Office (on behalf of the depositor) for allowing us to quote from some of the Austen-Leigh Papers; to the Harriet Beecher Stowe Center for permission to quote from an unpublished letter from Calvin Ellis Stowe to Harriet Beecher Stowe; to Manchester University Press for allowing us to quote from *The Letters of Mrs Gaskell* edited by J. A. V. Chapple and Arthur Pollard; to the New York Public Library for permission to quote from the originals of letters and diaries by Katherine Mansfield, Harriet Beecher Stowe, Mary Taylor, and Virginia Woolf held in their collections; to Oxford University Press for permission to quote from *Jane Austen's Letters* (fourth edition) collected and edited by Deirdre Le Faye, *The Letters of Charlotte Brontë* (volumes I–III) edited by Margaret Smith, and *The Collected Letters of Katherine Mansfield* (volumes I–IV) edited by

Vincent O'Sullivan and Margaret Scott; and to the Society of Authors as the Literary Representative of the Estates of Katherine Mansfield, John Middleton Murry, and Virginia Woolf for permission to quote from letters and diaries.

We also owe debts of gratitude to Keely Charlick, Catherine Cho, Leslie Frankel, Tony Gilbertson, Penny Gore, Patricia McVeigh, and Sarah Moore, all of whom helped us in important practical ways.

We were both very fortunate that Arts Council England awarded us Grants for the Arts, using public funding.

And though most of the words within these covers were written sitting at our own writing desks, between us we benefited from periods of intense creative focus at the following retreats: the Bread Matters Residency near Lisbon (thank you to Will and Inês Amado), Circle of Missé in the Loire (thank you to Aaron Tighe and Wayne Milstead), and Mill House Retreat in Devon (thank you to all the staff).

Just as Charlotte Brontë benefited from the sometimes stern, sometimes nurturing wisdom of her schoolteacher Margaret Wooler, and Fanny Austen would retain fond memories of her inspiring governess Anne Sharp, we are grateful to the many writing tutors and mentors who have guided us, in particular Jane A. Adams, Linda Anderson, Pat Borthwick, Andrew Cowan, Jill Dawson, Louise Doughty, Karen Maitland, Derek Neale, Gill Nuttall, and Michèle Roberts. We've also learned so much from our colleagues and students at City, University of London, and New York University London, as well as those we have worked with elsewhere over the years.

We couldn't ask for better literary agents than Veronique Baxter at David Higham Associates and Ariella Feiner at United Agents in the UK, and Michelle Tessler at the Tessler

Agency in the U.S.A. Your tireless work on our behalves has changed our lives in so many ways. We would also like to thank Max Edwards, Nikoline Eriksen, Sophie Scard, and Laura West.

A Secret Sisterhood has benefited enormously from the insightful editing of Nicole Angeloro at Houghton Mifflin Harcourt and Jennifer Barr at Aurum Press, who believed from the start that there was a story here worth telling.

Many thanks also to Susanna Brougham and Alison Moss for their careful copyediting. Also to Jessica Axe, Ann Barrett, Caroline Curtis, Richard Green, Liz Somers, Jessie Sullivan, and all at Aurum. And to Liz Anderson, Liz Deadrick, Sherri Dietrich, Dalia Geffen, Lisa Glover, Jackie Shepherd, and all at Houghton Mifflin Harcourt.

Thank you to all the guest bloggers and interviewees whose work has enriched our website SomethingRhymed .com, where we first began to write regularly about female literary friendship. Early on, we were also encouraged by the confidence of the readers of SomethingRhymed.com that this subject deserved to be explored in a full-length book. Particular mentions must go to Sarah Emsley, Naomi Frisby, Rohan Maitzen, and Andrea Stephenson.

Our writer and academic friends kept us going too, especially Susan Barker, Sarah Butler, Michael Caines, Michelle Carriger, Samantha Ellis, Miranda El-Rayess, Lauren Frankel, Edward Hogan, Antonia Honeywell, Ann Morgan, Irenosen Okojie, Julia Pascal, Emily Pedder, Elizabeth L. Silver, J. C. Sutcliffe, and Wendy Vaizey—some of whom commented on early drafts, and all of whom believed in us long before our words made it into print.

To our extended families, the Blanchards, the Prouts, and the Ruppins: we thank you for your good humor and unwavering support. To our first friends, our sisters, Erica, Louise, and Sarah, and to our parents, Elaine and Phil Sweeney and to both the late John Crump and Taeko Midorikawa Crump: we thank you for teaching us the enduring value of friendship and sisterhood.

Finally, to Jack Blanchard and Jonathan Ruppin—partners, allies, and friends—we thank you for always lending a sympathetic ear; for reading and rereading our multiple drafts; for keeping us well fed during long stints in our studies, and, most of all, never failing to be there when we emerged.

Notes

Authors' original spelling and punctuation have been retained in quotations, even when they have made errors.

We have usually referred to the book's central biographical subjects by first name. In the case of individuals not personally known to these central characters, we have most often referred to them by surname. Exceptions to these rules include teachers and doctors, referred to by their honorifics; George Henry Lewes, referred to as Lewes to avoid confusion with George Eliot; and John Middleton Murry, referred to as Murry, the name by which he was commonly known.

When we quote from an original manuscript, we include in the notes the institution where it is held. For ease of reference for future researchers, where possible we have also included publication details.

INTRODUCTION: IN SEARCH OF A SECRET SISTERHOOD

page

xviii *"in a fit of caution"*: Mary Taylor to Charlotte Brontë, June to 24 July 1848, The Morgan Library & Museum, Joan Stevens (ed.), *Mary Taylor, Friend of Charlotte Brontë: Letters from New Zealand and Elsewhere,* Auckland University Press, 1972, 75.

JANE AUSTEN & ANNE SHARP

The details included in this section are most often drawn from the letters and diaries of Fanny Knight, the letters of Jane Austen, and *A Memoir of Jane Austen* (1871) by James Edward Austen-Leigh. We consulted extant letters and other documents by Jane and Cassandra Austen at the Morgan Library and Museum. Manuscript sources were also consulted at Kent History and Library Centre, Hampshire Record Office, and the British Library. We also made substantial use of *The Jane Austen Files: A Complete Anthology of Letters and Family Recollections* (edited by Helen Amy) and *Jane Austen's Letters* (collected and edited by Deirdre Le Faye). We are indebted to Deirdre Le Faye for the painstaking work she undertook on the exhaustive *Chronology of Jane Austen and Her Family*. The biographies of Paula Byrne and Claire Tomalin were of regular assistance too.

Abbreviations

AS	Anne Sharp
BL	British Library
Byrne	Paula Byrne, *The Real Jane Austen,* HarperPress, 2013
CEA	Cassandra Elizabeth Austen
Chronology	Deirdre Le Faye, *A Chronology of Jane Austen and Her Family,* Cambridge University Press (second edition), 2013
DC	Dorothy Chapman
DLF	Deirdre Le Faye
FCK	Fanny Catherine Knight (née Austen)
Files	Helen Amy (ed.), *The Jane Austen Files: A Complete Anthology of Letters and Family Recollections,* Amberley, 2015
Household	Peggy Hickman, *A Jane Austen Household Book with Martha Lloyd's Recipes,* Readers Union, 1978
HRO	Hampshire Record Office
JA	Jane Austen
JEAL	James Edward Austen-Leigh
KHLC	Kent History and Library Centre
Letters	Deirdre Le Faye (ed.), *Jane Austen's Letters,* Oxford University Press (fourth edition), (© Deirdre Le Faye, 2011)
LMA	London Metropolitan Archives
Memoir	James Edward Austen-Leigh, *A Memoir of Jane Austen,* Richard Bentley and Son, 1871
ML	Martha Lloyd
Morgan	Department of Literary and Historical Manuscripts, The Morgan Library and Museum

pb   Fanny Catherine Knight (née Austen), Pocketbook, Kent History and
              Library Centre

Tomalin   Claire Tomalin, *Jane Austen: A Life,* Penguin, 2012

Uglow   Jenny Uglow, *In These Times: Living in Britain Through Napoleon's Wars,*
              1793–1815, Faber & Faber, 2014

1. A CIRCLE OF SINGLE WOMEN

page

3   *scoured Jane's personality:* JEAL, Memoir, 55.

4   *In the 1840s:* Caroline Austen, "My Aunt Jane Austen: A Memoir," 1867, *Files,*
    Helen Amy (ed.), 39.

    She refused to collaborate: Helen Amy (ed.), *Files,* 558; Lord Brabourne, "Letters
    of Jane Austen Edited with an Introduction and Critical Remarks," 1884, *Files,*
    Helen Amy (ed.), 426.

    Subtitled "Devoted Friends": "Jane Austen's Last Days: An Unpublished Letter,"
    The Times, 1 February 1926, 13–14.

    "my dearest Anne": JA to AS, 22 May 1817, Morgan, *Letters,* 355.

5   *"constituted the very class":* JEAL, *Memoir,* 9.

    The uptight tone: CEA to AS, 28 July 1817, Morgan, *Letters,* 362.

    But unpublished papers: FCK pb and letters to DC are all held at KHLC and have
    never been published in full.

    Anne was a writer: FCK to DC, 12 January 1806, KHLC.

    The child's entry: FCK, 21 January 1806, pb, KHLC.

6   *thirty-one years earlier:* Her age has been calculated according to her death cer-
    tificate, rather than the less reliable census returns. AS's birthday is recorded in
    FCK pb as 15 January. This is further supported by a baptismal certificate for
    Ann Sharp, daughter of Elizabeth and John in the St. Paul, Deptford, Composite
    register, LMA, dated February 1773.

    kindly condescension: Evident in the tone of FCK's letters to former governess
    DC.

    reached Godmersham Park: Details of Godmersham Park are drawn from FCK pb
    and letters; Historic England, Godmersham Park, List Entry number: 1000290;
    tour of Godmersham Park and materials supplied by Godmersham Park Heri-
    tage Centre; DLF, *A Chronology of Jane Austen and Her Family,* Cambridge Uni-
    versity Press (second edition), 2013; Nigel Nicolson, *Godmersham Park: Before,*
    During, and After Jane Austen's Time, Jane Austen Society, 1996.

    a woman who penned theatricals: FCK to DC, 12 January 1806, KHLC.

7 *were often paid little more:* Alice Renton, *Tyrant or Victim: A History of the British Governess,* Weidenfeld & Nicolson, 1991, 38.

"a kind of shuttlecock": "Jane Austen's Last Days: An Unpublished Letter," *The Times,* 1 February 1926, 13.

Jane's unfashionable attire: FCK to Marianne Austen, 23 August 1869, quoted in DLF, *Fanny Knight's Diaries: Jane Austen Through Her Niece's Eyes,* The Jane Austen Society, 2000, 38–39.

Fanny recorded: Details of AS's arrival and first days at Godmersham Park, including quotations, are drawn from FCK to DC, 25 January 1804, KHLC.

8 *disregard for consistent spelling:* JA's royalty check of 1816, for example, was made out to "Miss Jane Austin."

Elizabeth Sharpe: Elizabeth Sharpe, 20 April 1803, burial record, St. James Piccadilly, LMA.

dangerous bout of ill health: FCK to DC, 8 January 1804, KHLC.

delayed her arrival: FCK to DC, 27 November 1803, KHLC; FCK to DC, 8 January 1804, KHLC.

noisy newborn: FCK to DC, 13 December 1804, KHLC.

entrance hall forever rang: JA to Francis Austen, 25 September 1813, 240.

9 *Edward enjoyed his fortune:* JA to CEA, 2 June 1799, *Letters,* 44–45; JA to CEA, 30 June–1 July 1808, *Letters,* 144; JA to CEA, *Letters,* 17 May 1799, 41; FCK to Francis Austen, 25 September 1813, *Letters,* 240; FCK, 10 October 1805, pb, KHLC.

lady of the house invited: Details about Fanny's birthday are drawn from JA to DC, 25 January 1804, KHLC.

at ten o'clock: JA to CEA, 15–17 June 1808, *Letters,* 131.

fine china: JA to CEA, 16 September 1813, *Letters,* 233.

"a la Godmersham": JA to CEA, 15–17 June 1808, *Letters,* 132.

10 *"happy Indifference":* JA to Francis Austen, 25 September 1813, *Letters,* 239.

just such a decorative object: In vol. II, chapter XI, of *Sense and Sensibility,* the Dashwood sisters are snubbed by a snobbish man examining decorative toothpick cases. He turns out to be the brother of their sister-in-law — a woman who has convinced their own brother to neglect the sisters. JA, *Sense and Sensibility,* Penguin Classics, 1995, 186–87.

Her sister-in-law did not take kindly: Details of Elizabeth Austen's interests are drawn from FCK to DC, 27 November 1804, KHLC; FCK, 11 December 1805, pb, KHLC. Elizabeth Austen's attitude to intellectual conversation, including the quotation, is drawn from Anna Lefroy, "Recollections of Aunt Jane," 1864, *Files,* Helen Amy (ed.), 28.

11 *volunteer soldiers:* FCK, 17 September 1804, pb, KHLC; Claire Tomalin, *Tomalin,* 131–35.

the younger children: Most descriptions of the children are drawn from FCK to DC, 28 July 1805, KHLC.

breakfasting à deux: FCK, 1 December 1805, pb, KHLC.

The governess then heard: FCK to DC, 15 April 1806, KHLC; FCK, 5 July 1805, pb, KHLC.

12 *the child's great-aunt:* References to taking tea in Eggarton with AS appear throughout FCK's pb. For more information on "Mrs." Elizabeth Knight of Eggarton, see DLF, *Letters,* 599.

lured from their studies: FCK, 28 June 1804, pb, KHLC.

sharing her bed: FCK, 29 September 1805, pb, KHLC.

vast, empty room: JA to CEA, 3 November 1813, Morgan, *Letters,* 260.

13 *the British status quo:* In 1793 Wordsworth's brother urged him to "be cautious in writing or expressing your political Opinions," reminding him that by "the suspension of the Habeas Corpus Acts, the Ministers have great powers." Quoted in John Bugg, *Five Long Winters: The Trials of British Romanticism,* Stanford University Press, 2013, 145.

14 *a sum with which:* According to the historical UK inflation rates calculator, £10 in 1803 equals approximately £893 in 2017. JA wrote of using £10 for winter clothing in JA to CEA, 18–19 December 1798, *Letters,* 26: "I shall keep *my* ten pounds too to wrap myself up in next winter."

"putrid fevers": JA to CEA, 21–22 May 1801, Morgan, *Letters,* 90.

On June 19, the children: Anne's collapse, the lead-up, and its aftermath, including quotations, are drawn from FCK, 19–24 June 1804, pb, KHLC.

15 *high turnover of household staff:* FCK, Memorandums at the Beginning of the Year 1805, pb, KHLC.

16 *financial trouble:* Thomas Keymer, "*Northanger Abbey* and *Sense and Sensibility,*" Edward Copeland and Juliet McMaster (eds.), *The Cambridge Companion to Jane Austen,* Cambridge University Press, 2011, 21–38.

17 *Sense and Sensibility would later:* The Dashwood women in *Sense and Sensibility* were left to cope on £500 per year—more than the £460 household income that the Austen brothers considered sufficient for their mother and sisters.

25 Gay Street: DLF, 25 March 1805, *Chronology,* 308.

first crops up: JA to CEA, 21–23 April 1805, *Letters,* 109.

18 *an annotation tucked away:* In JA, *Letters,* 571, DLF claims: "The Miss Sharp whom

JA mentions as being in Bath in 1805 is clearly not the same as this Miss Anne Sharp."

away from home: "Papa, Anny and Henry set off at 8 in the morning for Town," FCK, 18 March 1805, pb, KHLC; "Papa, Edwd, George & Henry came home," FCK, 6 April 1805, pb, KHLC; "Miss Sharpe came home," FCK, 13 April 1805, pb, KHLC.

outside the schoolroom: FCK, 13 August 1804, pb, KHLC; FCK, 4 September 1804, pb, KHLC.

19   *about her eyes:* FCK to DC, 9 April 1805, KHLC.

outwardly reserved: Both Anna Lefroy and Caroline Austen remember JA as the more fun loving of the sisters. Anna Lefroy, "Recollections of Aunt Jane," 1864, Helen Amy (ed.), *Files,* 27; Caroline Austen, "My Aunt Jane Austen: A Memoir," Helen Amy (ed.), *Files,* 35.

Maria Edgeworth and Frances Burney: In vol. I, chapter V, of *Northanger Abbey,* novels by Frances Burney and Maria Edgeworth are singled out for praise. JA, *Northanger Abbey,* Penguin Classics, 1995, 34.

her new novel: JA's unfinished manuscript of *The Watsons* is written on paper watermarked 1803, and appears to have been started and abandoned in 1804–5. Like *Sense and Sensibility,* the novel is about a young woman left woefully unprovided for after the death of a family patriarch.

on April 9, 1805, Jane: Details of JA's return to Gay Street and Miss Colbourne's visit are drawn from JA to CEA, 8–11 April 1805, *Letters,* 103–7.

21   *"reduce her establishment":* Henry Thomas Austen to Frank Austen, 28 January 1805, HRO.

Martha to join their new household: JA to CEA: "I am quite of your opinion as to the folly of concealing any longer our intended partnership with Martha ... ," 21–23 April 1805, *Letters,* 109.

amateur cook and apothecary: Peggy Hickman, *Household,* passim.

"to take lessons of": JA to CEA, 21–23 April 1805, 109. AS had returned to Godmersham Park by this stage, but "to take" suggests that this is a plan for a future date.

2. REBELLION BEHIND CLOSED DOORS

23   *six o'clock in the evening:* Details of the Austen women's 1805 stay at Godmersham Park, including quotations, are drawn from FCK, 18 June to 15 September 1805, pb, KHLC; FCK to DC, 28 July 1805, KHLC.

24   *keep quiet about her past:* In response to *The Times's* 1 February publication of JA

and CEA letters to AS, Mrs. Creaghe-Haward wrote: "My aunt Miss Middleton (1817–94) knew her well and often spoke of her . . . From what she said I gather that Miss Sharp was a clever, rather dominant woman, much thought of in Everton society of her day. She was very reticent about her early life before coming to Liverpool, and also made a mystery of her age": Mrs. Creaghe-Howard, "Points from Letters, *The Times*, 12 February 1926, 8. In her will, Anne Sharp left "To Miss Mary Middleton ten pounds and Scotts bible. To Robina Middleton ten pounds and Milner's Church History. To Caroline Middleton ten pounds and four volumes of D'Aubigné on the Reformation." The Last Will and Testament of Anne Sharp, 11 January 1851.

baptismal ledger: St. Paul, Deptford, Baptismal Record, February 1773, LMA.

25 *As a writer herself:* FCK to DC, 12 January 1806, KHLC.

26 *Scotch reels:* JA's love of dancing is evidenced in JA to FCK, 20–21 February 1817, 345; Henry Austen, "Biographical Notice of the Author," 1818, Helen Amy (ed.), *Files*, 16.

satirical bent: For an example of Mrs. Austen's playful streak, see the letter and poem she wrote to a pupil, encouraging him to return to "the Mansion of Learning" where "we study all day, Except when we play," quoted in Claire Tomalin, Tomalin, 26. For more on Mrs. Austen, see Tomalin, 143–55.

secretly penned: The play described in FCK, 26 June 1805, pb, KHLC, is not attributed to AS. However, it includes several of the same characters as those in AS's play described in FCK to DC, 12 January 1806, KHLC. This suggests that AS did not own up to being its creator when it was first put on, redrafted the play during the intervening period, and then told the Godmersham Austens about her authorship when they staged the play "with a few more additions," as FCK put it, on 4 January 1806.

28 *great animation:* JA to CEA, 15–17 June 1808, *Letters*, 132.

ailing relatives: JA to CEA, 24 August 1805, *Letters*, 112.

29 *"pretty but not strikingly so":* FCK, 25 January 1804, pb, KHLC.

"Pray say everything kind": JA to CEA, 30 August 1805, *Letters*, 117.

A plan was already afoot: JA to CEA, 30 August 1805, *Letters*, 117.

for weeks on end: Details of the Worthing trip are drawn from FCK to DC, 15 September 1805, KHLC; FCK, 17–22 September 1805, pb, KHLC.

30 *"horridly affected . . . rather amusing":* JEAL to Anna Lefroy, September 1820, HRO.

a cheery woman: Peggy Hickman, *Household*, 34.

conversing late into the night: JA to CEA, 8 January 1799, *Letters*, 35.

31 *an all-time high:* William Playfair, "Price of Wheat: 1565–1821," 1821.

as many four-pound loaves: Earl of Suffolk, 25 April 1805, House of Lords debate, Hansard, vol. 4, cc374–75.

32 *for a while:* Details of DC's return to Godmersham Park are drawn from FCK to DC, 15 September 1805, KHLC; FCK, 25 September to 10 October 1805, pb, KHLC.

33 *upon her return:* Details of AS's return to Godmersham Park, including quotations, are drawn from FCK, 1 November 1805, pb, KHLC, and FCK to DC, 2 November 1805, KHLC.

attack by France: FCK, 30 September 1805, pb, KHLC; FCK, 11 December 1805, pb, KHLC.

a Gallic invasion: Jenny Uglow, Uglow, Loc 7407.

34 *rose before the rest of her household:* JEAL, *Memoir,* 50; Caroline Austen, "My Aunt Jane Austen: A Memoir," Helen Amy (ed.), *Files,* 36.

"paintress": Details of the portraiture, including quotations, are drawn from FCK, 5 November 1805, pb, KHLC; FCK, 14 December 1805, pb, KHLC; FCK to DC, 22 February 1806, KHLC.

35 *One of Anne's headaches:* Details of AS's operation and its aftermath, including quotations, are drawn from FCK, 15 November to 13 December 1805, pb, KHLC; FCK to DC, 22 November 1805, KHLC. The scene was also informed by William Lewis and John Aikin, *An Experimental History of the Materia Medica: Or of the Natural and Artificial Substances Made Use of in Medicine,* Johnson, 1784, 188–89; Coriann Convertito, *The Health of British Seamen in the West Indies, 1770–1806,* University of Exeter PhD, 2011, 44.

Trim Street in Bath: In 1801, JA wrote to CEA that Mrs. Austen "will do everything in her power to avoid Trim St." *The New Bath Directory* of 1805 shows that Trim Street was a commercial street.

36 *snow and melt:* Details of the festive games and theatricals, including quotations, are drawn from FCK, 18 December 1805 to 2 January 1806, pb, KHLC; FCK, 20 December 1805, pb appendix, KHLC; FCK, 4 January 1806, pb appendix, KHLC; FCK to DC, 12 January 1806, KHLC.

37 Evenings at Home: John Aikin and Anna Letitia Barbauld, *Evenings at home; or, the juvenile budget opened: Consisting of a variety of miscellaneous pieces,* vol. I, J. Johnson, 1792–96.

Mansfield Park: JA, *Mansfield Park,* Penguin Classics, 1996, vol. I, chapter XIV, 110.

poetry annuals: The Poetical Register and Repository of Fugitive Poetry for 1803, Rivington, 1805.

38 *"Anny":* It is clear that "Anny" refers to AS because in FCK's pocketbook she mentions "Anny's birthday" on 15 January 1806, which accords with her 15 January 1805 entry: "Miss Sharpe's birthday."

Pride and Prejudice: *Cecilia* by Frances Burney, 1782, ends with a paragraph in which the capitalized phrase "PRIDE and PREJUDICE" recurs three times. It is likely that this also informed JA's renaming of *Pride and Prejudice.*

come to an end: FCK, 18 January 1806, pb, KHLC.

"I assure *you":* FCK, 12 January 1806, pb, KHLC.

39 *family friend Martha:* DLF, *Chronology,* 327.

to offer opinions: Various authors, "Opinions by various people of Jane Austen's work," BL manuscript.

3. CLOSING RANKS

41 *putting pen to paper:* Evidence of lost correspondence between JA and AS appears regularly in JA's letters. For an example during this period, see JA to CEA, 1–2 October 1808, *Letters,* 147.

42 *"Panegyric on the Departed":* DLF, 13 October 1808, *Letters,* 152.

state of the corpse: JA to CEA, 15–16 October 1808, *Letters,* 155.

Mrs. Austen enjoyed: Details of life at Chawton Cottage are drawn from Constance Hill, *Jane Austen: Her Homes & Her Friends,* John Lane, 1902, 169–85.

43 *household chores:* Caroline Austen, "My Aunt Jane Austen: A Memoir," 1867, Helen Amy (ed.), *Files,* 36.

She confided in Jane: JA to CEA, 30 January 1809, *Letters,* 180.

44 *"eyes have been":* FCK to DC, 15 March 1807, KHLC.

"I can no more forget": JA to CEA, 25 April 1811, *Letters,* 190.

"magnificent project": JA to CEA, 31 May 1811, Morgan, *Letters,* 198–200.

45 *"I have given up":* JA to CEA, 6 June 1811, Morgan, *Letters,* 201.

August of 1811: Mary Lloyd Austen, 29 August 1811, pocketbook, HRO.

Collyer's public stagecoach: Caroline Austen, "My Aunt Jane Austen: A Memoir," 1867, Helen Amy (ed.), *Files,* 32.

46 *How glorious:* The description of Chawton Cottage is drawn from Constance Hill, *Jane Austen: Homes and Friends,* John Lane, 1901, 169–85.

47 *"the characters are":* Unsigned review, *Critical Review,* vol. IV, 1 February 1812, 149–57.

trip to London: Details of this trip, including quotations, are drawn from JA to CEA, 20 May 1813, *Letters,* 218–20; JA to CEA, 24 May 1813, Morgan, *Letters,* 220–23.

"as delightful a creature": JA to CEA, 29 January 1813, *Letters,* 210.

48 *"very superior":* Unsigned review, *Critical Review,* March 1813, 318–24.

"one of the cleverest things": Richard Sheridan, quoted in Park Honan, *Jane Austen: Her Life,* Weidenfeld & Nicolson, 1987, 318.

49 *share her children:* JA to CEA, 29 January 1813, *Letters,* 210.

"—Oh! I have": JA to CEA, 3 November 1813, Morgan, *Letters,* 260.

"Oh! Sir Wm": JA to CEA, 23 June 1814, *Letters,* 277. The full quotation raises questions about AS's relations with men: "She writes highly of Sir Wm—I do so want him to marry her!—There is a Dow: Lady P. presiding there, to make it all right.—The *Man* is the same; but she does not mention what he is by Profession or Trade.—She does not think that Lady P. was privy to his scheme on her; but on being in his power, yielded.—Oh! Sir Wm—Sir Wm—how I will love you, if you will love Miss Sharp!"

50 *"I know your starched Notions":* JA to CEA, 4 February 1813, *Letters,* 212.

wife of an Irish judge: JA to CEA, 3 November 1813, Morgan, *Letters,* 260.

"its good sense & moral Tendency": AS, "Opinions by various people of Jane Austen's work," BL manuscript.

51 *"fame nor profit":* Henry Austen, "A Biographical Notice," 1818, Helen Amy (ed.), *Files,* 17.

52 *James Stanier Clarke:* Details about JA's visit to Carlton House and its aftermath, including quotations, are drawn from the following exchange of letters: JA to James Stanier Clarke, 15 November 1815, HRO, *Letters,* 308; James Stanier Clarke to JA, 16 November 1815, Morgan, *Letters,* 309; JA to John Murray, 11 December 1815, *Letters,* 317–18; JA to John Murray, 11 December 1815, *Letters,* 318; JA to James Stanier Clarke, 11 December 1815, *Letters,* 319; James Stanier Clarke to JA, ?21 December 1815, *Letters,* 320.

Friendship Book: There is debate about whether this anonymous portrait is of Jane Austen. The president of the Jane Austen Society of North America makes a case for its authenticity: Joan Kingel Ray & Richard James Wheeler, "James Stanier Clarke's Portrait of Jane Austen," *Persuasions,* vol. XXVII, 2005.

presentation copies of Emma: DLF, *Letters,* 571.

plush Persian carpets: Jane Fawcett, *Historic Floors: Their History and Conservation,* Butterworth-Heinemann, 1998, 160.

crystal chandeliers overhead: W. H. Pyne, *The History of the Royal Residences,* vol. III, A. Dry, 1819.

53 *"because she is a woman":* JA to ML, 16 February 1813, Morgan, *Letters,* 217.

   each of his residences: JEAL, *Memoir,* 66.

   elegant double staircase: John B. Papworth, *Select Views of London; with Historical and Descriptive Sketches of Some of the Most Interesting of Its Public Buildings,* R. Ackermann, 1816.

   direction of the library: Augustus Pugin, plan of Carlton Palace, J. Taylor, 1821.

54 *library at Carlton House:* The presentation copy of *Emma* given by JA to the Prince Regent is now housed in the Royal Collection.

55 *her dozen copies:* DLF, *Chronology,* 525.

   literary acclaim and financial success: JA to FCK, 30 November 1814, *Letters,* 299: "tho' I like praise as well as anybody, I like what Edward calls *Pewter* too."

   "The authoress": Augustus Hare, *Life and Letters of Maria Edgeworth,* Houghton Mifflin and Company, 1895, 249, 260.

   "best-chosen language": JA, *Northanger Abbey,* Penguin Classics, 1995, vol. I, chapter V, 34.

   twelve recipients: John Murray's Archives record that presentation copies were sent to the following recipients: two to Hans Place (presumably for JA and Henry Austen); the Prince Regent's librarian; J. Leigh Perrot (the author's uncle); two for Mrs. Austen; Captain Austen (presumed to be JA's brother Charles); James Austen; H. F. Austen (presumed to be Frank); FCK; AS; Maria Edgeworth. A further two copies were given by the publisher to the Countess of Morley and Augusta Leigh. Augusta Leigh was the half-sister of Lord Byron, who, rumor had it, was having an incestuous affair with him. Augusta brought her copy of *Emma* with her when she went to stay at Byron's house to offer assistance during the confinement of his wife, who had her suspicions about the true nature of the siblings' relationship. But they did have something rather less inflammatory in common too. Lady Byron was also a great admirer of Jane Austen.

56 *for the spines and corners:* AS's presentation copy of *Emma,* 24 June 2008, Bonhams, Lot 107.

   "better than M.P.": AS, *Opinions of Emma,* BL.

   "human intellect": JA, *Emma,* Penguin Classics, 1996, vol. II, chapter 17, 247.

   "quite one of her Letters": JA to CEA, 8–9 September 1816, Morgan, *Letters,* 335.

57 *"nursing myself":* JA to CEA, 8–9 September 1816, Morgan, *Letters,* 335.

   resolved to write a letter: JA to AS, 22 May 1817, Morgan, *Letters,* 355–56.

58 *lock of Jane's hair:* All details about JA and CEA's interactions immediately following JA's death, including quotations, are drawn from CEA to JA, 28 July 1817, Morgan, *Letters,* 362.

59 *"starched Notions":* JA to CEA, 4 February 1813, *Letters,* 212.

 Anne returned to Chawton Cottage: Mary Lloyd Austen, 31 August 1820, pocket book, HRO.

 thirty pounds in her will: CEA to Charles Austen, 9 May 1843, Morgan.

 her own boarding school: DLF, *Letters,* 571; UK Census, Everton, 1841 and 1851.

60 *"She was very reticent":* Mrs. Creaghe-Howard, "Points from Letters," *The Times,* 12 February 1926, 8.

 far greater wealth: This is evidenced by the Last Will and Testament of Anne Sharp, 11 January 1851.

CHARLOTTE BRONTË & MARY TAYLOR

The details included in this section are most often drawn from the letters of Charlotte Brontë and Mary Taylor, and Elizabeth Gaskell's *Life of Charlotte Brontë*—particularly the two letters sent to her by Mary Taylor, sections of which are interspersed within the text of that book. Where possible (despite some of the factual inaccuracies mentioned in our notes), we have been guided by Mary Taylor's belief that the first edition of the *Life* was the truest one and have relied on that version where possible. When we have drawn on new information included in the revised third edition, we have stated this in our notes. The two letters from Mary Taylor to Elizabeth Gaskell no longer exist in their original form. We consulted original letters and other writings by Charlotte Brontë and Mary Taylor in the collections of the Brontë Parsonage Museum, the New York Public Library's Henry W. and Albert A. Berg Collection, and the Morgan Library and Museum. We made substantial use too of the published *Letters of Charlotte Brontë* (edited by Margaret Smith) and *Mary Taylor: Letters from New Zealand and Elsewhere* (edited by Joan Stevens). Juliet Barker's exhaustive biography, *The Brontës,* was also indispensable.

Abbreviations

Alexander	Christine Alexander (ed.), *Tales of Glass Town, Angria, and Gondal: Selected Writings,* Oxford University Press, 2010
Barker	Juliet Barker, *The Brontës,* Abacus, 2010
Bellamy	Joan Bellamy, *"More Precious Than Rubies": Mary Taylor, Friend of Charlotte Brontë, Strong-Minded Woman,* Highgate Publications, 2002
Berg	The Henry W. and Albert A. Berg Collection of English and American Literature, The New York Public Library
BPM	Brontë Parsonage Museum

CB   Charlotte Brontë

EN   Ellen Nussey

EG   Elizabeth Gaskell

LCB   Margaret Smith (ed.), *The Letters of Charlotte Brontë, with a Selection of Letters by Family and Friends,* Clarendon Press, vols. I–III, 1995–2004 (© Margaret Smith 1995, 2000, 2004)

Life (first)   Elizabeth Gaskell, *The Life of Charlotte Brontë,* Penguin, 1997 (based on the text of the first edition)

LMG   J. A. V. Chapple and Arthur Pollard (eds.), *The Letters of Mrs Gaskell,* Manchester University Press, 1966

Morgan   Department of Literary and Historical Manuscripts, The Morgan Library and Museum

MT   Mary Taylor

Reminiscences Ellen Nussey, "Reminiscences of Charlotte Brontë," *Scribners Monthly,* May 1871, II.i

RHJ   Roe Head Journal

SHB LL   T. J. Wise and J. A. Symington, *The Shakespeare Head Brontë, The Brontës: Their Lives, Friendships & Correspondence in Four Volumes,* Shakespeare Head Press, 1932

Shorter   Clement K. Shorter, *Charlotte Brontë and Her Circle,* Dodd, Mead and Company, 1896

Taylor   Joan Stevens (ed.), *Mary Taylor, Friend of Charlotte Brontë: Letters from New Zealand and Elsewhere,* Auckland University Press, 1972

4. THREE'S A CROWD

page

65   *ten or so pupils:* Juliet Barker, Barker, 199.

rosy cheeks: This detail is drawn from CB's description of Rose Yorke, the character based (in personality and appearance) on MT. CB, *Shirley,* Penguin Classics, 2006, chapter IX, 143.

"too pretty to live": From EN's account in Clement K. Shorter, Shorter, 234.

blue cloth coats they wore: All details about the Taylor sisters' clothing in this paragraph were drawn from an account by EN included in Clement K. Shorter, Shorter, 235.

other students assumed: From EN's account in Clement K. Shorter, Shorter, 235.

"a little old woman": EG, *Life* (first), 78.

the airy schoolroom: This schoolroom scene was drawn from a description by MT in a letter to EG, included in EG, *Life* (first), 78.

66 *reminiscent of an abbess:* Juliet Barker, Barker, 199.

67 *"You are very ugly":* This incident is related in one of MT's letters to EG: "I told her she was very ugly." EG, *Life* (first), 79.

untamed frizz of hair: EN, Reminiscences, 19.

68 *gauntness of her frame:* EN, Reminiscences, 19.

"a great deal of good": EG is quoting directly from one of MT's letters in EG, *Life* (first), 80.

"yield pleasure to Mary Taylor": CB to Mary Dixon, early 1843, *LCB* I, 313.

Ellen Nussey arrived: The following first encounter, including the quotation, is drawn from an account in EN, *Reminiscences,* 18–19.

69 *she would deride:* In this letter to her publisher, CB outlines what she believes are EN's strengths and weaknesses. CB to W. S. Williams, 3 January 1850, *LCB* II, 323.

Epistolary evidence suggests: In a letter from Martha Taylor to EN, after MT and CB had left the school, she asks if she may now sleep with EN—suggesting they are both without sleeping partners after their sister and friend have finished their schooling. Martha Taylor to EN, 17 May 1832, *SHB* I, 102.

70 *vied for first place:* From EN's account in Clement K. Shorter, Shorter, 234.

most coveted prizes: Martha Taylor to EN, 17 May 1832, *SHB* I, 102. This letter strongly suggests that EN won the prize.

71 *savagely split apart:* EN, Reminiscences, 24. Chapter 23 of *Jane Eyre* ends with the chestnut tree in the grounds of Thornfield being struck by lightning and split. CB, *Jane Eyre,* Penguin Classics, 2006, chapter 23, 296.

72 *none the wiser:* Clement K. Shorter, Shorter, 234.

73 *"bed-fellow . . . calm sleep":* CB to EN, ?26 October 1852, *LCB* III, 73. When EN transcribed this letter for publication, she replaced "bed-fellow" with "companion." *LCB* III, 74 (n5).

romantic friendships: Marilyn Yalom with Theresa Donovan Brown, *The Social Sex: A History of Female Friendship,* Harper Perennial, 2015, 143–44.

"My darling": CB to EN, ?October/November 1836, *LCB* I, 154–55.

74 *"I wish I could live with you always":* CB to EN, 26 September 1836, *LCB* I, 152.

75 *"Am I to spend":* CB, RHJ III, 11 August 1836, Bonnell Collection, BPM, Alexander, 162. Six individual pieces written by CB during her time as a teacher at Roe Head are known collectively as the Roe Head Journal.

76 *At one such private hour:* This scene, including quotations, is drawn from the first

of the pieces that make up the RHJ. CB, 4 February 1836, RHJ I, Morgan, Alexander, 158–60.

77 *Mary had been known to arrange:* Joan Bellamy, Bellamy, 10.

"How can you give so much": The dialogue within this scene is reconstructed from an extract from one of MT's letters to EG, included in the *Life*. MT wrote: "I went to see her, and asked how she could give so much for so little money . . . She confessed it was not brilliant, but what could she do?." EG, *Life* (first), 106.

79 *She broke the red sealing wax:* This scene, including quotations, is drawn from Robert Southey to CB, 12 March 1837, BPM, *LCB* I, 165–67.

"I must thank you": CB to Robert Southey, 16 March 1837, *LCB* I, 168–69.

heartily approve of: In reply to CB, Southey would write that "you have received admonition as considerately & kindly as it was given." Robert Southey to CB, 22 March 1837, *LCB* I, 170.

5. TWO ADVENTUROUS SPIRITS

81 *who had become reliant:* Barbara Whitehead, *Charlotte Brontë and Her "Dearest Nell": The Story of a Friendship,* Smith Settle, 1993, 85.

exacerbating existing tensions: Joan Bellamy, Bellamy, 25.

82 *a package received:* MT's letter to CB has not survived, but CB recounted its contents in EN, 7 August 1841, *LCB* I, 266. Most of the details in the following scene, including quotations, are drawn from this letter, written while CB was working for the White family at Upperwood House in Rawdon.

83 *"cast oil on the flames":* CB to EN, 2 November 1841, *LCB* I, 272.

jokingly offering: EN, Reminiscences, 26.

insisted on paying him: Rebecca Fraser, *Charlotte Brontë,* Methuen, 1988, 180.

an astute investment: Claire Harman, *Charlotte Brontë: A Life,* Viking, 2015, 156.

Charlotte told her aunt: All the following details and quotations are drawn from CB to Elizabeth Branwell, 29 September 1841, *LCB* I, 268–69.

84 *150 pounds of her savings:* Claire Harman, *Charlotte Brontë: A Life,* Viking, 2015, 135.

85 *The pair had quarreled:* CB to EN, 2 November 1841, *LCB* I, 271.

"quite enter": CB to EN, 20 January 1842, *LCB* I, 278.

86 *willowy Emily:* All these details about Emily Brontë's appearance are drawn from EN, Reminiscences, 26–27.

her clever older brother Joe: Joan Bellamy, Bellamy, 23, 28.

eleven-hour journey: Juliet Barker, Barker, 442.

Like Lucy Snowe: CB, *Villette,* Penguin Classics, 1985, chapter VI, 108.

St. Paul's was the one landmark: EG, *The Life of Charlotte Brontë* (third edition), Oxford University Press, 2009, 172. MT's account of the group's stay in London and arrival in Brussels, given in one of her letters to EG, does not appear in the original version of the *Life.*

gamely volunteered himself: Joan Bellamy, Bellamy, 29.

87 *arduous journey by stagecoach:* Juliet Barker, Barker, 444.

the British chaplain of Brussels: Helen MacEwan, *The Brontës in Brussels,* Peter Owen, 2014, 21.

female porter: Helen MacEwan, *The Brontës in Brussels,* Peter Owen, 2014, 35.

88 *dark, brooding mass of foliage:* Juliet Barker, Barker, 446.

A decade later: CB, *Villette,* Penguin Classics, 1985, chapter XII, 174.

Claire Zoë Heger: Helen MacEwan, *The Brontës in Brussels,* Peter Owen, 2014, 45.

stronger impression on Charlotte: CB to EN, May 1842, *LCB* I, 284.

permission of Madame and Monsieur Heger: Juliet Barker, Barker, 447.

a newsy letter to Ellen: The following scene, including quotations, is drawn from CB, MT, and Martha Taylor to EN, March–April 1842, Morgan, *Taylor,* 28–30.

90 *When Martha returned home:* Joan Bellamy, Bellamy, 30–31.

91 *allowing the director:* Claire Harman, *Charlotte Brontë: A Life,* Viking, 2015, 150.

93 *a strong constitution:* Juliet Barker, Barker, 474.

like Elizabeth Gaskell: EG, *Life* (first), 182–83.

given them a letter: Constantin Heger to CB (Margaret Smith's translation), 5 November 1842, *LCB* I, 299–300.

94 *the security of traveling:* This account, including quoted dialogue, covering CB's departure from Haworth and arrival in London, is drawn from what CB related to EG during the period of their friendship—EG later including the story in EG, *Life* (first), 184.

95 *In a letter to Ellen:* CB to EN, ?late June 1843, *LCB* I, 325.

96 *later destroy almost all:* MT to CB, June to 24 July 1848, Morgan, *Taylor,* 75. Just one of CB's letters to MT (4 September 1848, *LCB* II, 111–15) survives.

97 *an extant letter:* MT to EN, 16 February 1843, *Taylor,* 42–44.

Charlotte begged Ellen: CB to EN, 6 August 1843, *LCB* I, 327.

Another missive: This account of CB's walk and visit to the cathedral, including quotations, is drawn from CB to Emily Brontë, 2 September 1843, *LCB* I, 329–

30. The dialogue is adapted from this passage: "The priest asked if I was a Protestant then. I somehow could not tell a lie and said 'yes.'"

99 *had been discontinued:* The stopping of lessons, and limiting of contact between CB and Monsieur Heger, is suggested both by CB's letters of the time and the account of a former pupil at the pensionnat in Frederika Macdonald, *The Secret of Charlotte Brontë: Followed by Some Reminiscences of the Real Monsieur and Madame Heger,* T. C. and E. C. Jack, 1914, 61.

Mary . . . sent a letter: This letter from MT has not survived, but CB describes its contents in CB to Mary Dixon, 16 October 1843, *LCB* I, 336.

100 *"it is odd in a woman":* MT to EN, winter 1843, *Taylor,* 50.

a mournful letter to Ellen: CB to EN, 23 January 1844, *LCB* I, 340–41.

101 *Ellen would recall her feelings:* This scene, including the quotation, is drawn from EN to Mary Gorham, 21 May 1844, *LCB* I, 347–48.

102 *"a great planet":* CB to EN, c. 26 October 1844, *LCB* I, 372.

6. ONE GREAT MYTH

103 *On a mild winter's day:* Details about the likely date of Mary's climb, the local geography, and arrival in Wellington are drawn from Joan Stevens, *Taylor,* 57, 66–67, 73 (n2).

104 *The last time they'd met:* EG, *Life* (first), 206. EG gives the date of this meeting as January 1845, but it was in fact February. MT set sail on 18 March and arrived in Wellington on 24 July 1845.

105 *been afflicted by:* CB to Constantin Heger, 18 November 1845, *LCB* I, 437.

106 *this distant outpost:* MT to CB, June to 24 July 1848, Morgan, *Taylor,* 73–77. The letter was finished on 24 July 1848, but written over a period of several weeks, most likely beginning in June (second part of letter held at Berg).

an eighteen-gun sloop: Joan Stevens, *Taylor,* 73 (n2).

Charlotte read the letter: CB to EN, 10 December 1848, *LCB* II, 153 and 153 (n6); CB to EN, ?22 January 1849, *LCB* I, 172. In mid-December, a few days after the first of these two letters, Charlotte heard from Mary.

"much shattered": CB to EN, 28 July 1848, *LCB* II, 93.

107 *"we could not tell him of our efforts":* CB to W. S. Williams, 2 October 1848, *LCB* II, 123.

biggest disappointments came: All details about the letter, including quotations, are drawn from MT to CB, June to 24 July 1848, Morgan, *Taylor,* 73–76.

108 Quarterly Review *had attacked:* Elizabeth Rigby, "Vanity Fair—and Jane Eyre,"

Littel's Living Age, March 1849, 20, 503–7. The review was published in the *Quarterly Review* in December 1848, and subsequently reprinted in this American magazine.

110 *sink if she failed him:* CB to W. S. Williams, 25 December 1848, *LCB* II, 159.

By *the time Charlotte confided:* CB to EN, c. 12, 14 May 1849, *LCB* II, 208.

Written in April 1849: MT to CB, 10 April 1849, *Taylor,* 86 and 86 (n4).

111 *"writing it has been a boon":* CB to W. S. Williams, 29 August 1849, *LCB* II, 241.

112 *"Why do you like Miss Austen":* CB to George Henry Lewes, 12 January 1848, *LCB* II, 10.

113 *Charlotte's missive had not:* CB to EG, 17 November 1849, *LCB* II, 288.

"Boys! I have been dining with 'Jane Eyre'": Leonard Huxley, *The House of Smith Elder,* William Clowes & Sons, 1923, 68.

It was dark when: This scene, including quotations and EG's depiction of Patrick Brontë, is drawn from EG to Catherine Winkworth, 25 August 1850, *LMG,* 123–25.

114 *The consignment:* Details, including quotations, are drawn from MT's half of MT and Ellen Taylor to CB, 13 August 1850, Berg, *Taylor,* 96–98.

115 *an unenthusiastic assessment:* George Henry Lewes, "Shirley: A Tale. by Currer Bell, Author of 'Jane Eyre.' Smith, Elder, and Co. 1849," *Edinburgh Review,* January 1850, 153–73.

116 *comment to Ellen Nussey:* CB to EN, 26 February 1851, *LCB* II, 579.

By *the time that Charlotte voiced:* CB to EN, 6 January 1852, *LCB* III, 5.

In the early months of 1852: This scene, including the quotation, is drawn from MT to CB, 1852, Berg, *Taylor,* 107–10. The letter was most likely sent in the spring of 1852. The library record dates it to April 1852.

Charlotte had joked: CB to Margaret Wooler, 21 October 1851, *LCB* II, 705.

117 *feel that it would be best:* CB to EN, 31 October 1852, *LCB* III, 76.

persuading her publisher: CB to Elizabeth Smith, 30 December 1852, *LCB* III, 96.

"not the serious, grave, cool-headed": CB to Henry Nussey, 5 March 1839, *LCB* I, 185.

118 *"Could I ever feel":* CB to EN, 9 April 1851, *LCB* II, 599.

came to understand: This scene, including quotations, drawn from CB to EN, 15 December 1852, *LCB* III, 93. The dialogue is adapted from CB's description: "I asked if he had spoken to Papa. He said—he dared not."

120 *six sad letters:* Juliet Barker, Barker, 867.

"bearing" her current position: The following details, including quotations, are drawn from MT to EN, 24 February to 3 March 1854, *Taylor,* 120.

121 *"very stern & bigoted":* EG to John Forster, 23 April 1854, *LMG,* 280.

"narrow": EG to John Forster, 8–14? May 1854, *LMG,* 282.

persuaded her father to relent: EG to John Forster, 17 May 1854, *LMG,* 289.

Florence Nightingale: Juliet Barker, Barker, 900.

beginning of January 1855: EG to Catherine Winkworth, 1 January 1855, *LMG,* 327.

122 *"some beef-tea":* CB to EN, ?early March 1855, *LCB* III, 328.

courageous and dignified: Patrick Brontë to EN, 30.March 1855, *LCB* III, 329–30.

he contacted Elizabeth himself: Patrick Brontë to EG, 5 April 1855, *LCB* III, 335.

Here, at last: The following details about MT's thoughts, including the quotation, are drawn from MT to EN, 19 April to 10 May 1856, 126–28.

a letter long delayed: Joan Stevens, *Taylor,* 125.

123 *"bright little minds":* EG, *Life* (first), 70.

124 *"a vivid picture of a life":* George Henry Lewes to EG, 15 April 1857, Gordon S. Haight (ed.), *The George Eliot Letters* II, Yale University Press, 1954, 315.

"learn to rejoice that his wife": This comment by Sir James Kay-Shuttleworth is related in William Gaskell to EN, 15 April 1857, *SHB* IV, 222.

In July 1857: MT to EG, 30 July 1857, *Taylor,* 132–33.

"hasty, impulsive person": MT to EN, 28 January 1858, *Taylor,* 134.

125 *decidedly odd:* Joan Bellamy, Bellamy, 116.

Mary, on the other hand: Barbara Whitehead, *Charlotte Brontë and Her "Dearest Nell": The Story of a Friendship,* Smith Settle, 1993, 221–22. In 1878, for instance, Mary answered questions from the clergyman Altheus Wilkes, who wanted to write a book about the Brontës.

GEORGE ELIOT & HARRIET BEECHER STOWE

The details included in this section are most often drawn from the letters of George Eliot and Harriet Beecher Stowe, and the journal entries of George Eliot (in *The Journals of George Eliot,* edited by Margaret Harris and Judith Johnston). Whenever possible, we have viewed the pair's correspondence in its original form, in the collections of the New York Public Library's Henry W. and Albert A. Berg Collection, Harvard University's Houghton Library and Schlesinger Library, and the Huntington Library. We also relied on the published *George Eliot Letters* (edited by Gordon S. Haight) and Jennifer Cognard-Black's transcriptions of four letters by Harriet Beecher Stowe in *Kindred Hands: Letters on Writing by British and American Women Authors, 1865–1935* (edited by Jennifer Cognard-Black and Elizabeth Macleod Walls). Joan D. Hedrick's illuminating biography, *Harriet Beecher Stowe: A Life*, was another invaluable resource. Marlene Springer's essay "Stowe and Eliot: An Epistolary Friendship" (*Biography*, 9.1, Winter 1986, 59–81) provided an interesting introduction to the pair's relationship.

Abbreviations

Berg	The Henry W. and Albert A. Berg Collection of English and American Literature, The New York Public Library
GE	George Eliot (Marian Lewes).
GE Biography	Gordon S. Haight, *George Eliot: A Biography*, Oxford University Press, 1969
GE & JC	Gordon S. Haight (ed.), *George Eliot & John Chapman: With Chapman's Diaries* (second edition), Archon Books, 1969
GEL	Gordon S. Haight (ed.), *The George Eliot Letters*, Yale University Press, vols. I–VIII, 1954–78
GHL	George Henry Lewes
GHLD	George Henry Lewes Diary
HBS	Harriet Beecher Stowe
Hedrick	Joan D. Hedrick, *Harriet Beecher Stowe: A Life*, Oxford University Press, 1994
Henry	Nancy Henry, *The Life of George Eliot: A Critical Biography*, Blackwell, 2012
JC	John Chapman
JGE	Margaret Harris and Judith Johnston (eds.), *The Journals of George Eliot*, Cambridge University Press, 1998
Kindred Hands	Jennifer Cognard-Black and Elizabeth Macleod Walls (eds.), *Kindred Hands: Letters on Writing by British and American Women Authors, 1865–1935*, University of Iowa Press, 2006
LMG	J. A. V. Chapple and Arthur Pollard (eds.), *The Letters of Mrs Gaskell*, Manchester University Press, 1966
McCormack	Kathleen McCormack, *George Eliot in Society: Travels Abroad and Sundays at the Priory*, Ohio State University Press, 2013

Schlesinger   Beecher-Stowe family papers, Schlesinger Library, Radcliffe Institute, Harvard University

7. THE STUFF OF LEGEND

page

129   *A wonderful surprise:* In GE, 5 May 1869, *JGE*, 135, the author refers to the letter she received from HBS as "delightful," but she also mentions the bad health she has suffered on her travels, and it is clear that she is glad to be home.

     known off the page: Even in the 1871 UK Census, GE's surname was recorded as Lewes and she was listed as the wife of GHL.

     As the carriage reached the end: Kathleen McCormack, McCormack 27 (figure 7) and 31. Most details about GE's home are drawn from this book.

     high surrounding wall: This mention of the wall is included in Charles Eliot Norton's snobbish account of a visit to the Priory. Charles Eliot Norton, 29 January 1869, *GEL* V, 8.

130   *Amelia and Grace Lee:* UK Census, 1871.

     wallpaper custom-made: GHL, 13 November 1863, GHLD, *GEL* IV, 112.

131   *Marian had long admired:* George Eliot, "Harriet Beecher Stowe's *Dred*, Charles Reade's *It Is Never Too Late to Mend* and Frederika Bremer's *Hertha*," *Silly Novels by Lady Novelists*, Penguin Books, 2010, 93–94. In this anonymous review of HBS's latest novel, GE praised HBS's writing—especially with regard to her earlier book, *Uncle Tom's Cabin*.

     "Is this the little woman": Annie Fields (ed.), *Life and Letters of Harriet Beecher Stowe*, Houghton Mifflin and Company, 1898, 269.

     crowds turned up in droves: Joan Hedrick, Hedrick, 240.

     hosted by the Lord Mayor: Harry Stone, "Charles Dickens and Harriet Beecher Stowe," *Nineteenth-Century Fiction*, December 1957, 12.3, 197–99.

132   *a supposedly chance rendezvous:* Stanley Weintraub, *Victorian Yankees at Queen Victoria's Court: American Encounters with Victoria and Albert,* University of Delaware Press, 2011, 61–62.

     Edward Henry Corbould: These pictures form part of the Royal Collection.

     sold the exclusive serial rights: "Appendix I: GE's Literary Earnings," *GEL* VII, 361.

     Decades later, long after her death: Gordon S. Haight states that HBS wrote "Out of the blue," in Gordon S. Haight, *GE Biography,* 412.

133   *a kindly message:* HBS to GE, 15 April 1869, Berg, *Kindred Hands*, 25. HBS mentioned having received this message in her first letter.

Elizabeth Gaskell, for instance: EG to Grace Schwabe, 19 June 1853, *LMG,* 237; EG to George Smith, 2 November 1859, *LMG,* 587; EG to GE, 10 November 1859, *LMG,* 592. In the first of these letters, Elizabeth talks of meeting with Harriet twice on her first European tour.

"soiled" morals: EG to Harriet Martineau, 29 October 1859, *LMG,* 587.

intended initially: This background and the scene that follows, including the quotations, are drawn from HBS to GE, 15 April 1869, Berg, *Kindred Hands,* 25–27. HBS refers to GHL as GE's husband in the same sentence in which she introduces her own husband.

134 *and future tourists would pay:* Bill Belleville, *River of Lakes: A Journey on Florida's St. Johns River,* University of Georgia Press, 2000, 173.

135 *a hit with the literary establishment:* Gordon S. Haight, *GE Biography,* 404–5.

"heart soul & life blood": HBS to GE, 25 May 1869, Berg.

Worried that delivering her story: Joan D. Hedrick, Hedrick, 332.

136 *"so intensely American":* HBS to GE, 15 April 1869, Berg, *Kindred Hands,* 25.

"My dear Friend": GE to HBS, 8 May 1869, Schlesinger, *GEL* V, 29, 31.

137 *hunting big game:* Nancy Henry, Henry, 159.

written a pitiful letter: GHL to John Blackwood, 9 January 1869, *GEL* V, 4.

fast and loose with the truth: Kathryn Hughes, *George Eliot: The Last Victorian,* Fourth Estate, 1999, 388.

When, that day: GE to John Blackwood, 11 May 1869, *GEL* V, 34.

Later, he would sit down: GHL, 8 May 1869, GHLD, *GEL* V, 33.

138 *with two American friends:* Grace Norton and Sara Sedgwick accompanied Henry James that day. Rosemary Ashton, *George Eliot: A Life,* Hamish Hamilton, 1996, 299.

subsequent letter to his father: Unless otherwise stated, details, including quotations, in the following scene are drawn from Henry James to Henry James Sr., 10 May 1869, Leon Edel (ed.), *Henry James Letters, Volume I, 1843–1875,* Macmillan, 1974, 116–17.

artfully decorated drawing room: J. W. Cross, *George Eliot's Life as Related in Her Letters and Journals,* vol. III, William Blackwood and Sons, 1885, frontispiece illustration.

the armchairs carefully arranged: Kathleen McCormack, McCormack, 32.

written three reviews: Kathryn Hughes, *George Eliot: The Last Victorian,* Fourth Estate, 1999, 388. Henry James's verdict on *The Spanish Gypsy* appeared in the *North American Review* (Henry James, "The Spanish Gypsy. A Poem," *North American Review,* October 1868, 107.221, 620–35).

139 *During the gap in years:* Henry James, *The Middle Years,* W. Collins Sons & Co., 1917, 64–65.

140 *four times in the night:* GHL, 9 May 1869, GHLD, *GEL* V, 33.

   Harriet's description: HBS to GE, 25 May 1869, Berg.

   a Boston bookshop: Forest Wilson, *Crusader in Crinoline: The Life of Harriet Beecher Stowe,* J. B. Lippincott, 1941, 534.

141 *"sacred veil of silence":* HBS to Anne Isabella Byron, 17 December 1856, Charles Edward Stowe, *Life of Harriet Beecher Stowe Compiled from Her Letters and Journals,* Sampson Low, Marston, Searle & Rivington, 1889, 451.

   Over three weeks in June: Joan D. Hedrick, Hedrick, 356.

142 *As she made clear in her letter:* HBS to Oliver Wendell Holmes, June 1869, Charles Edward Stowe, *Life of Harriet Beecher Stowe Compiled from Her Letters and Journals,* Sampson Low, Marston, Searle & Rivington, 1889, 453–54.

   when the doctor returned it: Joan D. Hedrick, Hedrick, 357.

   she had been drawn: GE to HBS, 11 July 1869, Schlesinger, *GEL* V, 48.

143 *published simultaneously:* "The True Story of Lady Byron's Life" was published in the September issues of the *Atlantic Monthly* (24.143) and *Macmillan's* (20.119).

   remains unpublished: All of GE's known correspondence to HBS is published in *GEL.* A portion of these letters appears, in a less rigorously edited form, in *George Eliot's Life as Related in Her Letters and Journals,* edited by J. W. Cross. Three of HBS's letters to GE are published in *Kindred Hands,* edited by Jennifer Cognard-Black and Elizabeth Macleod Walls. Partial and at times inaccurate versions of the letters also appear in *Life and Letters of Harriet Beecher Stowe,* edited by Annie Fields, and *Life of Harriet Beecher Stowe,* edited by Charles Edward Stowe. One letter (viewable online) is held in the Amy Lowell Autograph Collection of the Houghton Library, Harvard University. The unpublished remainder of HBS's correspondence to GE (and also from Calvin Ellis Stowe to GE) is held in the collections of the Henry W. and Albert A. Berg Collection at the New York Public Library.

   Her letter goes on: Most details in this scene, including quotations, are drawn from HBS to GE, 3 August 1869, Berg.

   an alcohol addiction: Joan D. Hedrick, Hedrick, 140.

144 *Harriet too had been suffering:* Joan D. Hedrick, Hedrick, 362.

145 *significant number of his poems:* GE to Cara Bray, 23 August 1869, 54.

   "the novel of 'Romola'": HBS, "The True Story of Lady Byron's Life," *Atlantic Monthly,* September 1869, 24.143, 305.

wrote to other close friends: GE to Cara Bray, 23 August 1869, *GEL* V, 54; GE to Sara Sophia Hennell, 21 September 1869, *GEL* V, 56.

146 *the poems . . . were now finished:* GE, 1 August 1869, *JGE,* 137.

"this was always one of my best": GE to John Blackwood, 21 April 1873, *GEL* V, 403.

8. THE SPECTER OF SCANDAL

147 *"distressingly haggard":* GE, 17 September 1869, *JGE,* 138.

Though the new nurse: This refers to Thornton Lewes's second nurse. The first had left on 18 August 1869. GE, 19 August 1869, *JGE,* 137.

On at least one afternoon: GHL, 18 May 1869, GHLD, *GEL* V, 40 (n7).

148 *Back on January 1:* GE, 1 January 1869, *JGE,* 134.

"I do not feel very confident": GE, 11 September 1869, *JGE,* 138.

In mid-October, she recorded: GE, 13 October 1869, *JGE,* 139.

sometimes felt frustrated: Nancy Henry, Henry, 178.

"this death seems to me the beginning of our own": GE, 19 October 1869, *JGE,* 139.

149 *scale of the scandal:* Joan D. Hedrick, Hedrick, 364–65.

A Key to Uncle Tom's Cabin—a bestseller: Claire Parfait, *The Publishing History of Uncle Tom's Cabin, 1852–2002,* Ashgate, 2007, 109.

cherry-picking: Joan D. Hedrick, Hedrick, 231.

150 *"war to the knife":* HBS to J. R. Osgood, n.d., Joan D. Hedrick, Hedrick, 366. The letter from which Joan D. Hedrick quotes is in the collections of the Huntington Library (HBS to J. R. Osgood, n.d., Fields Papers, HL).

usual heartfelt greeting: Most details in this scene, including quotations, are drawn from GE to HBS, 10 December 1869, *GEL* V, 71–72. The original of this letter appears to be lost. Gordon S. Haight reproduces the copy from the Tinker Collection at Yale University Library.

"silent blue eyed golden haired boy": HBS to GE, 25 May 1869, Berg.

151 *New York City clinic of George Taylor:* Joan D. Hedrick, Hedrick, 367.

"clear as the sun fair as the moon": HBS to Hattie and Eliza Stowe, November to December 1869, Schlesinger.

152 *sheep grazing on the Green:* Roy Rosenzweig and Elizabeth Blackmar, *The Park and the People: A History of Central Park,* Cornell University Press, 1992, 252.

"ribbed & stretched & otherwise": HBS to Hattie and Eliza Stowe, November to December 1869, Schlesinger.

"paralysis of the sciatic nerve": HBS to GE, 3 August 1869, Berg.

153 *obliged with a long letter:* This letter no longer exists in its original form. Susan Belasco reproduces a copy from Dr. Williams's London Library. Most details in this scene, including quotations, are drawn from HBS to Eliza Lee Cabot Follen, 16 December 1852, Susan Belasco (ed.), *Stowe in Her Own Time: A Biographical Chronicle of Her Life, Drawn from Recollections, Interviews, and Memoirs by Family, Friends, and Associates,* University of Iowa Press, 2009, 62–69.

treated . . . to a reading: GE recalled her first impressions of HBS in GE to HBS, 8 May 1869, Schlesinger, *GEL* V, 29–30.

155 *"I am a little bit of a woman":* The wording of GE's letter, in which she also expresses her initial impressions of HBS, is slightly different from that which appears in the copy of the letter from Dr. Williams's London Library. GE to Cara and Charles Bray, 12 March 1853, *GEL* II, 92.

fearing that his daughter: Kathryn Hughes, *George Eliot: The Last Victorian,* Fourth Estate, 1999, 29.

156 *German and Italian, Greek and Latin:* Nancy Henry, Henry, 31.

job as a schoolmistress: Joan D. Hedrick, Hedrick, 54–57.

helping one of her brothers: Joan D. Hedrick, Hedrick, 89.

157 *"too great a sacrifice":* Cara Bray to Sara Sophia Hennell, 30 March 1845, *GEL* I, 184.

laughing at him up her sleeve: GE to Sara Sophia Hennell, 5 November 1846, *GEL* I, 225.

began to feel faint: GE to Cara Bray, 24 November 1843, *GEL* I, 166.

one he would never finish: Gordon S. Haight, *GE Biography,* 50–51. Gordon S. Haight quotes the words of Eliza Lynn Linton, writing about Dr. Brabant in her 1899 book, *My Literary Life.*

"in a little heaven here": GE to Cara Bray, 20 November 1843, *GEL* I, 165.

who grew suspicious: JC, 27 June 1851, GE & JC, 186.

John Chapman: Details about GE's relationship with JC, including the quotation, come from JC, 18–19 January 1851; 18–19 February 1851; 24 March 1851, *GE & JC,* 142, 133–34.

158 *leading many to assume:* Herbert Spencer, *An Autobiography,* vol. I, Williams and Norgate, 1904, 399.

Marian wrote to confess: GE to Herbert Spencer, 16? July 1852, *GEL* VIII, 56–57.

159 *enclosed a photograph:* HBS to GE, 8 February 1872, Berg.

Unable to bear: GE to HBS, 24 June 1872, *GEL* V, 281.

she'd seen the results: Both the sketch and a copy of the photograph (the latter produced much later, after GE's death) are part of the collections of the Herbert Art Gallery & Museum in Coventry. The sketch, by GE's friend Cara Bray, was drawn during a tour of Europe in 1849. The exact date of the original photograph is unknown.

first declared his affection: Joan D. Hedrick, Hedrick, 97.

160 *Prussian school system:* Details about Calvin Ellis Stowe's trip, HBS's pregnancy, and the birth of their twins are drawn from Joan D. Hedrick, Hedrick, 98–100, 112. The quotation is from a letter by Calvin Ellis Stowe, written on 7 June 1836, prior to his departure (held in the collections of the Harriet Beecher Stowe Center, Hartford, CT).

161 *introduced her to Lewes in 1851:* JC, 6 October 1851, *GE & JC,* 217; GE to Charles Bray, 8 October 1851, *GEL* I, 367.

long time later, in 1857: GE to Isaac Pearson Evans, 26 May 1857, *GEL* II, 331–32.

162 *just about possible:* Unlike earlier biographers, such as Gordon S. Haight, who suggests that it would have been out of the question for GE and GHL to marry, Nancy Henry makes the convincing case that such a union would not have been impossible. Nancy Henry, Henry, 98–101.

Unlike Arthur Bell Nicholls: CB to EN, ?20 October 1854, Margaret Smith (ed.), *The Letters of Charlotte Brontë with a Selection of Letters by Her Family and Friends,* vol. III, Clarendon Press, 2004, 295.

and the skullcap: Forest Wilson, *Crusader in Crinoline: The Life of Harriet Beecher Stowe,* J. B. Lippincott, 1941, 166.

163 *twinkling sense of humor:* CES to GE, 30 May 1869, Berg.

"a Christ in dwelling": CES to GE, 31 July 1872, Berg.

164 *several séances:* Joan D. Hedrick, Hedrick, 367.

ghost of a famed female author: This scene, including quotations, is drawn from HBS to GE, 25 May 1869, Berg; HBS to GE, 11 May 1872, Berg.

165 *must have gratified Harriet:* EG, *Life* (first), 1997, 410, 413.

166 *"deeply interested":* GE to HBS, 11 July 1869, Schlesinger, *GEL* V, 48–49.

the Charlotte Brontë episode: HBS to GE, 11 May 1872, Berg.

"whether rightly or not": GE to HBS, 24 June 1872, *GEL* V, 280.

167 *"comfort through love and care":* GE to HBS, 10 December 1869, *GEL* V, 71.

9. AN ACT OF BETRAYAL

168 *had not forgotten Harriet:* GE to Cara Bray, 3 August 1871, *GEL* V, 173.

"Dear Friend": Details of this letter from HBS, including quotations, are drawn

from HBS to GE, 8 February 1872, Berg. When mentioning the magazine, *Harpers Weekly* (as it was then), Harriet refers to it as "Harpers Monthly."

169 *"be so unreasonable as to expect"*: GE to HBS, 10 December 1869, *GEL* V, 72.

sent off promptly within days: GE to HBS, 4 March 1872, Schlesinger, *GEL* V, 252. Following the pattern of earlier letters between the pair, it is likely that HBS's letter of 8 February arrived at the Priory within a period of two and a half weeks.

170 *"without any very serious intention"*: GE, 2 December 1870, *JGE*, 141.

171 *"bits will be published right and left"*: Gordon S. Haight quotes from a letter by John Blackwood, written on 4 September 1871. Gordon S. Haight, *GE Biography*, 437.

As usual, Harriet had traveled: Details about HBS's travel arrangements and Fred's disappearance are drawn from Joan D. Hedrick, Hedrick, 382–83.

172 *"drawing-room scandal"*: "The Week," *Nation*, 6 January 1870, 10.236, 2.

"weak and trashy production": *Charleston Daily News*, 7 January 1870, 1.

"a turning over again": *Richmond Dispatch*, 6 January 1870, 2.

would have arrived: Both GE and HBS agree that there had been a gap of approximately two years since GE's letter of December 1869 (GE to HBS, 10 December 1869, *GEL* V, 71–72). HBS had already answered GE's previous letter sent over two and a half years earlier (GE to HBS, 11 July 1869, Schlesinger, *GEL* V, 47–49).

173 *about halfway through*: GE, n.d. 1872, *JGE*, 142.

With a frostiness: GE to HBS, 4 March 1872, Schlesinger, *GEL* V, 252–53.

174 *Treading carefully for now*: HBS to GE, 11 May 1872, Berg.

Since the revival: Most of this background plus the scene that follows, including quotations, is drawn from HBS to GE, 23 September 1872, Berg, *Kindred Hands*, 27.

first staying at a resort: Joan D. Hedrick, Hedrick, 383–84.

175 *presumably still mid-tour*: The address written at the top of the letter (seemingly in HBS's hand) reads "Hartford," but, as she was in Salem, Massachusetts, on 17 September and in Boston, Massachusetts, by 26 September, it seems unlikely that she returned to her home in Connecticut between those dates. HBS writes that she is "away from my papers," which further suggests that whoever wrote "Hartford" at the top of the letter was mistaken. Joan D. Hedrick lists some of HBS's tour dates in the section mentioned in the previous note.

176 *in no uncertain terms*: The original of this letter appears to be lost. Gordon S. Haight reproduces a fragment copy, which forms part of the Tinker Collection at Yale University Library. GE to HBS, October? 1872, *GEL* V, 322.

"shadow of old Casaubon": GHL to John Blackwood, 13 July 1872, *GEL*V, 291.

177 *On receipt of this second letter:* This background and the scene that follows, including quotations, are drawn from HBS to GE, 26 September 1872, Berg, *Kindred Hands,* 29–30.

178 *"Dear Love, did you think":* The letter has been incorrectly marked with the date 1831. From the context of its contents, it should be 1873. HBS to GE, 20 April 1873?, Berg.

179 *"rare genius":* George Eliot, "Harriet Beecher Stowe's *Dred,* Charles Reade's *It Is Never Too Late to Mend,* and Frederika Bremer's *Hertha,"* *Silly Novels by Lady Novelists,* Penguin Books, 2010, 94.

desired her friend's thoughts: The subject of anti-Semitism is one that GE talks of at some length in this letter. GE to HBS, 29 October 1876, Schlesinger, *GEL*VI, 301–2.

When Daniel Deronda *came out:* This background and the following scene, including quotations, are drawn from HBS to GE, 18 March 1876, Berg.

180 *"a splendid success":* HBS to GE, 25 September 1876, Berg, *Kindred Hands,* 33.

"the Jewish element": GE to HBS, 29 October 1876, *GEL*VI, 301.

her editor had expressed concern: John Blackwood to GE, 24 February 1876, *GEL* VI, 221–22.

"no existence outside of the author's study": Henry James, "Daniel Deronda: A Conversation," *Atlantic Monthly,* December 1876, 38.230, 686.

"warm appreciation": GE to John Blackwood, 2 September 1876, *GEL* VI, 275.

181 *Marian's subconscious prejudices:* George Eliot, *Daniel Deronda,* Penguin Classics, 1995, chapter 33, 383–84.

Harriet sent her friend the gift: The letter that accompanied this gift is held in the collections of the Amy Lowell Autograph Collection of the Houghton Library, Harvard University.

"had been gnawed by the rats": Gordon S. Haight quotes the words of Frances Anne (Fanny) Kemble. Gordon S. Haight, *GE Biography,* 512.

"thickening of the mucous membrane": Gordon S. Haight, *GE Biography,* 514.

182 *her anguished cries:* Gordon S. Haight, *GE Biography,* 516.

When, in April 1879: GE to HBS, 10 April 1879, *GEL*VII, 132.

This time, though, her letter: HBS to GE, 6 May 1880, Berg.

183 *"so fine and noble":* HBS to Annie Fields, 1 January 1881, Huntington Library, San Marino, California.

184 *"like falling stars":* Hattie Stowe to Annie Fields, January 1890, Huntington Library, San Marino, California.

"most delightful": Charles Edward Stowe, *Life of Harriet Beecher Stowe Compiled from Her Letters and Journals,* Sampson Low, Marston, Searle & Rivington, 1889, 459.

KATHERINE MANSFIELD & VIRGINIA WOOLF

The details included in this section are most often drawn from the letters, diaries, and journals of Katherine Mansfield and Virginia Woolf. Ida Baker's *Katherine Mansfield: The Memories of LM* is another chief source. We consulted Virginia Woolf's diaries and extant letters from Katherine Mansfield to Virginia Woolf in the New York Public Library's Henry W. and Albert A. Berg Collection. An unpublished letter from Virginia Woolf to Katherine Mansfield has been made available to view online by the Mortimer Rare Book Room, Smith College. We also made substantial use of the *Collected Letters of Katherine Mansfield* (edited by Vincent O'Sullivan and Margaret Scott); *The Letters of Virginia Woolf* (edited by Nigel Nicolson with Joanne Trautmann); *The Diary of Virginia Woolf* (edited by Anne Olivier Bell with Andrew Mc-Neillie); and *The Collected Works of Katherine Mansfield, vol. IV: The Diaries of Katherine Mansfield Including Miscellaneous Works* (edited by Gerri Kimber and Claire Davison with Anna Plumridge). The biographies of Kathleen Jones, Hermione Lee, and Claire Tomalin were of regular assistance too.

Abbreviations

Beginning   Leonard Woolf, *Beginning Again: An Autobiography of the Years 1911 to 1918,* Harvest/Harcourt Brace Jovanovich, 1975

Berg   The Henry W. and Albert A. Berg Collection of English and American Literature, The New York Public Library

CWKM   Katherine Mansfield, *The Collected Works of Katherine Mansfield,* vols. II–IV, Edinburgh University Press, 2012–16 (see Select Bibliography for editors)

DVW   Anne Olivier Bell with Andrew McNeillie (eds.), *The Diary of Virginia Woolf,* vols. I–IV, The Hogarth Press, 1978–84

Garsington   Ottoline Morrell, *Ottoline at Garsington: Memoirs of Lady Ottoline Morrell, 1915–1918,* Faber & Faber, 1974

IB   Ida Baker

JMM   John Middleton Murry

Journal	John Middleton Murry (ed.), *Journal of Katherine Mansfield,* Persephone Books, 2006
KM	Katherine Mansfield
Lee	Hermione Lee, *Virginia Woolf,* Vintage, 1997
LJMMKM	Cherry A. Hankin (ed.), *The Letters of John Middleton Murry to Katherine Mansfield,* Constable, 1983
LKM	*The Collected Letters of Katherine Mansfield,* vols. I–V, Vincent O'Sullivan and Margaret Scott (eds.), Clarendon Press, 1984–96. (© The Estate of Katherine Mansfield 1984, 1987, 1993, 1996, 2008)
LM	Ida Baker, *Katherine Mansfield: The Memories of LM,* Michael Joseph, 1971
LVW	Nigel Nicolson with Joanne Trautmann (eds.), *The Letters of Virginia Woolf,* vols. II–IV, 1976–78
LW	Leonard Woolf
Morgan	Department of Literary and Historical Manuscripts, The Morgan Library and Museum
OM	Ottoline Morrell
Smith	Frances Hooper Collection, Mortimer Rare Book Room, Smith College
Stories	Katherine Mansfield, *The Collected Stories of Katherine Mansfield,* Penguin Classics, 2007
Tomalin	Claire Tomalin, *Katherine Mansfield: A Secret Life,* Penguin, 2003
VB	Vanessa Bell
VW	Virginia Woolf

10. FRIENDS OR FOES?

page

187 *without feeling assured of success:* VW to VB, 26 April 1917, *LVW* II, 150.

"*utterly unscrupulous character*": VW to VB, 11 February 1917, *LVW* II, 144.

188 "*an ugly impassive*": Lytton Strachey to VW, 17 July 1916, Paul Levy (ed.), *The Letters of Lytton Strachey,* Viking, 2005, 310.

"*Katherine Mansfield has dogged*": VW to Lytton Strachey, 25 July 1916, *LVW* II, 107.

meet at Garsington: Details of the early days of KM's friendship with VW are drawn from LW, *Beginning,* 203–4.

any significant new work: JMM, *Journal,* ix.

189 *Women's Co-operative Guild:* VW to Margaret Llewelyn Davies, 22 February 1915, *LVW* II, 59.

After the arrival of the machine: VW to VB, 26 April 1917, *LVW* II, 150.

Four years earlier: Details of VW's mental health and its treatment during this period are drawn from LW, *Beginning,* 148–70.

As the train trundled east: VW's habitual mode of transport into London was by rail.

190 *Zeppelin raids:* Zeppelin raids in the area are detailed in John Hook, *London Air Raid Incidents,* 1990, London Metropolitan Archives.

Upon arriving at Katherine's studio flat: Descriptions of KM's living conditions and situation during this period are drawn from IB, *LM,* 101–5; KM to OM, 15 August 1917, *LKM* I, 325.

Lottie Hope, and . . . Nellie Boxall: Alison Light, *Mrs Woolf and the Servants,* Penguin, 2008, 167–68. Although Virginia Woolf referred to her as "Nelly," Alison Light has confirmed that her name was spelled "Nellie" on her birth and death certificates, and that she always referred to herself as "Nellie," xiii.

191 *outsider in literary London:* OM, *Garsington,* 150.

192 *The evening left:* Details of this evening are drawn from KM to VW, ?24 June 1917, *LKM* I, 313; VW to VB, 27 June 1917, *LVW* II, 159.

under the table: Barbara Bagenal, *Recollections of Virginia Woolf,* Joan Russell Noble (ed.), Peter Owen, 1972, 150. Barbara Bagenal recalls LW lying on the kitchen table while her bed was made up beneath it. Ordinarily, however, she would not have been with the Woolfs, so we've assumed that LW would more usually occupy the safer spot beneath the table.

193 *earliest sexual experience:* Details of VW's early experience of sexual abuse are drawn from VW, "Sketch of the Past," *Moments of Being,* Pimlico, 2002, 81.

"every sort of hog": VW to VB, 27 June 1917, *LVW* II, 159.

194 *"My God, I love":* KM to VW, ?24 June 1917, *LKM* I, 313.

"consider how rare": KM to VW, ?24 June 1917, *LKM* I, 313.

The first blow: VW to Clive Bell, 17 September 1917, *LVW* II, 179 (n2).

gather at the home: VW, "Sketch of the Past," *Moments of Being,* Pimlico, 2002, 50.

In early August 1917: VW to OM, 15 August 1917, *LVW* II, 174.

195 *But the particular incident:* VW, 10 October 1917, *DVW* I, 57; VW, 11 October 1917, Berg, *DVW* I, 58; VW, 27 October 1917, *DVW* I, 67 (n42); KM to VW, c. 23 August 1917, Berg, *LKM* I, 327.

Bertrand Russell: For more information on KM's interactions with Bertrand Russell, see Claire Tomalin, Tomalin, Loc 3022.

accusing Katherine of: OM, *Garsington,* 150 & 167. See also 185–92 for details of JMM's accusation that OM had fallen in love with him, and the fallout this caused between KM and OM.

Among her old friends: LW, *Beginning,* 30–31.

"Chaste & the Unchaste": VW, 11 October 1917, Berg, *DVW* I, 58.

196 *each guest's every whim:* OM, *Garsington,* 167.

through Garsington's host herself: KM and OM were in regular correspondence during August 1917, and KM knew of VW's gossip by c. 23 August 1917.

197 *"I do like her":* KM to OM, 3 July 1917, *LKM* I, 315.

Upon Katherine's return to London: the likely influence of KM on "Kew Gardens" by VW is drawn from VW to OM, 15 August 1917, *LVW* II, 174; KM to OM, 15 August 1917, *LKM* I, 325. For further analysis, see Katie Macnamara, "How to Strike a Contemporary: Woolf, Mansfield, and Marketing Gossip," Jeanne Dubino (ed.), *Virginia Woolf and the Literary Marketplace,* Palgrave Macmillan, 2010.

"Katherine Mansfield describes": VW to OM, 15 August 1917, *LVW* II, 174.

"write about that flower garden": KM to OM, 15 August 1917, *LKM* I, 325.

"The golden oranges: Most descriptions, including quotations, in this paragraph are taken from KM to OM, 15 August 1917, *LKM* I, 325.

198 *nights at Asheham:* VW's preferred spelling of Asheham rather than Asham has been used throughout.

The invitation arrived: KM to VW, mid-August 1917, Berg, *LKM* I, 324.

gonorrhea: For further detail on KM's likely contraction of gonorrhea, see Claire Tomalin, Tomalin, Loc 1426.

The lengthy delays: Details of this visit are drawn from VW, 18 August 1917, *DVW* I, 43; VW, 19 August 1917, *DVW* I, 43; VW, 21 August 1917, *DVW* I, 44; VW, 22 August 1917, *DVW* I, 44; KM to VW, c. 23 August 1917, Berg, *LKM* I, 327.

199 *behavior became guarded:* LW, *Beginning,* 204.

recurrent rheumatism: KM to VW, mid-August 1917, Berg, *LKM* I, 324.

"Night-Scented Stock": KM, *CWKM* III, 110–12.

After a promising start: JMM, "Introduction," KM, *Journal,* viii–ix.

200 *Katherine mulled over:* KM to VW, c. 23 August 1917, Berg, *LKM* I, 327.

tended to be defensive: OM, *Garsington,* 148–50.

"make our undiscovered": KM, *CWKM* IV, 191.

late August 1917: Quotations in the following three paragraphs are taken from KM to VW, c. 23 August 1917, Berg, *LKM* I, 327.

201 *And so Virginia tore up:* VW to Clive Bell, 17 September 1917, *LVW* II, 179.

202 *"many delicate things fall":* VW, 10 October 1917, *DVW* I, 58.

first page of Prelude: VW, 9 October 1917, *DVW* I, 56.

the meal came around: Details of this visit are drawn from VW, 10 October 1917, *DVW* I, 57; VW, 11 October 1917, Berg, *DVW* I, 58; KM to Dorothy Brett, 11 October 1917, *LKM* I, 330–31.

show of impassivity: OM, *Garsington,* 149.

"the living power": VW, 12 July 1918, *DVW* I, 167.

The new title: Georgina Joysmith, editorial note, IB, *LM,* 103.

203 *"Chaste & the Unchaste":* VW, 11 October 1917, Berg, *DVW* I, 58.

Burma and later Rhodesia: Georgina Joysmith, editorial note, IB, *LM,* 21; and IB, *LM,* 88.

minstrels' gallery: IB, *LM,* 102.

Aldous Huxley: Jeffrey Meyers, *Katherine Mansfield: A Darker View,* Cooper Square, 2002, 151.

204 *"formally buried":* VW to OM, 25 October 1917, *LVW* II, 190.

"I am sorry": KM to Dorothy Brett, 19 November 1917, *LKM* I, 334.

laboriously set the type: LW, *Beginning,* 237.

205 *"To Hell with other people's presses!":* KM to JMM, 29 May 1918, *LKM* I, 203.

Virginia holed herself away: Descriptions of the Woolfs' work on *Prelude* are drawn from VW, 9 July 1918, *DVW* I, 164; VW, 10 July 1918, *DVW* I, 165; LW, *Beginning,* 237.

"sell it on a barrow": KM to VW, 29 May 1918, Berg, *LKM* II, 200.

206 *pronounced it unremarkable:* JMM, "Introduction," KM, *Journal,* x.

She defended Prelude: VW to Clive Bell, 16 July 1918, *LVW* II, 262.

"doesn't set the Thames on fire": VW, 16 July 1918, *DVW* I, 168.

"one fine but very modest example": VW to Duncan Grant, 15 May 1918, *LVW* II, 241.

"afflicted with jealousy": VW to Roger Fry, 1 August 1920, *LVW* II, 438.

11. CAT-AND-MOUSE

207 *"marmoreal":* VW, 28 May 1918, *DVW* I, 150.

On January 7, Murry and Ida: Details of KM's journey and arrival are drawn from IB, *LM,* 106.

208 *no longer alone:* Details of IB's arrival and stay with KM are drawn from IB, *LM,* 107–8; KM to JMM, 12 January 1918, *LKM* II, 9; KM to JMM, 16 February 1918, *LKM* II, 74; 19 February 1918, *LKM* II, 79; KM to JMM, 24 May 1918, *LKM* II, 190.

"state of work": KM to JMM, February 1918, quoted in IB, *LM,* 107.

209 *"abject slave":* JMM to KM, 15 February 1918, *LJMMKM,* 122.

contrarian kind of love: KM to JMM, 24 May 1918, *LKM* II, 190.

"use her as a walking stick": KM to JMM, 16 February 1918, *LKM* II, 74.

purchase of a hand-press: JM to KM, 3 February 1918, Cherry A. Hankin (ed.), *Letters Between Katherine Mansfield and John Middleton Murry,* Virago, 1988, 106.

210 *hardly a sum to sniff at:* Kathleen Jones, *Katherine Mansfield: The Story-Teller,* The Book Mill, 2012, Loc 5195.

"It's the soberest": JMM to KM, 11 February 1918, *LJMMKM,* 119.

"her roof over her": KM to JMM, 30 November 1919, *LKM* III, 127–28.

a spot of exercise: Details of this walk and its aftermath are drawn from KM to JMM, 15 February 1918, *LKM* II, 73; *CWKM* IV, 19 February 1918, 421; IB, *LM,* 108.

211 *already regarded "Bliss":* KM to JMM, 26 February 1918, *LKM* II, 94; KM to JMM, 27 February 1918, *LKM* II, 98.

the English Review: British literary magazine, 1908–1937.

212 *Its readers would be treated:* All quotations from "Bliss" are taken from KM, *Stories,* 91–105.

sentimentally so: VW to Janet Case, 20 March 1922, *LVW* II, 514–15.

213 *Now that she had returned:* VW, 3 August 1918, *DVW* I, 177.

"marriage is of no more importance": VW to OM, 24 May 1918, *LVW* II, 243.

"get down to what is true rock": VW, 28 May 1918, *DVW* I, 150.

ahead of their guests: VW, 3 August 1918, *DVW* I, 177.

the Woolfs had traveled: Details of the train journey are drawn from VW, 31 July 1918, *DVW* I, 176.

opening up Asheham for their guests: Details of VW's arrival at Asheham are drawn from VW, 31 July 1918, *DVW* I, 176; VW to OM,? 1 August 1918, *LVW* II, 263. This date information is repeated as published in *LVW* II. However, 2 August 1918 is more probable, since VW wrote of expecting the Murrys tomorrow and KM wrote to OM on 3 August 1918 saying that they were supposed to go to the Woolfs' today.

214 *But the warm spell:* VW, 3 August 1918, *DVW* I, 177.

"beastly attack": KM's words in this and the subsequent paragraph are taken from KM to VW, 2 August 1918, *LKM* II, 263.

"may be rather hopelessly ill": VW, 3 August 1918, *DVW* I, 177.

215 *"We are supposed to have fought":* KM to OM, 3 August 1918, *LKM* II, 264.

rented bed-sit in Chelsea: IB, *LM, III.*

"merely greases": VW to Barbara Bagenal, 20 September 1918, *LVW* II, 277.

True, Virginia's inheritance: For further detail on the Woolfs' financial arrangements, see Hermione Lee, Lee, 325–26 and 560; for further detail on the Murrys' financial arrangements, see Kathleen Jones, *Katherine Mansfield: The Story-Teller,* The Book Mill, 2012, Loc 6294.

216 *In August 1918:* Descriptions of the weekend are drawn from VW, 3 August 1918, *DVW* I, 178.

But an intrusion: See KM to VW, mid-August 1917, Berg, *LKM* I, 324, for KM's depiction of VW's icy aloofness. See KM to VW, ?24 June 1917, *LKM* I, 313, for KM's portrayal of VW's air of mystery and for the gesture also accorded to Pearl in "Bliss." For further analysis of the possible influence of VW on "Bliss" by KM, see Katie Macnamara, "How to Strike a Contemporary: Woolf, Mansfield, and Marketing Gossip," *Virginia Woolf and the Literary Marketplace,* Jeanne Dubino (ed.), Palgrave Macmillan, 2010.

As she would recount: Details of VW's reaction to "Bliss," including quotations, are drawn from VW, 7 August 1918, *DVW* I, 179–80; VW, 8 August 1918, *DVW* I, 180; VW to Janet Case, 20 March 1922, *LVW* II, 514–15.

218 *"fish out of the Garsington pond":* KM to JMM, 28 February 1918, *LKM* II, 98.

"a little disturbed": VW to VB, 9 August 1918, *LVW* II, 266.

"one of those Dostoievsky": KM to OM, 3 July 1917, *LKM* I, 315.

take Virginia until 1921: Hermione Lee, "Introduction," *Moments of Being,* Jeanne Schulkind (ed.), Pimlico, 2002, xi.

A period of almost a decade: Jean O. Love, *Virginia Woolf: Sources of Madness and Art,* University of California Press, 1977, 200–201.

219 *"cuddling and kissing":* VW, "Old Bloomsbury," *Moments of Being,* Jeanne Schulkind (ed.), Pimlico, 2002, 44.

"sitting on the green": Quotations about VW's marriage in this paragraph are taken from VW, 14 June 1925, *DVW* III, 30; VW, 29 February 1936, *DVW* V, 13.

Not so very long into their marriage: VW to VB, 11 April 1920, *LVW* II, 428.

"never had understood": VB to Clive Bell, 27 December 1912, quoted in Hermione Lee, Lee, 331.

"fucks her once a week": Clive Bell to Mary Hutchinson, 7 May 1919, quoted in Hermione Lee, Lee, 331.

like Bertha: VW to LW, 1 May 1912, *LVW* I, 615.

220   *"made love to her"*: F.A. Lea, *The Life of John Middleton Murry*, Methuen, 1959, 31.

Her infatuation with: KM, 29 June 1907, *CWKM* IV, 52.

"more powerfully": KM, 1 June 1907, *CWKM* IV, 47–48.

221   *their unwise friendship:* IB, *LM,* 49.

a supposed lesbian affair: IB, *LM,* 54.

"every bit as sacred": KM to IB, 7 September 1921, *LKM* IV, 277.

"the Monster": VW, 9 November 1918, *DVW* I, 216.

Here, Virginia wrote of Ida: VW, 11 October 1917, Berg, *DVW* I, 58.

She recalled waiting: Details of KM and IB's visit to VW are drawn from IB, *LM,* 132–33.

222   *After the War Office:* JMM to KM, 20 May 1918, *LJMMKM,* 150; 2 June 1918, *LJMMKM,* 166.

took out a lease: Details of the household in Hampstead are drawn from IB, *LM,* 121–30.

"mine beyond words": KM to IB, 1 August 1918, *LKM* II, 262.

"were there for pleasure": KM to VW, 1 November 1918, Berg, *LKM* II, 286.

223   *When Virginia paid her first visit:* Details of this visit are drawn from VW, 16 January 1923, Berg, *DVW* II, 226.

On December 10, 1918: Details of this visit are drawn from VW, 10 December 1918, *DVW* I, 226–27.

224   *"there's room for everyone"*: VW to Roger Fry, 1 August 1920, *LVW* II, 438.

225   *"a pale shell"*: KM to IB, 8 March 1921, *LKM* IV, 188.

"lacerated feelings": VW, 24 April 1919, *DVW* I, 268.

she cared for her: VW, 16 January 1923, Berg, *DVW* II, 226.

12. LIFE AND DEATH

227   *Amid all this activity:* VW, 17 December 1918, *DVW* I, 228; VW, 22 January 1919, *DVW* I, 235.

cheerful presents: VW, 18 February 1919, *DVW* I, 243.

wine-fueled fun: KM to Dorothy Brett, 1 January 1919, *LKM* II, 298–99.

228   *no word of thanks:* Details of VW's foiled attempt to see KM are drawn from VW, 18 February 1919, *DVW* I, 243.

"quicksands": VW, 18 February 1919, *DVW* I, 243.

"brittle as barley sugar": VW to VB, 16 February 1919, *LVW* II, 331.

229 *"sailing on tropic seas—":* KM to VW, 20 February 1919, Berg, *LKM* II, 301.

feeling rather foolish: VW, 21 February 1919, *DVW* I, 243.

laden with gifts: Details of most of these gifts are drawn from KM to VW, 12 May 1919, *LKM* II, 318; KM to VW, 4 June 1919, *LKM* II, 323.

The pair plunged: Details of VW's visits and KM's situation are drawn from VW, 22 March 1919, *DVW* I, 257.

230 *"that no one else has ever":* VW to Lady Robert Cecil, 26? January 1919, *LVW* II, 321.

"a sense of ease": VW, 22 March 1919, *DVW* I, 258.

"apologies, or sense": VW, 22 March 1919, *DVW* I, 257.

By Easter Monday: Details of this Easter Monday walk are drawn from VW, 24 April 1919, *DVW* I, 268.

faintly ridiculous: LW, *Beginning,* 28–29.

231 *"haggard & powdered":* VW, 24 April 1919, *DVW* I, 268.

not attract many readers: Details of the success of *Kew Gardens* are drawn from LW, *Beginning,* 241; VW, 9 June 1919, *DVW* I, 278; VW, 10 June 1919, *DVW* I, 280.

232 *"a thing of original and therefore strange":* Harold Child, "Kew Gardens: Unsigned Review," 29 May 1919, *Times Literary Supplement.*

These sold at such a rate: LW, *Beginning,* 253.

"Night-Scented Stock": KM sent a copy of this poem to OM but it remained unpublished until 1923. Gerry Kimber & Angela Smith, *CWKM* III, 112.

William Heinemann, who rejected: VW, 17 April 1919, *DVW* I, 265.

"You must forgive": KM to VW, 4 June 1919, *LKM* II, 324.

Wrapped up: VW to VB, 6 June 1919, *LVW* II, 366.

233 *"The note-books":* Quotations from KM's review of *Kew Gardens* are taken from KM, "A Short Story," *Athenaeum,* 13 June 1919, 450, 459.

234 *on June 14, 1919:* Details of VW's visit, including quotations, are drawn from VW, 14 June 1919, *DVW* I, 281–82.

During the autumn of 1919: Details of VW's busy autumn are drawn from VW, 28 November 1919, *DVW* I, 313.

235 *The review of this:* Quotations from KM's review of "Night and Day" are taken from KM, "A Ship Comes into the Harbour," 1 *Athenaeum,* 4 November 1919.

"secret friend": KM, "Friends and Foes," *Athenaeum,* 3 December 1920.

feeling desolate: VW, 28 November 1919, *DVW* I, 314.

236 *"we have no right":* JMM to KM, 14 November 1919, *LJMMKM,* 212.

"something hard": JMM to KM, 23 November 1919, *LJMMKM,* 223.

the review's publication: All details of JMM's visit to VW are drawn from JMM to KM, 23 November 1919, *LJMMKM,* 223. Dialogue is reconstructed from the reported speech contained in this letter.

Just seven months earlier: VW, 17 April 1919, *DVW* I, 265.

237 *"Virginia's cry that she":* KM to JMM, 26–27 November 1919, *LKM* III, 122.

"a lie in the soul": KM to JMM, 10 November 1919, *LKM* III, 82.

Detecting anger: KM to JMM, 26–27 November 1919, *LKM* III, 122.

"scrupulously truthful": KM to VW, ?24 June 1917, *LKM* I, 313.

works of George Eliot: VW, 5 December 1919, *DVW* I, 315–16.

238 *"a decorous elderly dullard":* VW, 28 November 1919, *DVW* I, 314.

she now shuddered: VW, 10 April 1920, *DVW* II, 28.

She vowed to wait: VW, 5 May 1920, *DVW* II, 34.

within a fortnight: VW, 20 May 1920, *DVW* II, 41.

"I am grown very dull": KM to VW, 25 May 1920, *LKM* IV, 14.

stiff and formal: VW, 26 May 1920, *DVW* II, 43.

239 *On a cool day:* Details of this visit, including quotations, are drawn from VW, 31 May 1920, *DVW* II, 43–45. Dialogue is repeated from it verbatim and reconstructed from its reported speech.

240 *now haunted her:* KM to JMM, 17 November 1919, *LKM* III, 100.

early June day in 1920: Details about this visit, including quotations, are drawn from VW, 5 June 1920, *DVW* II, 45–46. Dialogue is repeated from it verbatim and reconstructed from its reported speech.

Times Literary Supplement: Harold Child, "Two Stories," *Times Literary Supplement,* 29 January 1920.

241 *"nothing but hate":* VW, 9 November 1920, *DVW* I, 216.

Constable & Co.: JMM to KM, 2 February 1920, *LJMMKM,* 261.

a war novel: VW, 26 January 1920, *DVW* II, 13.

other writer friends: VW, 26 September 1920, *DVW* II, 68.

242 *a luncheon hosted:* VW, 6 July 1920, *DVW* II, 52.

Katherine's Hampstead home: VW, 2 August 1920, *DVW* II, 61.

consider reviewing it: VW, 2 August 1920, *DVW* II, 55.

"if she's good then I'm not":VW, 28 November 1919, *DVW* I, 315.

In late August 1920: Details of this visit, including quotations, are drawn from VW to VB, 24 August 1920, *LVW* II, 441;VW, 25 August 1920, Berg, *DVW* II, 61; as well as from descriptions more generally of visits during this period from VW, 16 January 1923, Berg, *DVW* II, 226. Dialogue is reconstructed from reported speech.

244 *"insincere-sincere":* Details and quotations from this message are taken from VW, 19 December 1920, Berg, *DVW* II, 80.

*whether, like her, Katherine ever doubted:*VW, 25 August 1920, Berg, *DVW* II, 62.

Katherine replied swiftly: Details from this letter, including quotations, are taken from KM to VW, 27 December 1920, *LKM* IV, 154.

245 *The pair talked about Katherine:* Details of this conversation are drawn from VW, 16 February 1921, *DVW* II, 91.

Katherine had already learned: IB, *LM,* 154.

she put pen to paper: Details of this letter, including quotations, are drawn from VW to KM, 13 February 1921, Smith.

246 *Katherine was finally:* Details of KM's situation during this period are drawn from Georgina Joysmith, editorial note, IB, *LM,* 172; IB, *LM,* 206–9; KM to IB, 5 June 1922, *LKM* V, 193; KM to IB, 14 June 1922, *LKM* V, 201.

247 *"the small lies":*VW, 16 January 1923, Berg, *DVW* II, 227.

the drafting of Jacob's Room:VW, 20 May 1920, *DVW* II, 40.

*"sterile acrobatics":*VW, 14 February 1922, *DVW* II, 161.

*"soars in the newspapers":*VW, 12 March 1922, Berg, *DVW* II, 170–71.

By mid-August: Details in this paragraph are drawn from IB, *LM,* 209.

a mutual friend: Sydney Waterlow to VW, 21 August 1922, quoted in VW, 23 August 1922, *DVW* II, 194, and VW, 22 August 1922, *DVW* II, 192.

Virginia agonized: VW's attitude toward attending the salon, including quotations, are drawn from VW, 22 August 1922, *DVW* II, 192, and VW to Sydney Waterlow, 24 August 1922, *LVW* II, 553.

248 *could start afresh:*VW, 16 January 1923, Berg, *DVW* II, 227.

But the opinions: Details of KM's life at Le Prieuré are largely drawn from IB, *LM,* 211–26.

249 *"Mrs Murry's dead!":*VW's immediate reaction to KM's death is drawn from VW, 16 January 1923, Berg, *DVW* II, 225–27.

Katherine's obituary: "Death of Katherine Mansfield: A Career of Great Literary Promise," *The Times,* 12 January 1923, 6.

250 *"There's no competitor":* VW, 28 January 1923, Berg, *DVW* II, 228.

251 *would have made of them:* VW, 17 October 1924, Berg, *DVW* II, 317; VW to Dorothy Brett, 8 March 1929, *LVW* IV, 32.

may have deeply influenced: For further analysis of KM's influence on VW, see Hilary Newman, *Virginia Woolf and Katherine Mansfield: A Creative Rivalry,* Cecil Woolf, 2004.

"What odd friends": VW to Vita Sackville West, 5 August 1927, *LVW* III, 408.

252 *a matchless genius:* JMM, *Journal,* Introduction; JMM, *The Letters of Katherine Mansfield,* vol. I, Introductory Note, Constable & Co., 1928.

Eight years after Katherine's death: Descriptions of this dream, including quotations, are drawn from VW, 8 June 1931, *DVW* IV, 29.

EPILOGUE: A WEB OF LITERARY CONNECTIONS

253 *George Eliot read:* George Henry Lewes, [11]-18 May 1857, George Henry Lewes diary, Gordon S. Haight (ed.), *The George Eliot Letters,* vol. II, Yale University Press, 1954, 326. This entry mentions George Eliot reading *Emma* and *Sense and Sensibility* to George Henry Lewes while the couple was away from home during the spring of that year. George Eliot's travel journal, written some time after her trip—published in Margaret Harris and Judith Johnston (eds.), *The Journals of George Eliot,* Cambridge University Press 1998, 279—also mentions her reading *Persuasion* and *Northanger Abbey.*

A Room of One's Own: Virginia Woolf, *A Room of One's Own,* Penguin Books, 2012, 75–76, 81–82, 78.

255 *"Villette—Villette":* George Eliot to Cara and Charles Bray, 12 March 1853, Gordon S. Haight (ed.), *The George Eliot Letters,* vol. II, Yale University Press, 92.

marked by mutual distrust: Vera Brittain, *Testament of Friendship: The Story of Winifred Holtby,* Virago, 2012, 106.

repaired only when: Vera Brittain, *Testament of Youth: An Autobiographical Study of the Years 1900–1925,* Virago, 2004, 452.

256 *"travelling companion":* Vera Brittain, *Testament of Friendship: The Story of Winifred Holtby,* Virago, 2012, 130.

person who "made me": Jean E. Kennard, *Vera Brittain and Winifred Holtby: A Working Partnership,* University of New Hampshire by University Press of New England, 1989, xiv. Kennard is quoting from a letter from Winifred to Vera, written on 26 September 1935.

During the summer of 1937: Carol Angier, *Jean Rhys: Life and Work,* Faber & Faber, 2011, 361–62.

257 *continued to write to each other:* All details about the pair's correspondence are drawn from Michela Calderaro, "To be sexless, creedless, classless, free. Eliot Bliss: A Creole Writer," A Goodly Garlande. In onore di Sergio Perosa. Annali di Ca' Foscari, 42.4, 2003, 109–10.

invited Zora to tea the next day: Valerie Boyd, *Wrapped in Rainbows: The Life of Zora Neale Hurston,* Scribner, 2003, 15, 350–51.

refer to Marjorie as a "sister": Carla Kaplin (ed.), *Zora Neale Hurston: A Life in Letters,* Doubleday, 2002, 486.

When Zora visited: Anna Lillios, *Crossing the Creek: The Literary Friendship of Zora Neale Hurston and Marjorie Kinnan Rawlings,* University of Florida Press, 2011, 16–17.

258 *Marjorie subjected herself:* Anna Lillios, *Crossing the Creek: The Literary Friendship of Zora Neale Hurston and Marjorie Kinnan Rawlings,* University of Florida Press, 2011, 27–28.

against racial segregation: Rebecca Sharpless, "Neither Friends nor Peers: Idella Parker, Marjorie Kinnan Rawlings, and the Limits of Gender Solidarity at Cross Creek," *Journal of Southern History,* 1 May 2012, 346.

putting in a good word: Anna Lillios, *Crossing the Creek: The Literary Friendship of Zora Neale Hurston and Marjorie Kinnan Rawlings,* University of Florida Press, 2011, 32.

Jane Austen and Charlotte Brontë: Maya Angelou, *The Collected Autobiographies of Maya Angelou,* Virago, 2007, 75, 119, 123, 164.

find herself sharing the bill: Aisha I Jefferson, "In Conversation: Nikki Giovanni and Maya Angelou on Sisterhood, and Their Friendship with Toni Morrison," *Essence,* 15 February 2013.

Maya threw her a party: "Maya Angelou, Joanne Gabbin, and Nikki Giovanni," *Virginia Tech Videos* [audio], 16 October 2012.

259 *Toni's tribute speech:* "Ms. Toni Morrison presents the Literarian Award to Dr. Maya Angelou," *National Book Foundation* [video].

262 *sleeping on Alice's floor:* "Writers on Munro," *The New Yorker,* 10 October 2013.

formulated a theory: Lisa Allardice, "Nobel Prizewinner Alice Munro: 'It's a Wonderful Thing for the Short Story,'" *Guardian,* 6 December 2013.

heartwarming photograph: This can be seen in the background behind Alice during the video of the pair's "Google hangout," 22 January 2014.

Select Bibliography

In addition to the manuscript sources consulted (detailed in the Notes), the following publications were those most helpful to our research.

JANE AUSTEN & ANNE SHARP

Amy, Helen (ed.), *The Jane Austen Files: A Complete Anthology of Letters and Family Recollections,* Amberley, 2015

Austen, Jane, *Emma,* Penguin Classics, 1996

———, *Lady Susan / The Watsons / Sanditon,* Penguin Classics, 1974

———, *Mansfield Park,* Penguin Classics, 1996

———, *Northanger Abbey,* Penguin Classics, 1995

———, *Persuasion,* Penguin Classics, 1985

———, *Pride and Prejudice,* Penguin Classics, 1996

———, *Sense and Sensibility,* Penguin Classics, 1995

Austen-Leigh, James Edward, *A Memoir of Jane Austen,* Richard Bentley and Son (second edition), 1871

Bugg, John, *Five Long Winters: The Trials of British Romanticism,* Stanford University Press, 2013

Butler, Marilyn, *Jane Austen and the War of Ideas,* Oxford University Press, 2006

Byrne, Paula, *The Real Jane Austen: A Life in Small Things,* HarperPress, 2013

Harman, Claire, *Jane's Fame: How Jane Austen Conquered the World,* Canongate, 2010

Hickman, Peggy, *A Jane Austen Household Book with Martha Lloyd's Recipes,* Readers Union, 1978

Hill, Constance, *Jane Austen: Her Homes & Her Friends,* John Lane, 1902

Honan, Park, *Jane Austen: Her Life,* Weidenfeld & Nicolson, 1987

Kelly, Helena, *Jane Austen: The Secret Radical,* Icon Books, 2016

Lane, Maggie, *Jane Austen and Food,* Endeavour Press, 2013

Le Faye, Deirdre, *A Chronology of Jane Austen and Her Family,* Cambridge University Press (second edition), 2013

——, *Fanny Knight's Diaries: Jane Austen Through Her Niece's Eyes,* The Jane Austen Society, 2000

——, *Jane Austen: A Family Record,* Cambridge University Press (second edition), 2003

—— (ed.), *Jane Austen's Letters,* Oxford University Press (fourth edition), 2014

Nicolson, Nigel, *Godmersham Park: Before, During, and After Jane Austen's Time,* The Jane Austen Society, 1996

Renton, Alice, *Tyrant or Victim: A History of the British Governess,* Weidenfeld & Nicolson, 1991

Sutherland, Kathryn (ed.), *J. E. Austen Leigh: A Memoir of Jane Austen and Other Family Recollections,* Oxford University Press, 2002

Tomalin, Claire, *Jane Austen: A Life,* Penguin Books, 2012

Uglow, Jenny, *In These Times: Living in Britain Through Napoleon's Wars, 1793–1815,* Faber & Faber, 2014

CHARLOTTE BRONTË & MARY TAYLOR

Alexander, Christine (ed.), *Tales of Glass Town, Angria, and Gondal: Selected Writings,* Oxford University Press, 2010

Barker, Juliet, *The Brontës,* Abacus, 2010

Bellamy, Joan, *"More Precious Than Rubies" Mary Taylor: Friend of Charlotte Brontë, Strong-Minded Woman,* Highgate Publications, 2002

Brontë, Charlotte, *Jane Eyre,* Penguin Classics, 2006

——, *The Professor,* Penguin Classics, 1989

——, *Shirley,* Penguin Classics, 2006

——, *Villette,* Penguin Classics, 1985

Chapple, J. A. V., and Arthur Pollard (eds.), *The Letters of Mrs Gaskell,* Manchester University Press, 1966

Fraser, Rebecca, *Charlotte Brontë,* Methuen, 1988

Gaskell, Elizabeth, *The Life of Charlotte Brontë,* Penguin Classics, 1997 [based on the text of the first edition]

———, *The Life of Charlotte Brontë,* Oxford University Press, 2009 [based on the text of the third edition]

Gérin, Winifred, *Charlotte Brontë: The Evolution of Genius,* Clarendon Press, 1967

Gordon, Lyndall, *Charlotte Brontë: A Passionate Life,* Chatto & Windus, 1994

Harman, Claire, *Charlotte Brontë: A Life,* Viking, 2015

Macdonald, Frederika, *The Secret of Charlotte Brontë: Followed by Some Reminiscences of the Real Monsieur and Madame Heger,* T. C. and E. C. Jack, 1914

MacEwan, Helen, *The Brontës in Brussels,* Peter Owen, 2014

Shorter, Clement K., *Charlotte Brontë and Her Circle,* Dodd Mead and Company, 1896

Smith, Margaret (ed.), *The Letters of Charlotte Brontë, with a Selection of Letters by Family and Friends,* Clarendon Press, vols. I–III, 1995–2004

Stevens, Joan (ed.), *Mary Taylor, Friend of Charlotte Brontë: Letters from New Zealand and Elsewhere,* Auckland University Press, 1972

Taylor, Mary, *The First Duty of Women. A Series of Articles Reprinted from the Victoria Magazine, 1865 to 1870,* General Books, 2012

———, *Miss Miles, or A Tale of Yorkshire Life 60 Years Ago,* Oxford University Press, 1990

———, *Swiss Notes by Five Ladies,* Inchbold & Beck, 1875

Whitehead, Barbara, *Charlotte Brontë and Her "dearest Nell": The Story of a Friendship,* Smith Settle, 1993

Wise, Thomas James, and John Alexander Symington, *The Shakespeare Head Brontë, The Brontës: Their Lives, Friendships & Correspondence in Four Volumes,* Shakespeare Head Press, 1932

GEORGE ELIOT & HARRIET BEECHER STOWE

Ashton, Rosemary, *George Eliot: A Life,* Hamish Hamilton, 1996

Belasco, Susan (ed.), *Stowe in Her Own Time: A Biographical Chronicle of Her Life, Drawn from Recollections, Interviews, and Memoirs by Family, Friends, and Associates,* University of Iowa Press, 2009

Blind, Mathilde, *George Eliot,* W. H. Allen, 1888

Bodenheimer, Rosemarie, *The Real Life of Mary Ann Evans: George Eliot, Her Letters and Fiction,* Cornell University Press, 1994

Cognard-Black, Jennifer, *Narrative in the Professional Age: Transatlantic Readings of Harriet Beecher Stowe, George Eliot, and Elizabeth Stuart Phelps,* Taylor & Francis, 2004

———, and Elizabeth MacLeod Walls (eds.), *Kindred Hands: Letters on Writing by British and American Women Authors, 1865–1935,* University of Iowa Press, 2006

Cross, J.W. (ed.), *George Eliot's Life as Related in Her Letters and Journals,* vols. I–III, William Blackwood and Sons, 1885

Edel, Leon (ed.), *Henry James Letters,* vol. I, 1843–1875, Macmillan, 1974

Eliot, George, *Adam Bede,* Penguin Classics, 2008

———, *Daniel Deronda,* Penguin Classics, 1995

———, *Middlemarch,* Penguin Classics, 2003

———, *Romola,* Penguin Classics, 1997

———, *Silly Novels by Lady Novelists,* Penguin Books, 2010

———, *The Spanish Gypsy,* Pickering & Chatto, 2008

Fields, Annie (ed.), *Life and Letters of Harriet Beecher Stowe,* Houghton Mifflin and Company, 1898

Haight, Gordon S., *George Eliot: A Biography,* Oxford University Press, 1969

——— (ed.), *George Eliot & John Chapman: With Chapman's Diaries* (second edition), Archon Books, 1969

——— (ed.), *The George Eliot Letters,* Yale University Press, vols. I–VIII, 1954–78

Harris, Margaret, and Judith Johnston, *The Journals of George Eliot,* Cambridge University Press, 1998

Hedrick, Joan D., *Harriet Beecher Stowe: A Life,* Oxford University Press, 1994

Henry, Nancy, *The Life of George Eliot: A Critical Biography,* Wiley-Blackwell, 2012

Hughes, Kathryn, *George Eliot: The Last Victorian,* Fourth Estate, 1999

James, Henry, *The Middle Years,* W. Collins Sons & Co., 1917

Kohn, Denise, Sarah Meer, and Emily B. Todd, *Transatlantic Stowe: Harriet Beecher Stowe and European Culture,* University of Iowa Press, 2006

McCormack, Kathleen, *George Eliot in Society: Travels Abroad and Sundays at the Priory,* Ohio State University Press, 2013

Spencer, Herbert, *An Autobiography,* vol. I, Williams and Norgate, 1904

Stowe, Charles Edward, *Life of Harriet Beecher Stowe: Compiled from Her Letters and Journals,* Sampson Low, Marston, Searle & Rivington, 1889

Stowe, Harriet Beecher, *A Key to Uncle Tom's Cabin; presenting the original facts and documents upon which the story is founded together with collaborative statements verifying the truth of the work* (second edition), Sampson Low, Son & Co., 1853

————, *Lady Byron Vindicated,* Sampson Low, Son & Marston, 1870

————, *Oldtown Folks,* Harvard University Press, 1966

————, *Sunny Memories of Foreign Lands,* Routledge, 1854

————, *Uncle Tom's Cabin; or, Life Among the Lowly,* Penguin Classics, 1981

Uglow, Jenny, *George Eliot,* Virago Press, 2011

Wilson, Forest, *Crusader in Crinoline: The Life of Harriet Beecher Stowe,* J. B. Lippincott, 1941

KATHERINE MANSFIELD & VIRGINIA WOOLF

Baker, Ida, *Katherine Mansfield: The Memories of LM,* Michael Joseph, 1971

Bell, Anne Olivier (ed.), *The Diary of Virginia Woolf,* vol. I, 1915–19, The Hogarth Press, 1983

————, with Andrew McNeillie, *The Diary of Virginia Woolf,* vols. II–V, 1920–41, The Hogarth Press, 1978–84

Dubino, Jeanne, *Virginia Woolf and the Literary Marketplace,* Palgrave Macmillan, 2010

Hankin, Cherry A. (ed.), *Letters Between Katherine Mansfield and John Middleton Murry,* Virago Press, 1988

————, *The Letters of John Middleton Murry to Katherine Mansfield,* Constable, 1983

Jones, Kathleen, *Katherine Mansfield: The Story-Teller,* The Book Mill, 2012

Kimber, Gerri, and Vincent O'Sullivan (eds.), *The Collected Works, Volume 2: The Collected Fiction of Katherine Mansfield, 1916–1922,* Edinburgh University Press, 2012

————, and Angela Smith (eds.), *The Collected Works, Volume 3: The Poetry and Critical Writings of Katherine Mansfield,* Edinburgh University Press, 2014

————, and Claire Davison with Anna Plumridge (eds.), *The Collected Works, Volume 4: The Diaries of Katherine Mansfield Including Miscellaneous Works,* Edinburgh University Press, 2016.

Lea, F. A., *The Life of John Middleton Murry,* Methuen, 1959

Lee, Hermione, *Virginia Woolf,* Vintage, 1997

Levy, Paul (ed.), *The Letters of Lytton Strachey,* Viking, 2005

Light, Alison, *Mrs Woolf and the Servants,* Penguin Books, 2008

Love, Jean O., *Virginia Woolf: Sources of Madness and Art,* University of California Press, 1978

Mansfield, Katherine, *The Collected Stories of Katherine Mansfield,* Penguin Classics, 2007

Meyers, Jeffrey, *Katherine Mansfield: A Darker View,* Cooper Square, 2002

Middleton Murry, John (ed.), *Journal of Katherine Mansfield*, Persephone Books, 2006

Morrell, Ottoline, *Ottoline at Garsington: Memoirs of Lady Ottoline Morrell, 1915–1918*, Faber & Faber, 1974

Newman, Hilary, *Virginia Woolf and Katherine Mansfield: A Creative Rivalry*, Cecil Woolf, 2004

Nicolson, Nigel, with Joanne Trautmann, *The Letters of Virginia Woolf*, vols. II–IV, 1912–31, The Hogarth Press, 1976–78

Noble, Joan Russell (ed.), *Recollections of Virginia Woolf*, Peter Owen, 1972

Norburn, Roger, *A Katherine Mansfield Chronology*, Palgrave Macmillan, 2008

Orton, William, *The Last Romantic*, Cassell & Co., 1937

O'Sullivan, Vincent, and Margaret Scott (eds.), *The Collected Letters of Katherine Mansfield*, vols. I–IV, Clarendon Press, 1984–96

Schulkind, Jeanne (ed.), *Moments of Being*, Pimlico, 2002

Tomalin, Claire, *Katherine Mansfield: A Secret Life*, Penguin, 2003

Woolf, Leonard, *Beginning Again: An Autobiography of the Years 1911 to 1918*, Harvest/Harcourt Brace Jovanovich, 1975

Woolf, Virginia, *Jacob's Room*, Penguin Classics, 1992

———, *Mrs Dalloway*, Penguin Classics, 2000

———, *Night and Day*, Penguin Classics, 1992

———, *Selected Short Stories*, Penguin Classics, 2000

———, *To the Lighthouse*, Penguin Classics, 2000

EPILOGUE: A WEB OF LITERARY CONNECTIONS

Angelou, Maya, *The Collected Autobiographies of Maya Angelou*, Virago, 2007

Angier, Carol, *Jean Rhys: Life and Work*, Faber & Faber, 2011

Boyd, Valerie, *Wrapped in Rainbows: The Life of Zora Neale Hurston*, Scribner, 2003

Brittain, Vera, *Testament of Friendship: The Story of Winifred Holtby*, Virago, 2012

———, *Testament of Youth: An Autobiographical Study of the Years 1900–1925*, Virago, 2004

Grayling, A. C., *Friendship*, Yale University Press, 2013

Hurston, Zora Neale, *Their Eyes Were Watching God*, Virago, 1992

Kaplin, Carla (ed.), *Zora Neale Hurston: A Life in Letters*, Doubleday, 2002

Kennard, Jean E., *Vera Brittain and Winifred Holtby: A Working Partnership*, University of New Hampshire by University Press of New England, 1989

Lillios, Anna, *Crossing the Creek: The Literary Friendship of Zora Neale Hurston and Marjorie Kinnan Rawlings,* University of Florida Press, 2011

Morrison, Toni, *Beloved,* Vintage, 1997

Rhys, Jean, *Wide Sargasso Sea,* Penguin Modern Classics, 2000

Woolf, Virginia, *A Room of One's Own,* Penguin Books, 2012

Yalom, Marilyn, with Theresa Donovan Brown, *The Social Sex: A History of Female Friendship,* Harper Perennial, 2015

Index

Adam Bede (Eliot), 132, 163

Agnes Grey (Brontë), 104, 107

"Alfred" (play), 37

Angelou, Maya, 258–60

Angria (fictional kingdom), 76

Asheham House, 198–200, 213,
214–15, 227, 239

The Athenaeum
on Brontë, 104
luncheon at, 242
Mansfield in, 238, 244
Murry at, 228, 229
review of *Night and Day* in,
235–38
Woolf stories for, 239

Atlantic Monthly, 132–33, 135. *See also*
"The True Story of Lady
Byron's Life" (Stowe)
on *Daniel Deronda,* 180
Stowe's Byron article in,
141–46

Atwood, Margaret, 261–62

Austen, Anna, 25–27

Austen, Cassandra (mother), 13, 16–17,
42–43, 45

Austen, Cassandra (sister), 42
at Chawton, 42
at Godmersham, 23–24
jealousy of Sharp, 5, 45, 58–59
letters destroyed by, 4
reserve of, 19
sketch of Jane by, 3
in theatricals at Godmersham,
25–27

Austen, Charles (nephew), 11

Austen, Edward (brother)
holiday taken by, 36
lack of generosity of, 9–10, 16–17,
21, 30, 41
responsibilities of, 11, 33
on seaside holiday, 29–30
on Sharp's health, 19
wealthy lifestyle of, 8–10

Austen, Edward (nephew), 11

Austen, Elizabeth (sister-in-law), 8–9
  death of, 42
  on education, 11, 30
  holiday taken by, 36
  illness of, 28
  opinion of Jane of, 10–11
Austen, Fanny
  on arrival of Sharp, 6
  diaries of, 5–8
  gift for Sharp by, 33
  illness of, 28
  letters destroyed by, 4
  in plays at Godmersham, 25–27,
    36–38
  portrait of, 34–35
  routine of, with Sharp, 11–12
  on Sharp and Austen, 18
  on Sharp's departure, 38–39
Austen, Frank, 41
Austen, George (father), 13–14
  death of, 16–17
Austen, George (nephew), 11
Austen, Henry (brother), 44, 51–52
Austen, Henry (nephew), 11
Austen, Jane. *See also* Sharp, Anne
  anonymous publication by, 46–47
  Brontë on, 111–12
  at Chawton, 42
  clothing of, 7, 19–20
  correspondence with Sharp, 41–42
  on *Douglas,* 37
  father's death and, 16–17
  father's literary support for, 13–14
  George IV and, 52–54
  at Godmersham, 23–24, 28–29
  on the Godmersham lifestyle,
    9–11
  on her sister-in-law, 42

illness and death of, 57–58
impoverishment of, 16–18, 21,
    24–25
letters of, destroyed, 4
Mansfield on, 235
moves of, in Bath, 13, 14, 17, 18–19,
    24–25, 39
move to Chawton, 44–46
move to Southampton, 41
personality of, real vs. portrayed,
    3–4
as poor relation, 7
portraits of, 3, 34, 52, 53
presentation copies given by,
    54–57
prioritization of writing over ro-
    mance by, 16
profits of, 47
publishing efforts of, 13–14, 16,
    24–25, 44, 46–47, 51–52
on schools, 20–21
seaside holiday of, 29–32
shared literary ambitions of with
    Sharp, 5
on Sharp's health, 56–57
success of, 49–52
in theatricals at Godmersham,
    25–27
time for writing, 13, 24–25, 31–32,
    43
trip to London, 47–49
value placed on friendship with
    Sharp, 27
Woolf on, 235, 253–54
Austen, Lizzy (niece), 11
Austen, Louisa (niece), 11
Austen, Marianne (niece), 11
Austen, William (nephew), 11, 37

Austen-Leigh, James Edward
    (nephew), 3, 30, 112

Bailey, Miss, 41, 43
Baker, Ida Constance, 203–4, 210–11,
    224–25, 228
    in France, 207, 208–9, 243–44
    living situations of, 215
    Mansfield's animosity toward, 209
    Mansfield's death and, 249
    Mansfield's dependence on, 208–9
    Mansfield's relationship with,
        220–22
    move to Hampstead, 222
Battle of Passchendaele, 196
Battle of Trafalgar, 34
Battle of Waterloo, 51, 72
Beauchamp, Leslie Heron, 200, 223
Bell, Acton. *See* Brontë, Anne
Bell, Currer. *See* Brontë, Charlotte
Bell, Ellis. *See* Brontë, Emily
Bell, Vanessa, 227
Bendall, Edith, 220
Bennet, Elizabeth (character), 47,
    48–49
Bibesco, Elizabeth, Princess, 245
Blackwood's, 162
Bliss, Eliot, 256–57
"Bliss" (Mansfield), 208, 209, 211–13,
    217–18
Bliss and Other Stories (Mansfield),
    232, 241, 242–43, 244
Bloomsbury group, 194–96, 206
Bloomsbury Memoir Club, 218
Bonaparte, Napoleon, 11, 72
Boxall, Nellie, 190, 213–14, 216, 249
Brabant, Robert, 157
Branwell, Elizabeth, 83–85, 92–93

Brett, Dorothy, 247, 248
Brighton Pavilion, 31
Brittain, Vera, 255–56, 260
Brontë, Anne, 66, 93
    as governess, 101
    illness and death of, 111
    success of, 104
Brontë, Branwell, 66, 78, 93, 106–7
Brontë, Charlotte
    appearance of, 65–66, 67–68, 87,
        114
    arguments with Taylor, 72
    bed shared with Nussey and,
        68–69, 72–73
    in Belgium, 84, 86–100
    challenged by Taylor, 77–78
    creative childhood of, 66–67
    death of Aunt Branwell, 92–93
    education of, 66–67
    family demands on, 101, 106–8, 110,
        119–20, 254
    family ties vs. friendships of, 70,
        78, 93
    feelings of, for Heger, 90–91, 96,
        99, 102
    financial situation of, 85
    Gaskell on, 68, 122–24, 158
    Gaskell's friendship with, 113–14,
        117
    Glass Town stories, 66, 76
    as governess, 81–82
    on her father's decline, 100–101
    illness and death of, 121–22
    inner strength of, 79–80
    inspired by Taylor, 74–75, 77, 82–83
    intelligence of, 70
    isolation of, 95–100
    journey to Roe Head, 63–65

Brontë, Charlotte (*cont.*)
  at Lake Windermere, 112–14
  letters of, destroyed, 96
  letter to Southey, 78–79
  literary friendships of, 111–12
  in London, 86–87
  marriage of, 118–22, 162
  mythology about, 123–25
  personality of, 65–66, 72, 114
  plan to go to Europe, 83–85
  political interests of, 70, 108–9
  portrait of, 112
  proposals to, 117–18
  prospects of, 64
  publishing efforts of, 104–5
  quarrel with Nussey, 85, 89–90
  return to Belgium, 94–96
  return to Haworth, 100–101
  romantic friendship with Nussey,
    73–74
  on spinsterhood, 104, 117–18
  Stowe's contact with the spirit of,
    164–65, 166
  support for literary aspirations of,
    78–79
  talents of, 67
  as teacher at Heger-Parent, 91–92
  as teacher at Roe Head, 74–78
  vegetarianism of, 67
  visit to Gomersal, 101–2
  Woolf on, 253–54
Brontë, Elizabeth, 64, 92
Brontë, Emily, 64, 66
  appearance of, 87
  in Belgium, 84, 86–87
  death of, 116–17
  death of Aunt Branwell, 92–93
  illness and death of, 107, 109

  return to Haworth, 92–94
  at Roe Head, 75
  success of, 104, 106–7
  as teacher at Heger-Parent, 91–92
Brontë, Maria, 64, 92
Brontë, Patrick, 83
  on Charlotte's death, 122
  on Charlotte's marriage, 119, 120
  decline of, 100–101
  demands of, 106, 110, 119, 120
  education of his children, 64, 66
  Gaskell on, 114
  trip to Belgium, 86–87
Brookroyd, 81
"Brother and Sister" (Eliot), 146
Browning, Robert, 138
Byron, Anne Isabella, Lady, 141
Byron, George Gordon, Lord, 140–46,
  217

Cadell, Thomas, 13–14
Cadell and Davies, 13–14
Cage, Fanny, 25–27
Carlton House, 52–54
Chambers Edinburgh Journal, 110
Chapman, Dorothy, 32–33, 38–39
Chapman, John, 157–58, 161
Charleston Daily News, 172
Château de Koekelberg, 85, 87
  Brontës' visit to, 88–89
Chawton Cottage, 42, 44–46, 51, 59
Chevet Hall, 46
cholera, 91–92
Clarke, James Stanier, 52–54
Clergy Daughters' School, 63–64
Colbourne, Miss, 20–21
Collyer's stagecoach, 45
Conrad, Joseph, 217, 229

Constable & Co., 210, 241
Corbould, Edward Henry, 132
Creaghe-Howard, Mrs., 60
The Critic, 104
Critical Review, 47, 48
Crosby, Benjamin, 14
Crosby & Co., 14, 16
Cross, John Walter, 183, 184, 230
Crow, Miss, 34–35

Daily Lady's Companion, 38
Daniel Deronda (Eliot), 178–79, 180–81
*The Debatable Land Between This World
    and the Next* (Owen), 169
Dickens, Charles, 132, 138
Dixon, Mary, 96
Don Juan (Byron), 217
Dostoyevsky, Fyodor, 229
Douglas (play), 37
Duckworth, George, 218–19
Duckworth, Gerald, 193, 218
Duke of Wellington, 51, 72

Edgeworth, Maria, 46, 55
electrotherapy, 43–44
Eliot, George
    admiration of Stowe, 153–54,
        178–79
    appearance of, 139, 155–56, 159
    on Austen, 253
    belief in Stowe, 153–54
    biographical revisionism on, 158,
        183–84
    Bliss inspired by, 256
    Calvin Stowe's notes to, 162–64
    collected correspondence of, 143
    common ground with Stowe,
        136–37

conciliatory letters from, 173–74
courtships and proposals to, 156–59
death of, 183
death of Lewes and, 181–82
education of, 155–56
friendship with Stowe, 254–55
gaps in correspondence with
        Stowe, 167
health of, 152, 174
influence of, 136
Jewish stereotypes by, 180–81
on Lewes compared with
        Casaubon, 175–77, 178
on *Oldtown Folks,* 142–43
personality and temperament of,
        136–37, 139
portraits of, 159
the Priory and, 129–31, 138–39
professional identity of, 191–92
profits of, 130, 132
relationship with Lewes, 129–30,
        133, 134, 161–62
social norms ignored by, 157, 161–62
social ostracism of, 129–30, 133, 145,
        161–62, 254
sonnets by, 146
on spiritualism, 165–66, 173
stepson's death and, 147–48, 150,
        167, 168–69
stepson's illness and, 137–38,
        139–40, 143, 146, 147–48
Stowe's admiration of, 132
on Stowe's Byron article, 144–46,
        150–51, 172
success of, 162
Sunday afternoon gatherings of,
        138–39
Surrey home of, 181

Eliot, George (*cont.*)
　tone of correspondence with
　　Stowe, 166–67, 172–73
　on *Uncle Tom's Cabin,* 155
　Woolf essay on, 230, 237–38
　Woolf on, 253–54
　on writing, 140
Eminent Victorians (Strachey), 187
Emma (Austen), 51–52
　presentation copies of, 54–57, 60
English Review, 211–12, 213, 216
Evans, Marian. *See* Eliot, George
Evans, Robert, 155–56
Evenings at Home, 37

Fergusson, John Duncan, 204–5
Fields, Annie Adams, 132–33, 177
Fields, James T., 132–33, 177, 183–84
First Impressions (Austen). See *Pride
　and Prejudice* (Austen)
Fitzgerald, F. Scott, 258
Florida Normal and Industrial
　College, 257
Follen, Eliza Lee Cabot, 153–54, 155,
　159
*Footfalls on the Boundary of Another
　World* (Owen), 169
Forster, E. M., 246
friendship, 4–5
　of literary women, 253–63
　male literary, 255, 258
　romantic, 73–74
Friendship Book (Clarke), 52, 53

The Garden Party (Mansfield), 247
Garsington Manor, 187–88, 214
　garden story concept about,
　　196–98, 199–201

Gaskell, Elizabeth
　Brontë biography by, 68, 93,
　　122–24, 254
　on Brontë's marriage, 121
　on Eliot, 133
　friendship with Brontë, 113–14,
　　117
George Eliot's Life (Cross), 184
George IV, 31, 52–54
Glass Town saga, 66, 76, 94
Godmersham Park
　library of, 6–7
　portrait painter at, 34–35
　Sharp's arrival at, 5–6
　staff turnover at, 15
　the "Wilderness" at, 12
Goethe, Johann Wolfgang von,
　　163
Gondal saga, 94
Goodnestone Park, 8
governesses
　Brontë as, 81–82, 84–85
　Sharp as, 5–8
　status of, 7
Great Reform Act of 1832, 178
Guiccioli, Teresa, Countess, 141–42
Gurdjieff, George, 248–49

Haight, Gordon S., 132
Hallé, Charles, 100
Halle, Friedrich, 100
Harpers Weekly, 170, 171
Hartford Female Seminary, 156
Haworth Parsonage, 63
　Charlotte and Emily's return to, 93,
　　100–101
　creative atmosphere in, 66
　school at, 82, 101

Heger-Parents, Claire Zoë and
    Constantin, 85–86, 93–94
  Brontë's relationship with, 90–91,
    96, 99, 100, 102, 123
  Brontë writings based on, 104–5
  descriptions of, 88
Heinemann, William, 229, 232
Hemingway, Ernest, 258
Henry W. and Albert A. Berg
    Collection, 143
Heron Press, 223–24, 228, 229
HMS *Fly*, 106
Hogarth House, 190, 200, 235
  Murry published by, 223–24, 234
Hogarth Press, 188–89, 229
  Kew Gardens, 231–33
  Mansfield published by, 192, 202,
    204–6
  subscription method of, 210
  success of, 209
  Woolf published by, 248
Holmes, Oliver Wendell, 142, 149
Holtby, Winifred, 255–56, 260
Hope, Lottie, 190, 213–14, 216
Hôtel Beau Rivage, 208
Huard, Monsieur, 89
Hunt, Thornton Leigh, 161
Hurston, Zora Neale, 257–58
Huxley, Aldous, 203

I Know Why the Caged Bird Sings
    (Angelou), 258
Institute for the Harmonious
    Development of Man, 249

Jacob's Room (Woolf), 241, 247–48
James, Henry
  on *Daniel Deronda,* 180

Mansfield and Woolf on, 203
  at the Priory, 138–39
Jane Eyre (Brontë), 63–64, 105
  inspirations for, 71, 115
  reviews of, 108–9
Je ne parle pas français (Mansfield),
    240–41
Journal of Katherine Mansfield, 251–52

Kay-Shuttleworth, James, Sir, 112–14,
    124
Kay-Shuttleworth, Janet, Lady,
    112–14, 124
Kew Gardens (Woolf), 231–33
"Kew Gardens" (Woolf), 198, 199
  Mansfield on, 201
A Key to Uncle Tom's Cabin (Stowe),
    149–50
Knight, Catherine, 28–29
Knight, Thomas, 8–9

Lady Byron Vindicated (Stowe), 151–52,
    172
Lady Susan (Austen), 32
Lascelles, Mr., 35–36
Lee, Amelia, 130
Lee, Grace, 130
lesbianism, 217, 220–22, 224, 225
Lewes, Agnes, 161–62
Lewes, George Henry, 167
  Brontë and, 111–12
  Eliot's correspondence vetted by,
    168
  on Gaskell's biography of Brontë,
    124
  health of, 174
  illness and death of, 181–82
  marriage of, 133, 161–62

Lewes, George Henry (*cont.*)
    relationship with Eliot, 129–30
    on *Shirley*, 115
    on spiritualism, 166
    stepson of, 137–38
    Stowe on, 175–76
    Surrey home of, 181
    Woolf on, 230
Lewes, Thornie
    death of, 148
    Eliot on the death of, 150
    illness of, 137–38, 139–40, 144, 146,
        147–48
The Life of Charlotte Brontë (Gaskell),
        122–24, 165
    on Heger, 158
Lincoln, Abraham, 131
Lloyd, Martha, 20, 39
    at Chawton, 42
    jealousy of Sharp, 45
    move to Bath, 21
    seaside holiday of, 30–31

Macmillan's, 143
Mahupuku, Maata, 220
Mandarin, Florida, 134, 169–70,
        171–72, 174, 179–80
Mansfield, Katherine
    appearance of, 231
    biography of, 251–52
    brother's death and, 200
    character of, 187, 207, 231, 239
    Christmas of 1918, 227–28
    connection with Woolf, 241–42,
        243–45
    conversational style of, 191, 193
    death of, 248–49
    desire for creative ally, 193–94

    envy of the Woolfs' homes, 211, 215
    in France, 207–11, 243–47, 248–49
    garden story concept of, 196–98,
        199–201, 232
    on the Garsington gardens, 196–98,
        199–201
    health issues of, 198–99, 207–8,
        210–11, 214, 220, 222–23,
        228–29, 234, 238, 243–44, 246,
        248–49
    at Hogarth House, 192–93
    Hogarth Press publications, 192,
        202, 204–6
    in Italy, 234
    journalism by, 216
    on *Kew Gardens*, 232–34, 239
    lack of response from, 228–29
    as literary outsider, 191
    literary productivity of, 208–9,
        244–45, 246
    literary successes of, 199–200
    marriage of, 213
    meeting with Woolf, 187–88
    move to Hampstead, 222
    on *Night and Day*, 235–38, 240
    obituary of, 249–50
    personality of, 193
    praise for, 246
    relationship with Baker, 203–4,
        225
    relationship with Murry, 219–20
    resentment of, 232, 233–34, 237,
        240–41
    return to London, 247
    rivalry with Woolf, 188, 206, 251
    self-protection by, 202
    sexual history of, 193, 195–96,
        201–2, 219–21

sexuality of, 220–21, 225
short stories by, 229, 237
social ostracism of, 230
studio of, 189–92
success of, 238, 240–41
visits between Woolf and, 194
visit to Asheham, 198–200, 213,
    214–15
on the war, 237
on Woolf's fragility, 218
Woolf's snide remarks about,
    194–96, 200–202, 204
Mansfield Park (Austen), 37, 50–51, 52
Mary Barton (Gaskell), 113
A Memoir of Jane Austen, 3, 5
Middlemarch (Eliot), 132, 148, 152–53
Eliot's attitude toward, 170–71
Stowe on, 170, 171, 174–78
Midorikawa, Emily, xiv–xvi, 260–61
Military Library Whitehall, 44
Milles, Molly, 28–29
Miss Miles (Taylor), 89, 125–26
Morrell, Ottoline, 197–98, 204, 215,
    218
Morrison, Toni, 258–60
Mrs. Dalloway (Woolf), 212, 251
"Mrs. Dalloway in Bond Street"
    (Woolf), 248
Munro, Alice, 262
Murray, John, 51–52, 54
Murry, John Middleton, 190, 201–2,
    205, 243
affair of, 245, 246
at Asheham, 213, 214
autobiographical novel by, 210
at Hogarth House, 192–93, 235–36
journalism by, 216
Mansfield biography by, 251–52

Mansfield on being let down by,
    241
Mansfield's death and, 249, 250
marriage of, 213
move to Hampstead, 222
on *Night and Day,* 236
physical aversion to Mansfield,
    220–21
poetry by, 223–24, 234
printing press of, 209–10, 223–24,
    228
self-absorption of, 203
in the War Office, 207
My Recollections of Lord Byron
    (Guiccioli), 141–42

The Nation, 172
Nelson, Horatio, 34
New Age, 200
New York Public Library, 143
New York Sun, 172
Nicholls, Arthur Bell, 118–22, 124, 162
Night and Day (Woolf), 204, 227, 230,
    234, 235–38, 241
Nightingale, Florence, 121
"Night-Scented Stock" (Mansfield),
    199–200, 232
Northanger Abbey (Austen), 14, 16, 55
Nussey, Ellen, 68–69
background of, 71
bed shared with Brontë, 68, 72–73
Brontë biography by, 125
Brontë's death and, 122
at Brontë's wedding, 120–21
at Brookroyd, 81
comfort from, 76
decline of friendship with
    Taylor, 125

Nussey, Ellen (*cont.*)
  intelligence of, 70
  Mary's letters to, from Belgium,
    88–90
  Nicholls on letters to, 162
  portrait of, 68
  quarrels with, 85, 89–90
  on spinsterhood, 120
  as third wheel, 84, 85
  on trip to Belgium, 96
  visit to Gomersal, 101–2

Oldtown Folks (Stowe), 135–36,
    140–41
  Eliot on, 142–43
Owen, Robert Dale, 169

Paget, James, 140
Pamela (Richardson), 108
Pensionnat de Demoiselles Heger-
    Parent, 85–89, 90–91
  Brontë as teacher at, 95–100
  Brontës' adjustment to, 90–91
  in *Villette,* 88
Persuasion (Austen), 55
Pilkington, Lady, 46, 59
Pilkington, William, 49
Prelude (Mansfield), 202–3, 232, 240
  reviews of, 206
  typeset by Woolf, 204–6
Pride and Prejudice (Austen), 13–14, 38,
    44, 47, 52
  Brontë on, 112
  portrait of Elizabeth Bennet and,
    47, 48–49
  reviews of, 48, 50
Pride Punished or Innocence Rewarded
    (Sharp), 38

Priory, 129–31
  Sunday afternoons at, 138–39
  Thornie's illness and upheaval at,
    144, 147–48
The Professor (Brontë), 104–5, 115

Quarterly Review, 108–9

Raikes, Mrs., 41
Rawlings, Marjorie Kinnan, 257–58
Red House, Gomersal, 71–72, 77,
    101–2
Reform Bill of 1831, 70
Rhys, Jean, 256–57
Richardson, Dorothy, 229
Richardson, Samuel, 108
rivalry
  between Austen and Sharp, 49
  benefits of female, 259–60
  between Brontë and Taylor, 70–71,
    73
  between Woolf and Mansfield, 188,
    224, 251, 252, 255
Roe Head School, 66–70
  Brontë as teacher at, 74–78,
    95–96
  journey from Haworth to, 63–65
Romola (Eliot), 132
A Room of One's Own (Woolf),
    253–54
Royal Academy Exhibition Room,
    48–49
Russell, Bertrand, 195
Ruth (Gaskell), 117
Rydings, 71

Sackree, Susannah, 15
Sackville-West, Vita, 224, 251

Semi-Colon Club, 160
Sense and Sensibility (Austen), 10, 17,
   43, 44, 46–47, 52
   reviews of, 47, 50
seton stitch, 35–36, 43
sexuality
   in "Bliss," 216–18, 219
   Brontë and Nussey and, 73–74
   of Mansfield, 193, 195–96, 201–2,
      220–21, 224
   of Woolf, 193, 217, 224, 251
Sharp, Anne
   appearance of, 8, 29
   arrival of, at Godmersham, 5–7
   attempts to replace as governess,
      32–33
   Austen's death and, 58–59
   Austen's search for employment
      for, 21–23
   background of concealed, 24,
      59–60
   boarding school of, 59–60
   correspondence with Austen,
      41–42
   departure of, from Godmersham,
      39–40
   duties of, 18–19
   employment at Chevet Hall, 46
   employment at Godmersham ter-
      minated, 38–39
   family's secrecy about, 4–5
   friendship with Austen, 18–19
   on the Godmersham lifestyle, 9–10
   health problems of, 8, 14–15, 19,
      33–36, 43–44, 56–57
   literary support for, 39
   loss of family, 7–8
   on *Mansfield Park,* 50–51

omission of, 254
operation on, 35–36
plays put on by, 25–27, 36–38
portrait of, 34–35
presentation copy of *Emma* to,
   55–56, 60
relationship with Austen
   children, 11
routine of, with Fanny, 11–12
seaside holiday of, 29–32
sent to Bath, 18–19
time for writing, 12–13, 31–32
value placed on friendship with
   Austen, 28
visit to Chawton, 44–46, 59
Sharpe, Elizabeth, 8
Shirley (Brontë), 111, 113
   Taylor family as inspiration for,
      115–16
   Taylor on, 114–15
Snowe, Lucy, 86
Southey, Robert, 78–79
The Spanish Gypsy (Eliot), 134–35, 138
Spencer, Herbert, 158–59
spinsterhood
   Brontë and, 103–4, 117–18
   Eliot and, 156–59
   Nussey on, 120
   Stowe and, 156
spiritualism, 135–36
   Calvin Stowe and, 163–64
   Stowe and, 163–66, 169, 174
Stanton, Elizabeth Cady, 149
Steventon Rectory, 13
St. Gudule's Catholic church, 97–99
Stowe, Calvin Ellis, 154, 159–60
   decline of, 182
   on ghosts, 163–64

Stowe, Calvin Ellis (*cont.*)
  notes of, to Eliot, 162–64
  Stowe on, 175–76
Stowe, Catherine, 156
Stowe, Charles Edward, 154–55,
  184
Stowe, Fred, 171–72
Stowe, Harriet Beecher
  appearance of, 155, 156, 159
  on biography of Eliot, 183–84
  collected correspondence of, 143
  common ground with Eliot,
    136–37
  courtship of, and husband of,
    159–60
  on *Daniel Deronda,* 179, 180–81
  defense of *Uncle Tom's Cabin* by,
    149–50
  education of, 156
  on Eliot and Lewes's relationship,
    133–34, 162, 184
  Eliot's books read by, 133–34
  on Eliot's works, 134–35
  faith of, 154
  fame of, 153
  first letter to Eliot, 131–36
  on Florida, 134, 169–70, 171–72,
    174, 179–80
  friendship with Eliot, 254–55
  gaps in correspondence with El-
    iot, 167
  on husbands, 175–76
  lack of response from, 167–69,
    172–73
  on Lord Byron, 140–46, 148–51,
    172
  marriage of, 159–60
  on *Middlemarch,* 170, 171, 174–78
  motivation for friendship with
    Eliot, 134, 135–36
  personality and temperament of,
    136–37
  physical collapse of, 144
  portraits of, 159
  pregnancies of, 160
  retreat from painful memories by,
    182
  as schoolmistress, 156
  sons' deaths and, 154–55, 172–73
  son's disappearance and, 171–72
  son's illness and, 143, 150
  spirit contact with Brontë, 164–65,
    166
  spiritualism and, 135–36, 163–66,
    169, 174
  stereotypes by, 181
  Swedish Movement Cure and,
    151–52
  writing voice of, 153–55
Strachey, Lytton, 187–88, 198, 199
stream-of-consciousness technique,
  229
Sunny Memories of Foreign Lands
  (Stowe), 179
Swedish Movement Cure, 151–52, 164
Sweeney, Emma Claire, xiv–xvi,
  260–61
Swift & Co., 199–200
Swiss Notes by Five Ladies (Taylor),
  125

Tait's Edinburgh Magazine, 110
Taylor, Ellen, 110, 116–17
Taylor, George, 151–52, 164, 169
Taylor, James, 117–18
Taylor, Joe, 86, 87

Taylor, Martha, 65, 81, 97
  in Belgium, 85
  illness and death of, 91–92
  on Mary, 90
Taylor, Mary
  arguments with Brontë, 72
  background of, 71–72
  in Belgium, 82, 86
  on Belgium, 88–89
  on Brontë's biography, 122–24
  Brontë's death and, 122
  on Brontë's marriage, 120–21
  on Brontë wasting her life, 103–10
  challenges to Brontë by, 77–78
  common interests with Brontë,
    69–70
  condescension of, toward Brontë,
    65–68
  cousin's move to join, 110, 116–17
  on the drudgery of teaching, 77–78
  earthquake and, 110
  envy of Brontë, 73
  feminism of, 89, 109, 125–26
  financial situation of, 81, 85
  on Gaskell's biography, 123–24
  independence of, 103–4
  influence of, on Brontë, 108–9, 254
  inspiration from, 74–75
  intelligence of, 70–71
  on *Jane Eyre,* 106, 107–9
  lack of information about, 78
  letter destroyed by, 96
  literary efforts of, 109–11, 116,
    125–26
  in London, 86–87
  on marriage, 120
  in New Zealand, 102–4, 108–12,
    113, 116–17, 123

  return to Yorkshire, 124–25
  on *Shirley,* 114–15
  trip to Germany, 90, 92, 96–97,
    99–100
Taylor, Waring, 81, 104
The Tenant of Wildfell Hall (Brontë), 107
Tennyson, Alfred, Lord, 138
Testament of Friendship (Brittain), 256
Testament of Youth (Brittain), 256
Thackeray, William Makepeace, 111,
    112, 113, 165
Their Eyes Were Watching God
    (Hurston), 257
Ticknor and Fields, 132–33
The Times (London)
  Austen letters in, 4
  Mansfield's obituary in, 249–50
  on Sharp, 60
  on the status of governesses, 7
Times Literary Supplement, 231–32, 234
  on *Je ne parle pas français,* 240–41
  on *Prelude,* 240
To the Lighthouse (Woolf), 251
"The True Story of Lady Byron's
    Life" (Stowe), 141–46
  Eliot on, 144–46
  repercussions from, 148–51, 153
tuberculosis
  in Anne Brontë 111, 116
  in Branwell Brontë, 106
  in Charlotte Brontë, 121
  in Emily Brontë, 109
  in Mansfield, 211, 220, 229
  in Maria and Elizabeth Brontë, 64

Uncle Tom's Cabin (Stowe)
  Brontë on, 165
  criticisms of, 149–50

Uncle Tom's Cabin (cont.)
  Eliot on, 254–55
  fame of, 153
  gift of, to Eliot, 181, 182
  religion in, 154
  on separation of families, 154–55
  stereotypes in, 181
  success of, 131–32

Victoria, 125
Victoria, Queen, 99, 132, 140
Villette (Brontë), 86, 88, 117
  confessional scene in, 97–99
  Eliot on, 255
  Heger in, 96
Virtue Rewarded (Sharp), 26–27, 38
The Voyage Out (Woolf), 187–88, 189,
    217

The Watsons (Austen), 25
Westminster Review
  Chapman and, 153, 157–58
  Eliot in, 191–92
Wide Sargasso Sea (Rhys), 256
William Heinemann, 229, 232
Williams, William Smith, 111
Wilson, William Carus, 124
Women's Co-operative Guild, 189
Wooler, Margaret, 67, 75, 96, 120, 122
Woolf, Leonard, 189
  at Asheham, 199, 213–14
  income of, 215–16
  journalism by, 216
  marital relationship of, 219
  meagre hospitality of, 202, 215
Woolf, Virginia
  admiration of Mansfield, 187–88
  appearance of, 221, 230–31

  on Baker, 203–4, 221
  on "Bliss," 216–18, 219, 222
  on *Bliss and Other Stories,* 242–43
  Christmas of 1918, 227–28
  connection with Mansfield,
      241–42, 243–45
  dream of Mansfield, 252
  education of, 191
  on Eliot, 230, 237–38
  envy of Mansfield, 238, 244, 250
  on ethics of literary criticism, 242
  fears of abandonment, 228–29,
      246–47
  feelings of, toward Mansfield,
      224–26
  first visit to Mansfield's studio,
      189–93
  garden story concept, 196–98,
      199–201
  health of, 210
  income of, 215–16
  journalism by, 216
  on Mansfield's character, 187, 207,
      230, 239
  Mansfield's death and, 249–50
  on marriage, 213
  meagre hospitality of, 202, 215
  meeting of, with Mansfield,
      187–88
  mental health of, 189
  personality of, 193
  praise for, 246
  praise of Mansfield by, 245–46
  on *Prelude,* 202–3
  Prelude typeset by, 204–6
  printing press work by, 188–89, 192
  profits of, 232
  publication of, 200

relationship with servants,
190
rivalry with Mansfield, 188, 206,
224, 251
sexual history of, 193, 218–19
sexuality of, 217–18, 251
snide remarks of, to Bloomsbury
friends, 194–96, 200–202
South Downs home of, 198,
227–28

visits between Mansfield and, 194,
224–26, 229–30
on woman writers, 253–54
World War I, 190, 192, 197, 200, 223,
255
Wuthering Heights (Brontë), 104, 106–7

Yeats, William Butler, 212
York and North Midland Railway
Company, 83